A Broadcast News MANUAL OF STYLE

Second
Edition

A Broadcast News MANUAL OF STYLE

Ron MacDonald
Washington and Lee University

Longman
New York & London

A Broadcast News Manual of Style,
second edition

Copyright © 1994, 1987 by Longman Publishing Group.

Longman, 10 Bank Street, White Plains, N.Y. 10606

Associated companies:
Longman Group Ltd., London
Longman Cheshire Pty., Melbourne
Longman Paul Pty., Auckland
Copp Clark Pitman, Toronto

Acquisitions editor: Kathleen Schurawich
Production editor: Victoria Mifsud
Cover design: Joseph DePinho
Production supervisor: Anne Armeny

Library of Congress Cataloging-in-Publication Data

MacDonald, R.
    A broadcast news manual of style / by Ron MacDonald.—2nd ed.
       p.   cm.
    Includes bibliographical references and index.
    ISBN 0-8013-1110-1
    1. Broadcast journalism—Authorship.   2. Journalism—Style
manuals. I. Title.
PN4784.B75M24   1994
808' .02—dc20   93-6072
                                           CIP

1 2 3 4 5 6 7 8 9 10-MA-9897969594

CONTENTS

A Broadcast News MANUAL OF STYLE

INTRODUCTION

In the years since the first edition of this book, it has been adopted as a standard usage and style guide in numerous schools of journalism. The time has come for an update to recognize changes in the way things are done, notably because of the introduction of computers to many newsrooms and college newswriting laboratories, the improvements in electronic cameras and tape editing equipment and the widespread use of satellites in news gathering. This is also an opportunity to expand the usage guide and to include materials suggested by reviewers and users.

Many newsrooms rely on the usage guides published by The Associated Press or the United Press International. Those, however, were written for those people who work for the wire services, or work primarily in editing wire service copy, and therefore tend to perpetuate the peculiarities of wire service style and usage. This is not to say the AP or UPI usage guides are poor. They are, in fact, excellent in most cases and I can't imagine a good newsroom without one or the other. However, they were adapted partly from style and usage guides that were developed for the newspaper wires where a quite different approach to newswriting is recommended.

In addition, we find that most broadcast newswriting texts deal with broadcast style, not necessarily good writing. They tend to concentrate on snappy leads, brief storytelling and writing to video. That's all to the good, but stories still need serious treatment and precise language. Some texts also seem to dwell on details of reporting techniques and mechanical skills, such as tape editing. That information is important, but may not be appropriate for a broadcast newswriting course.

What the reader will find here are discussions of what we are calling "style" for want of a better word. Style here includes such things as page formats, how to cue tapes and the like, for both radio and television. It must be understood that what we present here are examples of just one way to construct script pages. There are nearly 15,000 radio and TV stations in this country and perhaps dozens of different ways of formatting a page. What we present here is probably conventional enough to be acceptable in most places. But anyone contemplating going to work in any newsroom must be ready to adapt to its way of doing things. Where there are areas of difference or disagreement, we have tried to so note.

The author entered TV news in its infancy when there were no "right" or "wrong" ways to do things. We were "inventing" TV news and learned by experimenting. Most newsrooms in the early to mid-1950s developed independently. Consequently, many different methods of handling copy and conventions of usage emerged.

What you will find here is the evolved result of that experimenting, now augmented by the experience of others and practiced in many newsrooms. The result is a set of "rules" that may differ in detail from those presented in some texts. However, the intent and, I hope, the result will be very similar. Audience understanding and ease of handling copy are the goals. I believe the practices I recommend here meet those goals. Classroom instructors and professionals who may use this guide are certainly free to adjust its recommendations to suit their own preferred way of doing things. Broadcast news is still an evolving craft. Each new piece of electronic magic that enters the newsroom has the potential of fundamentally changing the way things are done. The advent of portable videotape machines and electronic cameras and tape editing had profound effects, as has the development of news gathering by satellite and the rapidly spreading introduction of computers in newsrooms. Future advancements certainly have that same potential. Rules evolve with the craft and change is inevitable.

As you get into the following pages keep in mind that although things seem to be presented as dicta from on high, very little in this business is cast in concrete (please note I did not say "cement"--*see* Part Four, "Usage Guide"). Newsrooms have their little quirks and pet ways of doing things. Anchors have preferences as to how things ought to be done to suit their particular ways. And in some cases we shall see that methods of handling things change with circumstance.

Broadcast newswriting needs to be precise and unmistakably clear. Careful use of the language is essential to that process. To that end this book contains an extensive usage guide.

Some of the conventions we'll discuss may seem unnecessary, but there is a reason for everything. Those reasons most often can be traced to the desire to help the listener understand. Listener understanding is, after all, what we must be most concerned about. Some rules, however, are intended to help you and your colleagues do a better job. An example is the differing ways numbers are handled in different circumstances. Many of the "rules" we will be discussing have exceptions. The rules and exceptions are all intended to make the news and other information we broadcast easier to comprehend.

Conventional style is extremely helpful in newsrooms with several writers working toward the same news program. There would be chaos if the anchor person were forced to wade through the differing styles, formats and spellings of a half-dozen writers, each with a different rule book. If the anchor gets confused, listener misunderstanding is likely to follow.

It is not considered a crime to break style for good reason. But to break style because of ignorance or carelessness is not easily forgiven. The writer who consistently misspells or ignores the conventions of page format is considered an unreliable co-worker and a poor journalist.

On another level, we broadcasters have delivered news to the public for well over half a century now, and people have become accustomed to hearing certain information presented in certain ways and they simply comprehend things better that way.

Even though we're dealing with the spoken language, correct spelling remains of major importance. Among the reasons are the obvious problems misspellings will cause people reading someone else's writing aloud. In addition, problems of pronunciation and inflection arise when sound-alike or look-alike words are misspelled. For example, to write "trusty" when you mean "trustee" can cause a great deal of embarrassment. Do doctors have "patients" or "patience" or both?

You need to be aware that regional idiom varies widely across the nation, so adjust your usage of some terms to fit the region in which you may find yourself. A perfectly good expression in the Mid-South might mean something entirely different in New England. An example is the noun variant for *burlap bag*. In the South and elsewhere they may be called a "tow sack" or "croker sack," in the West a "gunnysack" and in New England a "bran sack." There are numerous examples of these regionalisms and quirks of usage that you must make it your business to learn as you settle into a new locality and attempt to communicate with its people.

We will also deal with punctuation and how it differs from everyday use. The broadcast writer never writes anything that cannot be pronounced. Therefore, most of the symbols on the top row of your keyboard are useless to you. Everything you want said on the air must be written out in full. The broadcast writer will rarely use semicolons or colons. Instead, his copy will be sprinkled liberally with dashes--like that. Some writers will use the ellipsis (. . .) to indicate slight pauses. I don't recommend it, because it really indicates that something has been left out of the text. Differing punctuation in broadcast newswriting is a purely mechanical thing. The divergence from "standard" punctuation is designed to help the copy reader. The differences should never be translated into formal writing. Most students of broadcast newswriting will spend most of their college careers in courses that demand correct, standard punctuation. Keep this specialized form in the broadcast newsroom. Much non-standard punctuation develops as the individual preference of the newsreader and is later formalized in a newsroom "stylebook." Such is what is presented here. The purpose is to aid the reader in smoothing delivery, looking for inflection traps, emphasizing key words and making a point.

Done properly, non-standard punctuation can go a long way toward our goals of clarity and precision of understanding.

The section on editing is brief, because there's not much to it. Generally, if a script page needs much editing, it should be rewritten. Newsroom computers make editing, rewriting and polishing almost painless.

The usage guide makes up the greater part of this book. It is arranged alphabetically with cross-references. You will find common words that are frequently either mis-pronounced or mis-used. You will also find the pure opinion of the author as to which words are "better" for broadcast usage where there is a choice of two or more to express a thought. In many cases troublesome words are included with a suggestion that preference be given to words that are "better" for broadcasting, although there may be perfectly good substitute words. The preference is usually based on how the word sounds when spoken, but sometimes there are words that may confuse the anchor and lead to inflection problems.

You will find that many entries in the usage guide are not necessarily specific to broadcast newswriting, but apply to all good writing. I have relied on *Webster's Tenth New Collegiate Dictionary* as my authority, even though it tends to be somewhat permissive.

It may come as a surprise to some that dictionaries frequently disagree, especially on matters of pronunciation and usage. There are some instances where Webster's and I do not agree. I have so noted.

No usage guide can ever be complete, unless it becomes a fully developed dictionary, and that's not what we're after here. I have relied on years of collecting misusages and mispronunciations which I find to be commonly heard and read, as well as on such excellent works as *Harper Dictionary of Contemporary Usage* by William and Mary Morris, *The Writer's Art* by James J. Kilpatrick, *A Treasury for Word Lovers* by Morton Freeman, *Dictionary of Problem Words and Expressions* by Harry Shaw, *Words on Words* by John Bremner, *American Regional Dialects* by Craig M. Carver and two wonderful and painstakingly researched books on pronunciation by Charles Harrington Elster, *There Is no Zoo in Zoology* and *Is There a Cow in Moscow?* All are exhaustive, authoritative and witty examinations of our language. I highly recommend them for any writer's bookshelf.

Our language has been called the "glue of our society." Language should be carefully protected--especially by those who make their living from its use.

The author is a journalist who has spent his entire career working with words and shades of meaning, and attempting, through precision of language, to make understandable the daily events of our times. Precise language has power. Someone has said than an adequate word is like a lightning bug, the precise word is like lightning.

There are some great writers working in broadcast newsrooms--but not many. For most, the pressures of hourly deadlines and demands for ever briefer stories make graceful and precise writing impossible. But those very pressures make precision necessary. When you have only a fraction of a minute to tell a complex story, precision of language is essential--using the exact word to convey the precise thought.

In broadcast writing we try to use conventional words--words our listeners are accustomed to hearing and using in their daily lives. This means broadcast news writing tends to the casual rather than the formal.

You will find this a straightforward approach to the subject of broadcast newswriting practices. There is no attempt to make this a scholarly document. In fact, students of language and usage may very well take issue with some of the proclamations. That is one of the risks in writing about writing. There's always someone out there who's better at it and will find the lapses and errors.

The author's career has carried him from his beginnings in radio in a New England town of 1,500 to a major metropolitan area and finally to a smaller city where he spent the larger part of his 18 professional years as a TV reporter, assignment editor, anchor and news director. He has been teaching broadcast newswriting at the university level for more than 20 years.

Included here are the inevitable appendixes (is *appendixes* now acceptable? *See* **Latinates** in the usage guide) at the end of the book. These contain the code of ethics of the Radio-Television News Directors Association, a look at the wire services, the real meaning of "ten-four, good buddy," standard patient condition definitions, comparative military ranks, a list of state capitals, a listing of the nations of the world and their capitals, telephone area codes by state and numerically, and foreign telephone codes.

Lexington, Virginia, 1993

ADVANCING TECHNOLOGIES

In the past five years there have been two major technological advancements in television news gathering. One has been a new generation of lightweight self-contained field units combining a camera and a recorder, called *camcorders*, that have freed camerapersons from the cumbersome separate recorder unit and done away with the awful umbilical cable that greatly hindered movement. This development has also made more practical the "one-man band" field operation, in which the reporter is also expected to act as camera operator. This is seen as a great breakthrough by those who have to pay salaries, but as a major step toward diluted news coverage by those who are concerned about journalism. The problem they see is that a single person is expected to concentrate on serious journalism while at the same time being concerned about operating the camera and recorder. It may be the wave of the future, at least in smaller, non-union operations. It's a rare wave of the future, indeed, that brings only good things.

The second technological advance has been the emergence of the age of satellite news gathering. SNG, too, promises to pose problems as well as to open new vistas. Those of us who came into broadcast journalism just as television emerged had only to deal with already existing technologies in new ways. Broadcast news had been around for 20 years or so and motion pictures were downright elderly. It was just that the two had never been put together before, except in the stylized newsreels. We married the two with many successes and many failures and the result was TV news.

Now comes SNG. A whole new generation of bright young TV journalists now has the opportunity to "invent" its own form of journalism. This is not intended to be an exhaustive discussion of the uses, technology or journalistic implications of SNG. There are entire books on the subject, and my guess is the whole business has a lot of innovating, evolving and developing yet to do. There is no question the use of satellites has already had profound effect on the way local news is produced and the role of the networks in broadcast journalism.

The satellites have been in orbit for a relatively long time. We have been getting news feeds from foreign lands for a number of years. Those feeds have been arranged primarily by the networks to enhance their daily news programs.

A few years ago one of our local stations sent a reporter and camera crew to England to cover complicated maneuverings in a notorious local murder trial. Other stations sent their own reporters to international hot spots, to tailor their

7

reports for their local audiences. Critics say those hit-and-run reports from local newsmen cannot possibly be based on the same sort of insight that experienced foreign correspondents can bring to a story. Today, many of those same stations have their own satellite uplink trucks to bring live reports to newscasts from virtually any location in North America and elsewhere. And virtually all stations each day receive satellite news feeds from news gathering consortia, networks and other sources.

This has resulted in the creation of an entirely new production position in the newsroom: satellite coordinator. It's a busy, full-time and major newsroom job. The details of the position are complex, but include videotaping feeds from a variety of sources and arranging satellite "windows" for live feeds.

A window is a pre-arranged segment of time, usually five minutes, during which a station's uplink truck has exclusive use of a satellite transponder. That means the production team in the newsroom must coordinate its story line-up to allow the feed to be received during that time frame. If the story is likely to be a lead or at least in the opening segment of the program, the window will be the first five minutes. If it's a feature story, the window can be placed later in the program.

Satellite technology is complex. But it is a part of news gathering that will surely grow in importance as time goes on.

During the Persian Gulf War we were transfixed by the live reports from the area--all by satellite. That took a very complex arrangement of multiple satellite "hops" to bring off. A satellite can "see" only as far as its horizon. A feed from the other side of the globe requires a series of relays from ground to satellite to ground and back again. Each step is about 45,000 miles round trip. Several hops can require sufficient time that a perceptible lag is created. This is especially noticable when, for example, an anchor in the U.S. is questioning a reporter in Saudi Arabia. It takes the question about an extra second to reach the reporter, who seems to hestitate a moment in response. This probably has nothing to do with journalism, but is an interesting side-line look at the technology.

Not every local station is yet equipped for satellite news gathering. Most are able to receive feeds, but not originate them. An uplink truck is very expensive, but it can be a valuable asset for the news operation which, in most stations, is a profit center.

The emergence of satellite news feeds from foreign countries that can be accessed by local stations is seen by some as calling into question the central role of network news divisions as the primary source of international news. Local stations or consortia are able to cover and select for their special audiences their own foreign news.

One more word on satellite news feeds: They are not protected from pirating. We like to think journalists don't steal from one another, but the temptation is enormous when a spectacular piece of video is being transmitted by satellite that anyone with a receiver is fully capable of taping. This is a matter of ethics that has yet to be adequately addressed.

Any young journalist must be aware there's a satellite in the future. Be prepared.

STYLE AND FORMATS

FORMATS

The conventions of copy formats are by no means universal. Most newsrooms use similar rules for designing the different kinds of script pages, but the individual variations seem almost endless. Most have been developed through use and are almost traditional. What we present here is a set of conventions that seems to be widely accepted and certainly would cause little problem. However, you must realize that when going to work in any newsroom, you must be ready to adapt to its way of doing things.

We will proceed on the assumption that the newsroom in which you find yourself is still using typewriters. There is a rapid move toward computerized broadcast newsrooms, in which cases page formats will be automatically decided. Your first step, whether dealing with a typewriter or a computer terminal--infantile as it may seem--is to become thoroughly familiar with the machine. You must know how to set margins and tabular stops, how to change the ribbon and so on. I have found that most students have great difficulty with unfamiliar typewriters. Get to be a friend of yours.

Even though there is probably a computer in the future of every broadcast journalist, the move is by no means complete. About half of the TV newsrooms today are equipped with computers. The figure is much lower for radio. In journalism education, computer-equipped laboratories are widespread, leading some to suggest we not deal with typewriter formats. However, teachers need to be aware that most of their students will find entry-level jobs in smaller stations, which are the least likely to have computers, or have systems that are far less sophisticated than those in their labs. Therefore, we will continue to include the following section on the use of typewriters.

1.1 *Setting Margins and Tabular Stops for Radio Scripts*

A typical page of radio news copy is put together as follows:

First, set the paper guide on the top of your typewriter to zero. That's usually as far to the left as it will go. Then, set the first tabular stop at 10. We'll come back to this later. Set the left margin at 20 and another tab stop at 25. Still another tab stop should be set at 40 and the right margin at 80. This results in a 60-character line with a five-space indentation for paragraphs and a tab stop at about midpage which is useful for end marks and other purposes. This 60-character line takes about 3 seconds to read, so 10 lines equal 30 seconds--making timing easy. Timing, of course depends on the reader. Some people simply read faster or slower than others.

1.2 *Setting Margins and Tabular Stops for TV Scripts*

A page of TV news copy looks somewhat different. The demands of television are so much greater than radio that more information needs to be put on the page--not to be read on the air but to tell the director and other production people what to do and when. In some TV newsrooms producers decide on visual effects and other such things, but often the writers are expected to turn in copy complete with all audio and video directions.

For a TV news script, again set the paper guide at zero and a tab stop at 10, just as with radio. However, now we get into a quite different form. Set the left margin at 40 and the paragraph indent at 45; the midpage tab stop is set at 60 and the right margin at 80. This gives us a 40-character line which takes about 2 seconds to read--still useful for timing as 10 lines equal 20 seconds.

The extrawide left margin is used to write in video and audio directions. Some newsrooms provide copy paper that has a vertical ruling to set off the left margin.

1.3 *Carbon Copies*

Most newsrooms will want multiple copies of news stories. Sometimes carbon paper is used, but often "books" of carbonless, color-coded paper are provided. There may be six or more pages in the book to be distributed to the variety of people who need them. Those people would include the producer, director, audio operator, prompter operator, graphics operator, and floor director, among others, including, of course, the anchor. The presence of the prompter does not offer enough comfort for the anchor to dare go on the air without a paper script in hand. In radio a single carbon for file purposes may be all that is needed.

1.4 *The "Slug," Writer's Name and Date*

Before you begin to write a story, you must identify it. In most newsrooms a story is given a "slug," or name when it is assigned to a reporter and will carry that same identifying label through the entire news process from assignment to the final air script. The story slug is usually determined by the assignment editor. As you begin to write your story, type in the one- or two-word slug in ALL CAPS in the upper left corner of the page. Immediately below that type in your name (just the last name will usually do) and below that, the date (just the day and month).

Some editors prefer to have the slug, name and date typed as a single line across the top of the page, but that leaves little room for tape information, which we'll get to shortly. Yet others say to put it in the upper RIGHT corner. It depends on how your newsroom prefers it. For now, we'll use the upper left.

Now, space down about two inches before you start to write. This is very important because that room at the top of the page is needed for possible written instructions to be added later.

1.5 *Using Normal Upper- and Lowercase*

Write in normal upper- and lowercase. Some newsrooms prefer all uppercase while still others use special typewriters with larger-than-normal typefaces. Most, however, use normal capitalization. The copy is easier to read, it prevents confusion between common words and names (Green, for example), and signals the reader that a name is coming up to avoid getting caught in an inflection trap.

1.6 *Triple Space*

Set your typewriter for TRIPLE space. All broadcast copy is triple-spaced to leave room for written corrections between the lines. With computers, this is not necessary because there normally would be no handwriting on a script.

1.7 *Using Capital Letters Freely*

Certain key words and titles, which ordinarily might not be capitalized, can be in broadcast copy. The word *federal*, for example, ordinarily is used lowercase unless in a formal title, but I have found it helps to capitalize it, because very often you will want stress on *Federal*, and the capital letter signals the reader that an inflection change is coming up. In fact, capitalize freely to help the reader smooth out delivery. That's just a matter of personal preference. Some readers might object to the practice.

1.8 *One Story on a Page*

A couple of other simple-minded things: Type only on one side of the paper and put only one story on a page, no matter how short it is or how closely it might be related to another story. That allows you to rearrange your copy if needed. The exception would be when writing briefs or headlines that you know will air in the order in which you have written them.

Now that you have your book of copy paper in your typewriter and have set the machine on triple space, and have written your slug and other information and have left a two-inch margin at the top of the page, you are ready to begin writing. Push your tab key to indent five spaces and go to it.

1.8 *End Marks*

When you have written your story be sure to put some sort of end mark on it. That's where your center-of-page tab stop comes into use. You will find different writers using distinctive end marks. The most common are *-30-*, *-0-*, *XXXX* or *END*. You should pick one and stick with it.

1.10 *Going to Page Two*

If your story is long and goes to a second page, you must type at the bottom of page one: ((MORE)). Note that the word *MORE* is in caps and enclosed in double parentheses. This gives the reader an instant clue that the word is not to be read on the air and that the story goes to page two.

Many broadcast writers will circle by hand any material not to be read on the air. I've always found that the double parentheses and caps has the same effect and eliminates one step in the process. However, follow the practice of your newsroom.

1.11 *End Every Page with a Complete Sentence*

Always end page one with a COMPLETE sentence. NEVER break a sentence when going to page two. What if page two gets lost? Or if time is running low and you decide to drop page two? Disaster!

At the top of page two type the same slug word or phrase you used to identify page one. It is not necessary to write in your name or the date on page two. Just the slug and a string of four twos: 2222. As in: INTERSTATE CRASH 2222. The same form is used for page three (3333) and so on.

There is one school of thought that says to call page two ADD ONE. I have always found that to be confusing and do not recommend it. It's a holdover from newspaper copy formats where it may have been useful in the scissors-and-paste days.

Don't go to page two for just one more line. Try to leave about a one-inch margin at the bottom of the page, but go ahead and put in an extra line if that's all you have.

1.12 *Timing or Line Count*

When your story is complete, pencil in the approximate time or line count, depending on how it's done in your newsroom, at the top right of page one. If the story contains a tape insert, the running time of the tape should be written in.

Other than the differing margin and tab settings, all of the above applies to both radio and TV scripting. Study the examples of "typical" radio and TV script formats and see how they differ. See Sections 1.20, 1.21 and 1.22.

Now, the differences become more dramatic.

1.13 *Writing a Tape Cue for Radio*

Cueing a tape for a radio newscast is a reasonably simple procedure. You simply note at the top of the page that a tape goes with the story, and at the point where the tape is to be used move the typewriter carriage to the right to tab stop 10 (there it is, I told you we'd get to this), and type in the "roll cue" in ALL CAPS. The sample copy coming up will show you how this looks. A roll cue consists of the phrase "TAPE ON HERE" (or something similar), the timing of the tape and the last three or four words it contains. And that's about it for radio. See Section 1.23.

1.14 *Writing a Tape Cue for TV*

Television presents a somewhat more complicated problem, largely because there are so many people involved and they all must know what's to happen. Furthermore, the medium is so much more complex than radio that a lot of additional information has to be available to the production team.

1.15 *Visual Effects*

For television, of course, we must deal with both audio and video cues and with a variety of visual enhancements, such as superimpositions (supers), squeeze zooms, slides, chroma keys and so on. All these, if you want to use them, must be indicated on the script exactly the way you want them to appear on the screen and at the precise moment you want them. Sometimes, however, it is not the writer but the producer who decides on video effects.

At the top of page one indicate that a videotape goes with the story and give its timing and whether it is a voice-over (VO), which will probably be a silent (SIL) tape; that is, one with no sound track or with background sound only. If there is a voice track on the tape, that is called sound-on-tape (SOT).

1.16 *"On Camera"*

To begin, space down two inches and at tab stop 10 write "OC" followed by a string of dots. That means "on camera," and tells the director that the anchor should be seen on the screen. At one time (and probably still showing up in many places) the command was "man on camera," or MOC. Recently, as more and more anchors are female, "man on camera" is looked on as sexist. I've seen it suggested that MOC now means "mike on camera" in reference to the microphone. Today, OC is the genderless command gaining popularity. Another is POC (person on camera). That's a matter of individual newsroom style. In any case, it means the anchor is to be shown on the TV screen.

1.17 *Videotape Without Sound*

The anchor reads the lead-in to the story and introduces the tape. At that point, you write (beginning at tab stop 10 again) TAPE ON HERE . . . VO . . . and the anchor continues to read as the picture shows what is on the tape, as illustrated in Section 1.24.

1.18 *Videotape with Sound*

If there is a voice track on the tape, say an interview, that comes up after the anchor has read his or her portion, you write (at tab stop 10): SOUND UP HERE . . . :43 . . . "THE LOUSY CREEP." That tells the director to have the audio controller to bring up the sound track for 43 seconds until the "Out Cue" is heard, at which point he or she will "kill" the sound.

If at the end of the tape you wish to go back to the anchor's face, you once again write OC . . . beginning in the far left margin. See Section 1.25.

1.19 *The "Super" and Other Effects*

There are so many gimmicks available to enhance a video story it is almost impossible to list them all and new ones appear frequently. Probably the most commonly used is the "super." With an interview you will almost always want to super the subject's name. That needs to be indicated in detail in that wide left margin. Sometimes you will want to "key" in a piece of tape or a slide behind the anchor. That needs to go there, too. Just remember, EVERY-THING you want on the screen must be described in exact detail in the margin of the script, or it won't show up--at least not where or in the form you want it.

One of the great horrors of working in television is the number of hands that are in the soup. Each one is capable of the grossest sort of error. As a writer, you are the first in a long line of people in a position to damage a perfectly good story. If you do your job well, it will lessen the chances of others down the line botching theirs.

1.20 Typical Radio Script Format

SLUG   TAPE TIMING
NAME
DATE
10   20   25   40   80

                    ((THIS GIVES THREE SECONDS A LINE--
                       TEN LINES = 30 SECONDS))

AUDIO CUES GO   ALL COPY GOES IN THIS SPACE
IN THIS SPACE

          ALL BROADCAST COPY IS **TRIPLE=**
          SPACED. NEVER WRITE TO THE END
          OF A PAGE--LEAVE AT LEAST A
          ONE-INCH MARGIN--GO TO NEXT
          PAGE WITH ((MORE)).
          NEVER BREAK A SENTENCE AT THE
          END OF A PAGE.
          ALWAYS USE SOME SORT OF END
          MARK.
          -30-, -0-, ---, XXXX OR -END-.

1.21 Typical TV Script Format

SLUG   VIDEOTAPE AND TIME
NAME
DATE

10   20 25   40   80

                        THIS GIVES A
                        TWO-SECOND LINE--
                        10 LINES = 20 SECONDS

ALL VIDEO AND   ALL NARRATION GOES IN
AUDIO DIRECTIONS   THIS COLUMN.
GO IN THIS COLUMN.

1.22 Sample Radio Script

BURGLAR
MACD
9/13

A 30-year-old Smallville man is under arrest in connection with a series of household break-ins.

Gaylord Swann of the 25-hundred block of Pelham Place was arrested late this morning on a warrant issued by Judge Charles Guernsey.

The warrant charges Swann with seven counts of breaking and entering over a period of four weeks.

In the past month, at least eleven local homes have been burglarized. Police estimate the total value of stolen goods to be in excess of 25-thousand-dollars.

A preliminary hearing for Swann has been set for tomorrow afternoon.

-0-

1.23 Sample Radio Script with Tape

BURGLAR   TAPE :15
MACD
9/13

A 30-year-old Smallville man is under arrest in connection
with a series of household break-ins.

Gaylord Swann of 25-38 Pelham Place was arrested late this
morning on a warrant issued by Judge Charles Guernsey.

Police Chief Sensor Calderara outlined the charges contained
in the warrant . . . .

TAPE ON HERE . . . RUNS :15 . . . "THE LOUSY CREEP."

Calderara said there have been eleven burglaries in the last
four weeks--the total value of stolen property is estimated at
more than 25-thousand-dollars.

A preliminary hearing for Swann is set for tomorrow
afternoon.

-0-

1.24 Sample TV Script with Silent Tape

BURGLAR   TAPE-SIL :30
MACD
9/13

OC . . .   A 30-year-old Smallville man is being held in
                  connection with a series of household break-ins.

TAPE ON HERE VO :30 . . .

                  Gaylord Swann of 25-38 Pelham Place was arrested
                  this morning on a warrant issued by Judge Charles
                  Guernsey.
                  Swann was taken into custody at his home by Police
                  Chief Sensor Calderara and several other officers. Swann
                  offered no resistance.
                  A police spokesman said the warrant charges Swann
                  with seven counts of burglary over the past four weeks.
                  In all, there have been eleven household break-ins during
                  that period.
                  Total property loss is estimated at more than 25-
                  thousand-dollars.

OC . . .

                  A preliminary hearing for Swann is set for tomorrow
                  afternoon.

                              -0-

                  (Shown single-spaced for clarity)

1.25 Sample TV Script with Sound on Tape and Super

BURGLAR   TAPE-SOT :54
MACD
9/13

OC. . .   A 30-year-old Smallville man is under arrest in

                     connection with a series of household break-ins.

TAPE ON HERE VO :09 . . .

                     Police arrested Gaylord Swann at his Pelham Place

                     home this morning. Chief Sensor Calderara told a news

                     conference about the charges.

SOUND UP HERE RUNS :45 . . .

"THE LOUSY CREEP"

((SUPER:

CHIEF S. CALDERARA))

                              ((MORE))

BURGLAR 2222

OC . . .   A preliminary hearing for Swann is set for tomorrow

                     afternoon.

                              -0-

(Two-page story shown on one page for convenience and clarity.)

1.26 *Newsroom Computers*

As stated earlier, these guidelines refer to the use of typewriters in the newsroom. The rapid introduction of computers in newsrooms is changing many of the "traditional" ways of doing things. For example, line length is determined by the machine. It is set by a person called the "SYSOP," or system operator. Computers not only handle the copy for you, they also drive the prompter, and it is possible to adjust the line length to suit individual anchors. The shorter the line, the less likely eye movement will be detected by viewers. The speed of the prompter scroll can also be set to fit the reading speed of individual readers. And, in most cases, the anchor is able to control the speed of the scroll either with a hand device or a foot pedal.

Special encoding keystrokes while writing on a terminal assure that the slug and other information at the top of the story show up on the printed script, but not on the prompter. The same is true of tape and other cues within the body of the story. Some of the more sophisticated computer systems automatically seek out stored and indexed video effects when the writer calls for them. They will bring up on the screen supers and other matter just by indicating them in the script. Soon to come, I'm told, is computer software that will allow marking up a prompter script for emphasis, pauses and so on.

Computer systems and what they can do vary widely with the sophistication of the programs. They have in some ways simplified and speeded up the newswriting process, but in other ways have complicated things as well. Such is the nature of progress.

1.27 *Databases*

One other wonderful feature of computers in the newsroom is that they contain an array of databases that may be created locally or obtained from other sources. These range from dictionaries and pronunciation guides to lists of important phone numbers. Some provide maps showing the locations of even small towns. I believe we are at just the beginning of the computer age in our newsrooms. The future will be filled with "gee whiz!" innovations.

GETTING WORDS ON PAPER

Many new writers find getting started somewhat intimidating. It's really not hard. We'll try to lead you through the preliminary steps. There are lots of "rules" that you may find confusing at first. Don't worry too much about them--eventually, they'll come naturally.

2.1 *Indenting for Paragraphs*

Indent normally for paragraphing. Again, some newsrooms prefer not to indent, but leave an extra blank line between paragraphs. That's probably OK, but the practice uses up a lot of paper. Where computer-driven prompters are in use, the extra line can be a serious problem. That blank line has to scroll up before the next line can be read. For our purposes, we indent. Indenting probably helps the reader.

2.2 *Avoid Hyphenating Words Between Lines*

There are some things we do in normal writing that we never do in broadcast newswriting. We NEVER, for example, hyphenate a word at the end of a line. If you are running out of room, strike out the word and start anew on the next line. With a computer system, you don't have to worry about this. A feature called "word-wrap" automatically drops to the next line without hyphenating. Computer-generated hyphenation can lead to some hilarious (mans-laughter, fig-urine) or dangerous (the-rapist) results.

2.3 *Avoid Hyphenating Groups Between Lines*

You will find, however, we use a lot of hyphens in broadcast writing--in forming number groups and combination phrases, for example ("three-million," "politically-correct"). It's not always possible, but try to avoid breaking a hyphenated group between lines. Again, prompters driven by a computer will not adhere to this rule.

2.4 *Clear and Concise Sentences*

Remember, we are not interested in how the copy looks here; we are interested in making it easy to read and easy to understand. One thing that helps both is keeping paragraphs short so each one contains one clear and concise thought. Many broadcast writers will suggest making each sentence a paragraph all by itself. That certainly would make the editing process simpler and probably help reading as well.

2.5 *Simplifying Numbers*

If there is a key word in broadcast newswriting it is *simplify*. Make things as easy to understand as you can without getting simple-minded. Not everything, of course can handily be made simpler. Don't strain to do it; you'll just sound silly.

Simplification is especially important with large numbers that have a way of piling up in the ear and never reaching the brain. If you can express a number in such a way as to make it easier to understand, you have gone a long way toward the goal of helping your listeners.

Sometimes an exact number is necessary--in which case, use it. Most often, however, you can simplify numbers for your audience in one of several ways.

2.6 *Rounding*

Rounding: 1,348,975 is "more than one-and-one-third million." See how easy it is?

2.7 *Analogy (Comparison)*

The analogy we use so much it's a cliché is the comparison of the length of something to that of a football field, where the playing area is 100 yards or 300 feet long. With analogy, however, you have to be careful that the object you are using for comparison is fully familiar to your audience. Aunt Tillie may not have the faintest idea what a football field even looks like, much less how long it is. Remember, too, that only the playing area is 300 feet--that doesn't count the end-zones or stadium seats beyond. Analogy depends heavily on the images we have in our heads relative to the world around us, and on the commonality of those pictures--do we all share the same images? If the image is not widely shared, analogy won't work.

Sports people, pay attention to this.

2.8 *Approximation*

Approximate when possible. "Albany is about 150 miles from New York City." Actually, mileage charts say it's 156, but 150 is close enough for most uses.

2.9 *Conventions of Number Use*

There are certain conventions for the use of numbers in broadcast news copy that make them easier to read and understand.

Again, I will point out there are some areas of disagreement among professionals on details of number usage, but most are matters of personal style and not of great substance. What we present here will generally be accepted as competent usage.

2.10   *Spell Out One through Eleven*

We prefer, for example, to spell out numbers one through eleven and one-hundred-eleven. Ordinal numbers are spelled out through eleventh, as in: first, second, third, fourth, etc. For higher numbers use 12th, 32nd, 43rd, 51st.

2.11   *Use Numerals 12 through 999*

All other numbers are expressed as numerals up to 999. Some writers suggest writing out only single-digit numbers--that is, one through nine. I think getting rid of the somewhat startling 11 and 111 is worth the slight additional effort.

2.12   *Exceptions*

As with so many rules there are exceptions to the above. When using numbers in compounds such as ages, always use the numeral: "6-year-old child." The same is true of street addresses and time: "5 o-clock," "3-57 14th Street"; but it is "five 13th Avenue." I know it's inconsistent. Another inconsistency occurs when a number begins a paragraph. In that case, the number should be spelled out, even though "normally" it should be written as a numeral. For example: "Thirty-year-old Sam Smith has been arrested . . ." But: "A 30-year-old Smallville man . . ."

2.13   *Hyphenating Number Groups*

Please notice the hyphenations in the preceding paragraph. Hyphens play a heavy role in broadcast newswriting style. They are used to link the several connected parts of compounds, such as "two-million-dollars," "four-and-one-half-percent," "15-cents." Because these are compounds (that is, the linked group of words and numbers expresses a single idea), they should not be broken at the end of a line when possible.

2.14   *Alphanumeric Groups for Large Numbers*

Notice, too, that as we get into larger numbers--those above 999--we move into what our computer friends would call "the alphanumeric mode." We use a combination of words and numerals in order to express numbers the way we speak. It is considered poor style, although entirely correct, to write "two-million-500-thousand" or "two-point-five-million." Instead, use "two-and-one-half-million." It's more conversational and much easier to read and understand. For 3,010, write "three-thousand-ten." For 568,000, write "568-thousand." For 18,300, write "18-thousand-300." Do not write "three-hundred."

2.15   *Avoid Use of "Point" in Decimals*

Avoid using the word *point* where possible in dealing with decimals, especially when the decimal is less than one. A phrase like "point-seven-percent" is jarring. Such expressions are ugly and are remote from conversational speech. Write "seven-tenths-of-one-percent" or, better yet, if the number is not really critical, "more than two-thirds."

Notice we say ". . . of one percent," not ". . . of a percent." That can be mistaken for eight percent. This old rule may be a holdover from AM radio days when the quality of the broadcast was not always great. With today's high-fidelity sound, it may be an anachronism. We include it here just because it's in all the rule books.

2.16   *Express Decimals as Fractions*

Where possible, express decimals as fractions. So .75 becomes "three-fourths" (not three-quarters, by the way), .48 becomes "nearly half" and .55 is "slightly more than half." Don't strain to make that change. It's better to sound natural than to reach too far for the conversion.

2.17   *Exceptions*

Certain things, such as stock market reports, are often expressed as decimals and should be, because that's the way listeners are accustomed to hearing them and the precise numbers are very important to some people.

2.18   *Age Comes Before Name in Identifiers*

Ages normally come before the name in a combined identifier: "23-year-old Sue Jones." However, to vary things you might write "Sue Jones, who is 23," or where the age is important, "Sue Jones received her first book contract at the age of 23." Some writers now say that "23-year-old . . ." is old newspaper style and should be avoided by broadcasters. I don't find it objectionable. It is, indeed, an older style and perhaps not very conversational, but it is a widely understood usage and unmistakably clear.

Age is not always important to a story. When it is not, leave it out. It may be only unnecessary baggage. Generally age is considered important when, for example, a very young or very old person is a crime or accident victim. Age may not be important in a story about, for example, a school bus driver or whatever, unless the person is very young or very old.

2.19   *Street Addresses Expressed as Numerals*

Street addresses should always be expressed as numerals: "5-23 Walnut Avenue"; "43-27 Holmes Street." *See* 2.12 Exceptions.

2.20   *Years Usually Written Normally*

Years should be as normal: "1993." Some writers prefer "19-93." That's OK if your news reader doesn't object. It's certainly the way we say it. I personally find it a bit jarring. Many times stating the year is not necessary; in fact, it may be extra baggage. You can say "last December . . ." or "next year."

2.21   *Road and Highway Designations*

You should make yourself familiar with the conventions of road and highway designations in your area and the local idiom used to refer to them. "Rural route" for example, doesn't mean the same thing everywhere. In copy one would write "I-81," "U-S route 2-20," "state route 6-46" or "Virginia 6-46 " (it's ROOT, by the way, not ROWT), according to local custom.

2.22   *Phone Numbers and Auto Licenses*

We are rarely, but occasionally, called upon to put such things as phone numbers or auto license numbers in our copy. Here you want each numeral pronounced as a word, so you hyphenate. Write: "That number is 4-6-3-8-4-3-5," or if local custom permits: "4-6-3-84-35." "The license number is Virginia J-Z-R-4-0-4." Some writers would express that number as "J-Z-R-4-0H-4." Whichever you feel most comfortable with is OK. The point here is that the hyphens tell the newscaster that each unit of the number is to be pronounced as an individual word. When giving a phone number it's a good idea to warn your listeners they may want to jot something down, and then repeat the number at least once.

2.23   *Simplifying Names*

As with numbers, try to simplify names as well. You might wonder how that can be done. In many instances there's not much you can do, but there are also numerous cases where certain elements of individual names are not needed.

2.24   *Avoid Full Names of the Very Prominent*

It's not necessary to use the full name of the President of the United States, the Secretary General of the United Nations or the governor of the state where you're working. Often, there will be persons locally who are well-enough known to be referred to only by title and last name in a strictly local context.

2.25   *Avoid Junior, Senior, Third, etc.*

We usually drop Junior, Senior, Third, etc., unless there is a real possibility of confusing the subject of the story with a relative of the same name. Often you have no way of knowing, and neither does your audience. Other elements of identification, such as occupation or age, are usually sufficient to make clear who you are talking about.

2.26   *Exceptions*

However, we once again run into exceptions to our rules: Sammy Davis Junior was not simply Sammy Davis--the Junior was needed there because it became part of his full name through repeated use. There are other similar cases.

2.27   *Avoid Middle Names and Initials*

We normally dispense with middle names or initials.

2.28   *Exceptions*

Again exceptions loom large. No one would recognize Robert Lee as being anyone special until he is called Robert E. Lee. John Foster Dulles was not simply John Dulles. When a person's name is especially well-known, we must follow the common use of that name. Jerry Lewis and Jerry Lee Lewis are two very different persons.

2.29   *The Lesser-Known*

However, lesser-known individuals' names lend themselves to simplification. This is especially true in police and court cases where the individual involved is almost always referred to in official documents by all the names he has: Billy Rayjoe Huntsbarger, Junior. In most cases you will be on safe enough ground just calling him Billy Huntsbarger along with the other usual identification.

2.30   *Don't Use Both Full- and Nickname*

There's one other way a name can be simplified--or at least shortened. In cases where a person is known by both a formal first name and a nickname: Former Congressman Thomas P. "Tip" O'Neill, for example. In broadcast news copy we would refer to him as either Thomas or Tip, but not both. Pick one and stick with it.

2.31   *Second References*

Normally, the subject of the story or quoted source is referred to by first and last name and title, if any, on first reference, then by last name only in subsequent references. In the case of women, this becomes somewhat awkward. Notice that an unknown woman, Mrs. Blanche Smith, will be referred to on second and subsequent references as Smith, if it doesn't endanger the understanding of the story. However, well-known women such as former British Prime Minister Margaret Thatcher, will almost always be referred to by title or as Mrs. in later references. It's considered a mark of respect for the title, but it does create an inconsistency.

2.32   *Use of Abbreviated Titles*

All titles are spelled out fully except Mr., Mrs. and Ms. We use Mr. because it cannot be confused with anything else; we use Mrs. because it is an abbreviation of mistress and you certainly would not want to use that, and we use Ms (no period, note) because it stands for nothing and cannot be spelled out. Some writers say Dr. is OK. I disagree. I once met a Doctor Drive whose name could be abbreviated as "Dr. Dr." That can be rough on copy readers. We rarely use Mr. because it is a title of respect, not simply a statement of marital status, as is Mrs.

All titles except Mr., Mrs. and Ms should be spelled out. That includes Professor, Doctor, Lieutenant Colonel, Private First Class and The Reverend.

2.33   *The Clergy*

And that brings us to the clergy. We will not attempt here to get into the complexities of forms of address and titles of the various denominations. Both the AP and the UPI stylebooks have excellent discussions of the form for clerical titles. If in doubt, call the man or woman in question and ask. Remember, forms of address vary widely from one denomination to another, and it is possible to offend deeply by using the wrong form of title or address. Another thing to remember: Reverend is an honorific denoting a member of the clergy, not part of the person's name, so reference is always to "The Reverend."

2.34   *Acronyms*

We live in a world of acronyms--a word made up of the first letters of a longer title, such as "NATO." Acronyms are fine in broadcast copy as long as they are well-enough known to the public at large. Deciding to use them is usually a matter of your own familiarity with the name. "NATO" certainly is OK to use on first reference; so is "RADAR." The audience might be less well-informed if you used "North Atlantic Treaty Organization" or "radio detecting and ranging device. To be a true acronym the formation must be a pronounceable word.

2.35   Non-acronymic Abbreviations

There are many groups of initials we frequently use that cannot be pronounced, but they are to be preferred over the full name of the organization: "N-double-A-C-P" is an example. However, AFL-CIO is considered an exception to the hyphenation rule because it is difficult to write and to read when it is written as "A-F-L--C-I-O."

2.36   Use of Hyphens and Periods in Abbreviations

Note the hyphenation when you want each letter pronounced as a separate word and the lack of hyphens in the true acronyms where the whole group of letters is pronounced as one word. Note, too, the use of hyphens where in normal writing there would be periods. Another rule exception: Only in the case of a person's initials do we use periods, otherwise use hyphens. It is "H.L. Mencken," but "U-S," "U-N" and "P-M." It has been suggested that P-M can be confused with Prime Minister. I think the possibility of confusion is very small because either would be used in such different contexts. But we all know about Murphy's Law . . . if something can be confused, it will be.

2.37   The Abbreviation of State, City and Street Names

We've already discussed the nonabbreviation of most titles. The same rule applies to just about everything else that you want pronounced fully. Do not abbreviate the words *Street*, *Place*, *Drive* and so on. Do not abbreviate the names of the states. Do not abbreviate directions such as West or North. Intermediate compass points are written as one word: Northwest, but it is East Southeast. Do not abbreviate the names of cities such as Saint Louis or Fort Worth.

I must admit some writers claim "St." is all right because it is so well known. But it can be confused with street. *See* Murphy's Law in 2.36.

2.38   The Use of A.M. and P.M.

Some writers, in an effort to be more conversational, advise us to avoid the use of a.m. and p.m. and instead say "this morning" or "tomorrow afternoon." I really don't object to A-M and P-M, but they must be written in CAPS and with a hyphen. *See 2.36.*

2.39   *The Use of Contractions*

There are also differing schools of thought on the use of contractions. Some writers believe the use of contractions makes the copy less formal and more conversational. That may be true, but it can also lead to misunderstanding. It is especially true of negative contractions where the *n't* can easily be missed by either the reader or the listener. "Can't" can be confused with "can"--"cannot" cannot. Often, too, you will want to use the "not" for emphasis. I find no trouble with some contractions such as that's, there's, there'll and so on. "Won't" is probably the only negative contraction that's safe. It cannot be confused with its positive form, "will." But there are parts of the country where "want" sounds just like "won't."

2.40   *Collective Nouns*

Collective nouns give many writers special problems. Again, it probably has to do with the emphasis on colloquial and conversational style rather than on literary correctness. There is the argument that certain constructions, although grammatically correct, sound horrid when spoken. An example is the treatment of the word *couple* as a collective noun. In some instances it must be a collective, but in others it is strained, at best. "The couple are going," is clearly wrong. However, listen to this: "The couple is going; it will arrive in an hour." Now, that's just awful. "The couple is going" is just fine and is correct. But to refer to the couple as "it," in the second part of that sentence, although correct in agreeing with the first phrase, is grating on the ear and so far from colloquial speech as to make the meaning unclear. If the collective noun in that example were *family* or *team*, however, it would be treated as a singular all the way. Go for what sounds best, and poses the least threat to the sentence.

Other collective nouns that should be treated as singulars unless the meaning of the sentence is endangered are such words as *dollars* (when referring to a bulk of money), *miles, council* and *committee.*

2.41   *Singulars That Look Like Plurals*

The special problems brought up by collective singulars that look like plurals cause real trouble: "One-million-dollars has been spent." Here, "dollars" looks plural, but it's really singular because what we are talking about is a single unit of one million dollars, not one million individual dollars. The same reasoning holds true for the other examples above and many others.

2.42   *Proper Names Ending in "S"*

Also troublesome for broadcasters are proper names that end with *s*. Dealing with plurals and possessives of such names can be maddening. Let's use Jones as an example. The plural of Jones is Joneses. The singular possessive can be either Jones' or Jones's, both pronounced Joneses. The plural possessive is Joneses'. Got that?

Also when dealing with names that end in *s* keep in mind how they will sound on the air. "Hodges's body" sounds terrible--rewrite. "The victim's body . . ." sounds much better. The name and body don't have to go side by side.

2.43   *Avoid Writing What the Audience Must Figure Out*

Never write anything the listeners have to figure out. They don't have time. Remember, listeners have no way of knowing where your sentence is going until they hear it all.

If they have to stop listening part way through to dope out some math problem or figure out what you mean by "two days later," they'll lose the sense of what you're trying so hard to tell them.

2.44   *Avoid Math Problems*

Always do the math. Often stories will appear with a lead like "Six men have been named to the Island Pond Chamber of Commerce Committee on Roach Control." Then in the body of the story, seven men are named. This is so common a fault, as is the genetic inability of reporters to add columns of figures, that every time numbers appear in a story they should be checked. Take no one's calculations for granted. Always do the math.

2.45   *Punctuation*

Proper punctuation is just as important in broadcast news copy as in any other form of writing. It is necessary for the writer to learn its somewhat different form, and to recognize that news anchors frequently have personal preferences on sentence structure.

Punctuation in broadcast news copy is somewhat modified from normal usage, to help the person who has to read the copy on the air.

2.46   *Use of Dashes*

Use periods normally at the end of sentences. However, use many dashes rather than commas and semicolons. Set off phrases--such as this one--with dashes. A dash on a standard typewriter or computer terminal is formed by using a double hyphen--like that. Dashes tell the reader that a slight pause is needed, or inflection might need to be altered. Dashes can also be used where a comma normally would be placed in order to help the flow of the story. Use lots of dashes.

Use commas normally in separating words in a series and to separate the names of cities and states, as in "Helena, Montana."

2.47   *Avoid Parentheses*

NEVER use a parenthetical phrase. Parentheses are used only to set off material in the body of the story that is not intended to be read on the air--((PAUSE)), for example. Note the parentheses are doubled and the instruction to the reader is written in all CAPS to further assure it will not be read aloud. If you must use a parenthetical phrase--and usually you should not--set it off with dashes. If you find you have written a sentence that needs a parenthetical phrase to explain it, you have written a bad sentence for broadcast news use and you should start over. Remember: Simplify. Keep your sentences short, clean, direct and uncomplicated.

2.48   *Avoid Direct Quotations*

Do not use quotation marks. In fact, avoid using direct quotations wherever possible. There are times, of course, when a person's exact words are necessary. In those cases, use the exact words, but precede them with some sort of introductory phrase, such as "These were the mayor's exact words," or something similar. If the quotation is long, it's a good idea to interject a phrase such as "still quoting" somewhere midway. Do not EVER say "quote" and "unquote." That's a holdover from the ancient days of sending news by telegraph when the sending operator needed to be certain the receiving end knew the limits of the quoted material. And, for heaven's sake, don't write the inanity: "He said in his words." He can't say it in anyone else's.

2.49   *Avoid First-Person Quotations*

NEVER use a personal quotation--that is, a quotation including personal pronouns or references such as "I," "We" and "You." That can confuse the listener as to just who is saying it--you or the person quoted--as in "According to Mayor Blatz, 'I have no plans to seek re-election.'" Paraphrase all personal quotations. "Mayor Blatz says he has no plans to seek re-election." Of course, use exact words when they are needed to avoid confusion or are so outrageous it's the only safe way to put them on the air. "As Mayor Blatz put it: Sam Schlotz is a total jerk."

2.50   *Symbols Have No Use*

Most other punctuation marks are to be avoided in broadcast copy. ! @ # $ % & * - + = have no place in what we're doing. They cannot be pronounced.

2.51   *Editing*

Even though you may be a whiz on a keyboard, you're bound to make mistakes. There are ways to correct them--but your anchor isn't going to tolerate very much messy copy. "Dirty" copy is considered a sign of an unreliable writer. There's no time in broadcasting to do much rewriting, so the trick is to make the copy as clean as you can the first time through. The presence of computer terminals in broadcast newsrooms should make editing almost painless--but they also leave no excuse for copy errors. Some people seem unable to spot their own typos on a computer screen--but they glare out in copy or on the prompter. Not all errors are as simple as typos, of course--mistakes in facts or omissions are not easily forgiven by either your audience or your co-workers.

2.52   *Relatively Simple*

Copy editing for broadcast news is relatively simple beside the complexities of print media editing. There is one basic idea to keep in mind: some poor soul--you or someone else--is going to have to read this mess aloud before an audience. Therefore, keep your editing as clean and simple as possible. We're dealing here, of course, with typed copy, not computer-generated. No such on-paper editing should occur with computers.

2.53   *Avoid Proofreader's Marks*

Never use those newspaper editing marks you may have learned in journalism school. They mean nothing to a broadcaster and just mess up the copy.

2.54   *Correcting an Error*

If you have made an error--a typo or the wrong word or whatever--COMPLETELY OBLITERATE the entire offending word and write the correction in block printing above the error. NEVER change just one or two letters in a word--change the whole word. Never assume the reader is going to figure out the typo--always fix it. If you catch the error while the story is still in your typewriter, of course, you can X-out the bad word and type in the correction above it.

2.55 *Exceptions*

If you fail to indent for a paragraph, forget it--don't use a proofreader's graph mark. If you type a lowercase letter where you want a capital, go ahead and block print the capital over the little letter (see, I told you these rules are not carved in stone), so long as it is clearly legible.

2.56 *Inserting Omitted Material*

If you have left out some material that needs to be inserted into the body of a story, print it in between the lines if it's only a few words. If it's going to take more than one line, start the whole story over. Any time you are penciling in something to be read, make certain it can be read. That is, use block printing that is clearly legible.

2.57 *Pronouncers*

Pronouncer is the term commonly used to describe phonetically written pronunciation guides in broadcast copy. The guides are usually ad hoc--that is, made up by the writers as they go along--but they do emerge remarkably alike from various writers.

2.58 *Use of Guides*

Every newsroom should have a pronunciation guide to unusual (or unusually pronounced) local family and place names. USE THE GUIDE.

2.59 *Effects of Mispronunciations*

There is nothing that will damage the reputation and credibility of a news operation more quickly and more thoroughly than the mispronunciation of well-known local names. How can the audience depend on the accuracy of the facts of your story if you don't even know basic things like the pronunciation of local names? Correct pronunciation--that is, "correct" in your locality--is crucially important. This cannot be stressed too strongly.

2.60 *Watch for Local Anomalies*

Near the locality where this is written, for example, there is a city named Buena Vista. Every person who knows anything about language recognizes it as a Spanish name, meaning roughly "Pretty View." And in Spanish it is pronounced BWAYN-uh VEES-tuh. But here it is pronounced BYOO-nuh VIHS-tuh.

2.61   *Writing Pronouncers in Copy*

Note how the pronunciation guide is written in the above paragraph. It is called phonetic spelling and that is the way all pronunciation guides should be written for broadcast--in such a way as to provide the actual sound of the word. This is the ONLY way to write pronouncers for broadcast news copy. Do not underline stressed syllables. Do not use dictionary-style diacritical marks. Do not--as the wire service broadcast circuits do--use an apostrophe to indicate stress. (The wire service broadcast news circuits are transmitted in all-uppercase, so they cannot use upper- and lowercase to indicate stressed syllables.) Sometimes it is helpful to the reader to use the "rhymes-with" approach to pronunciation. You might write "Wythe ((RHYMES WITH SMITH))." Note that in all cases, the pronouncer is enclosed in double parentheses following the troublesome word. Especially when you are writing for someone else, use pronouncers freely. It is not necessary, except in very difficult cases, to write in a pronouncer more than once. If the word or name is that difficult, it's probably better to work around it on subsequent references.

2.62   *Wire Service Pronunciation Guides*

The AP and UPI both have pronunciation guides in their style handbooks. In addition, they provide pronouncers for unusual names that come into the news on a day-to-day basis.

When you are rewriting wire copy, however, you should convert their method of depicting pronunciation to the method we have discussed here, which is simply showing stressed syllables in uppercase and unstressed ones in lowercase, and showing vowel sounds phonetically--the way they sound.

You will find a phonetic spelling guide at the beginning of Part Four, "Usage Guide."

2.63   *Pronunciation*

It has been suggested that there be a section on "performance" included in this manual. I believe such a subject to be beyond the scope of what we're discussing here. There are a number of books on the subject. However, there are certain commonly occurring language flaws that could come under the heading "performance." These fall in the general area of lazy or careless pronunciation. Some of them also appear in the usage guide section. These problems do not stem from accent, although some of them seem to occur more frequently in certain regions of the country. Professional speakers--those who make their living speaking the language aloud--absolutely must use it correctly, not only finding the right words, but speaking them as they should be spoken. Let's look at a few of them to give you the general idea.

Also is a two-syllable word: ALL-soh. Many younger radio and television people say AW-so. Learn to get your tongue around that *l*.

Temperature must be fully pronounced--not TEM-puh-chur.

Words with the -LE ending often get pronounced as if they ended in -OH. Peanut BRITT-oh. Again, it's the lazy *l*.

Days of the week should, for broadcast purposes, be fully pronounced. *Monday* is MUHN-day, not MUHN-dee. Dictionaries disagree on this. Broadcasters do not--universally saying -DAY.

The lazy *t* is a problem. A few years ago there was a commercial for a toothbrush said to have been "invenned by a dennis."

Some words are hard to say--but say them we must. Both *r's* in *February* and *library* are pronounced.

Some people toss in extra letters, such as an *r* in *Washington* so it comes out *Warshington*. In parts of Massachusetts and elsewhere your male parent is called your *farther*.

Texans and others substitute *i* for an *e* or *a* in many words: the U.S. *Sinit* (Senate).

The lazy *l* strikes again in *million* when it comes out MEE-yun.

A recent change that Elster claims emerged in the '80s is pronouncing *negotiate* as neh-GOH-see-ate. It's neh-GOH-shee-ate. He blames broadcasters for the "oh-so-precious" SEE.

We include *sandwich* in the Usage Guide as being mispronounced SAN-widge, SAN-witch, SANG-widge and so on. It is SAND-witch.

Here's a lazy *u*. MAN-uh-FAC-chur. It's MAN-yoo-FAC-chur.

Ours often comes out of midwestern mouths as ARS.

It's a *miracle* that so many people say MEER-kul.

Also in the Usage Guide is *diphtheria* and its cousins with the *phth* combination. It is fully pronounced: diff-*THIR*-ee-uh.

2.64   *The Weather*

What is it about the weather? We hear more barbarous use of language in TV weather programs than in almost any other instance, except in the sports and that's a lost cause, I fear. The weather may be, too. Weatherpeople on radio and television, apparently trying to be informal or cute, come up with some real whoppers. It seems they're not thinking about the logic of what they are saying. Yes, in most cases, they are ad-libbing, working without a script. But that does not excuse a professional broadcaster from the responsibility of using grammatical and logical language.

2.65   *Mangled Language*

"Three inches of rainfall has fallen." "We can expect a 40-percent chance of rainfall tomorrow." No. A chance of rain, perhaps, but not rainfall.

Rainfall is rain that has already fallen. We predict rain, we measure rainfall. "Rain shower activity." A shower is by definition both rain and an activity. That's a double-headed redundancy. OK, there is talk of snow "showers" but what they really mean is snow flurries.

2.66   *Some Examples*

How often have you heard it said that the thermometer is falling? It'll break. It's the temperature that's falling, not the thermometer. What about "temperatures will warm up"?   No. The weather will warm up, the temperature will rise.

There is one accepted use in which a weather instrument is said to be moving: the old sea-dog who says "The glass is falling (or rising)" as he looks at his barometer. That's informal, at best.

How's this for mind-bending logic? "We can expect a widely scattered shower." How can one shower be scattered, even widely? Think about what you are saying--make sense.

A few other weather observations: Celsius is dead. Has been since 1744. It confuses a lot of people to have to deal with two sets of temperature figures, one of which is generally meaningless. On the other hand, we must recognize that the United States is home to many people who have emigrated from foreign lands where the metric system--including Celsius temperature measurement--is in use. There is disagreement among newspeople whether to use the Celsius reading. A lot may depend on where you are. In a major metropolitan area with significant foreign population, its use might be advisable, as it would be were you located near a national border where you may have a significant audience in Canada or Mexico.

The word *presently* is not synonymous with *currently*. To say "the temperature is presently 60 degrees" is nonsense. *Presently* means "soon," "in the near future." Some authorities have caved in on this one and are saying *presently* means both "now" and "soon." That, too, is nonsense.

"The winds are calm." Think about it. If the air is calm, there is no wind, so winds cannot be calm. There may be no wind, in which case say there is no wind, or the air is calm.

Only when referring to wind do we use the compass point it is coming FROM. In all other references to direction we speak of the point toward which something is moving. A northerly wind blows a boat in a southerly direction.

2.67   *Chamber of Commerce Mentality*

Finally, on a somewhat different plane, serious thought needs to be given to what might be called the Chamber of Commerce approach to weather: sun is good, rain is bad, hot is bad, cold is bad, mild is good. Radio and TV weatherpeople speak of the "threat" or "risk" of rain or snow. Surely, there are few times when the words *threat* or *risk* are not overstating the case. This is not to say that weather warnings should be avoided--but let's save some words for when we really need them.

PART THREE

THE LAW

3.1   *The Law*

I preface this section with a caution: I am not a lawyer. What I present here is my understanding of some of the law of broadcasting and of journalism that weighs on the news department and individual journalists. Your news department should have, at the very least, a company lawyer on retainer who is familiar with communication law. This section is intended to raise your consciousness about legal problems that might arise. It is not intended as a field guide to safe and happy broadcasting.

3.2   *The FCC and News*

The Federal Communications Commission has very little in its rules, regulations and policies impinging directly on the content of news programs because the First Amendment says government may not get involved in such things. But there are some areas where the FCC's rules, regulations and policies do seem to violate the First Amendment's intent. Such things as the prohibition against reporting lottery information, and the use of indecent, profane or obscene language is in the law or rules.

On the other hand, the political access rules (Section 315) and the at least temporarily defunct Fairness Doctrine, as well as a few other rules and regulations, require that broadcasters put things on the air they may not wish to. That, too, is seen by some to be an infringement of the broadcast journalist's constitutional protection from government interference.

It is a fact that the U.S. Supreme Court has opined that broadcasting does not enjoy the same full protection of the First Amendment as do the printed media, because it is so "pervasive." That argument is not accepted by many broadcast journalists. The Radio-Television News Directors Association and other groups wage a continuing battle to establish parity with the print media.

Until that takes place, however, the broadcaster must adhere to the FCC's "rules and regs," as they are known. For the front office in a broadcasting station, the ever-changing FCC directives can be maddening. For the news room, it's not quite such a burden. The recent atmosphere favoring deregulation has seen the abolition of the Fairness Doctrine but not the political equal time rules. Such rules must still be the concern of the news department as well as other departments of a broadcast station. The news operation also plays a major role in the station's "promise versus performance" equation.

3.3   *Promise Versus Performance*

Broadcasting stations must file with the FCC on a regular basis statements indicating community problems the station has identified and what it intends to do about them through its programming. The news department, wearing its public affairs hat, will often get involved in that process. The "performance" may take the form of a series of feature stories, a documentary or other special programming to address community problems. How well a station follows through on its promise of meeting community needs may be taken into account at license renewal time.

3.4   *Section 315*

Section 315 of the Federal Communications Act of 1934, as amended, contains the political equal time rules. Stated very simply, the section says that when a broadcaster provides air time, free or paid for, to one candidate for a given public office, he must make equal time available to all other candidates for that same office. Bona fide news stories and events are exempt from the rule, as are documentaries where the candidate's appearance is incidental to the content of the documentary. A broadcaster may, in the case of local and state elections, decide not to provide time to any candidate. But in the case of federal elections, which include elections for Congress, the broadcaster must provide time if the candidates request it, and must provide that time at the lowest possible cost on the station's rate card.

Broadcast journalists in the day-to-day reporting on politicians will worry very little about Section 315. They will, however, be aware of balance in the coverage of rival candidates as a matter of journalistic fairness.

3.5   *The Fairness Doctrine*

The FCC has declared the Fairness Doctrine to be null and void on constitutional grounds. The commission was upheld by the courts. However, there is a strong movement in Congress to legislate broadcast fairness. Broadcasters will need to keep a close eye on such activity.

While Section 315 deals with people--candidates for public office--the Fairness Doctrine dealt with issues, specifically controversial issues. It was intended to ensure that "controversial issues of public importance" are addressed fairly by broadcasters. It said--again to be very simple about it--that whenever broadcasters allowed one side of a controversial issue of public importance to be aired, they had a positive obligation to seek out responsible spokesmen for all other sides of that issue and provide them with equivalent opportunity. (Note the difference between "equal time" and "equivalent opportunity.") Most broadcasters recognize their own self-interest in being fair. To act otherwise would alienate portions of their audience. The demise of the Fairness Doctrine does not seem to have had great effect on the airing of public issues. To be sure, some broadcasters prefer not to get involved in controversial issues.

3.6   *Personal Attack Rule*

Within the Fairness Doctrine there was also a "personal attack rule" which provides reply opportunity for a person who may have been attacked on the air--but it must have been an attack within the context of a controversial issue of public importance. To say John Jones is a jerk is not, in the meaning of the Personal Attack Rule, a personal attack.

However, to say John Jones is a jerk because he does not believe in the death penalty, probably would count as a personal attack. And when such an attack does take place on your station, the station must make time available to Jones to reply, if so desired. The Personal Attack Rule survived the nullifying of the Fairness Doctrine, as did the following item.

3.7   *Editorial Endorsements of Candidates*

Like the Personal Attack Rule, this rule was originally to be found in the Fairness Doctrine. Included are provisions for reply when a broadcaster editorially endorses or comes out opposed to a candidate for public office. Here is the gray area where the Fairness Doctrine and Section 315 seem to overlap. But notice that in this rule the reply is to a statement by the broadcaster, while under Section 315, the reply is to a statement by a rival candidate. The preceding discussions of Section 315 and the remaining features of the Fairness Doctrine are bare bones. These can be very complicated issues, and you will find more thorough treatment of them in basic   texts   on   broadcast   newswriting,   telecommunications   or communications law.

3.8   *Rebroadcasting Signals*

Generally, it is a violation of the law to rebroadcast an intercepted radio signal, such as police dispatchers talking to patrol cars. Such intercepted information may be used as tips for news coverage, but may not be used as a primary source of news.

There is an exception to the prohibition against using intercepted radio signals. In emergency situations, radio messages sent by amateur (ham) radio operators may be used by news broadcasters--either directly, on tape, or the information used to develop a story. You must use caution. Many times the hams will be relaying information they have received from someone else--second, third or more hands away. There is no assurance their information is correct, not exaggerated or timely. However, many hams are organized into one of several groups trained to handle emergency "traffic" in and out of areas where normal means of communications are disrupted. Those direct reports from the scene are generally accurate, timely and reliable. Hams, you should know, are also licensed by the FCC after a difficult examination. There's a good chance one or more of your station's engineers will be licensed hams. They can give you a great deal of information. Citizens Band operators are not required to take examinations nor to be truly "licensed." There is some question as to the legality of using intercepted CB signals. I would avoid them.

3.9   *Taping Telephone Interviews*

Many radio reporters rely very heavily on their telephones both for routine reporting and for getting interviews. It is perfectly all right to tape record a telephone interview IF you have first obtained the permission of the subject.

The best way to do that is to make the call with the tape recorder running, and ask if it's all right to tape the conversation for possible use on the air. If the subject agrees, you have that agreement on tape. If the subject disagrees, my advice would be to stop the tape and continue with taking notes. Telephone taping laws vary from state to state. In some states, all parties to a taping must, by law, know what's going on. In other states, only one party needs to be aware that a tape is being made. Those laws are intended to prevent illegal wiretaps, but they also apply to all telephone taping.

3.10   *Obscenity, Indecency, Profanity*

Social values change rapidly, and this is one area where change is very apparent. I don't think I've ever heard what I would consider a true obscenity deliberately uttered in a news program. But what many people think of as profanities are being allowed to air daily. These are usually uttered by interview subjects or people making statements, but there have been cases where correspondents--that is, professional, trained broadcasters--have been heard to spill some pretty rotten stuff on the air.

My personal beliefs in this area go back to my training in early 1950s radio where "darn" was forbidden and where we were not permitted to play even an instrumental version of a record the vocal version of which contained "questionable" lyrics. I still have trouble with the deliberate airing of profanity. Just call me old-fashioned.

3.11   *Lotteries*

Comes now a complicated issue. A lottery is illegal, unless sponsored by a state or somehow otherwise exempt from the law. A broadcaster is not permitted by law to knowingly promote any criminal act. So, it is illegal to promote a lottery--EXCEPT where the station is located in a state that has its own legal lottery. Then the station may broadcast advertisements, information and winning ticket numbers for its home-state lottery. Stations in adjacent states may also broadcast that information, even though they may be licensed to another state. It is unclear whether the state of license must also conduct a lottery. The wording of the law is ambiguous on that point. Some communications lawyers have said that the state of license must also have its own lottery. If, however, your state does not have a legal lottery, nor does an adjacent state, you will be in violation of federal law, and probably your own state law, to in any way promote a lottery, no matter how worthy the organization conducting it. As a journalist, you might get caught on this one by running a feature story on a church conducting a lottery.

So, how do you know when a lottery is a lottery and not just an innocent contest? There are three elements that must be present to constitute a lottery: consideration, chance and prize.

That may sound pretty simple, but it can get messy. "Consideration" is anything a person must pay or do to enter the lottery or collect the prize. Simply being present usually does not constitute consideration, unless the admission price was uncommonly high. A requirement that one must be present to win may constitute consideration.

Definitions of consideration vary from state to state. If in doubt, check with your local counsel. "Chance" is self-explanatory--there must be an element of chance in the awarding of the prize. And the "prize" is similarly not troublesome. There must be a prize or there's no lottery. Even charity raffles can be lotteries. Take care.

3.12   *Emergency Announcements*

The station's programming and traffic people and engineers need to be concerned about compliance with the Emergency Broadcast System requirements. Those requirements include visual (in television) captioning of the EBS message for the hearing-impaired. EBS originally was intended to warn of enemy attack. Today its use is pretty much limited to severe weather warnings. Every station is required to periodically conduct a test of the system. I'm sure you've all heard the familiar complex tone that is broadcast prior to an announcement that usually begins "This is only a test . . . ." I believe it's a good idea for the news department to provide visual captioning for any important announcement. You can imagine the fear that would be struck into the hearts of the deaf to see something on the screen that read: "WEATHER ALERT" and not have any idea what was happening. Most TV stations today have some sort of character generator that can be used to quickly create a written message to air along with the aural announcement. It's a rare emergency announcement that cannot wait two minutes to be captioned before airing. There's one more requirement related to this. TV stations broadcasting primarily in a foreign language must caption emergency messages in both English and the foreign language.

3.13   Other Legal Matters

There are other laws affecting the practice of all journalism, not just broadcast, which are not part of the Federal Communications Act. They come generally under the heading of freedom of information and shield laws.

3.14   Freedom of Information

Sometimes called sunshine laws, Freedom of Information laws in all states provide in various ways that meetings of public bodies be open to the public (and the media) to assure that governing bodies are accountable to the public and that the public's business is conducted openly. These laws vary greatly among the states and it is beyond the scope of this discussion to get into detail. In some states the sunshine law is absolute--nothing is exempted. In others, there may be a long list of exceptions. The laws differ in significant detail, specifying just what constitutes a governing body, what constitutes a "meeting," what subjects may be exempted and what recourse the public and the media have when improper secrecy is practiced. It is perhaps unfortunate that some, especially local, governing bodies seem to believe that they can deliberate "more efficiently" out of the public's view. They have devised ingenious ways to avoid having the public and the press viewing their decision making, including "informal information sessions," telephone conference calls, having staff people do the actual negotiating and so on. As a journalist, it is up to you to assure that these bodies conduct public business in public.

3.15   Open Records Laws

In addition, there are open records laws on the state and federal levels under which the public may request specific documents held by the government. The ways in which this may be accomplished are, as with open meetings laws, varied and in some cases complex and time-consuming.

It is the responsibility of individual journalists to know the details of these laws in the states where they may be working, and to know how to go about invoking them and challenging undue official secrecy.

3.16   *Shield Laws*

About half the states have shield laws designed to prevent journalists from being forced to disclose their confidential sources, notes and tape outtakes. The shield laws are not always effective nor are they universally endorsed by journalists. Some experienced reporters prefer to rely on the protection of the First Amendment rather than on an imperfect shield law. Generally, the shield laws protect journalists from enforced disclosure subject to a three-pronged test: (1) The journalist must possess information that is relevant to a violation of the law, (2) the information cannot be obtained in any other way and (3) there must be a showing of a compelling and overriding interest in the information. All three must be present for a shield law to be set aside and the journalist be required to disclose the information or testify before a grand jury or at trial as to confidential information. These conditions having been met, however, a journalist who continues to refuse to disclose confidential information is subject to being found in contempt of court and would likely be jailed and fined for an indefinite period.

3.17   *Libel and Privacy*

In areas of law directly affecting journalists and their work, the laws of libel and privacy are the most likely to change over the next few years. It seems nearly every major case that comes before the U.S. Supreme Court makes some change in the interpretation of the laws of libel. Currently, *New York Times v. Sullivan* of 1964 still sets the guiding principle of "actual malice." However, any time a test of that principle comes before the courts, there is a chance it could be changed, possibly to the detriment of journalism.

The following is derived from the "Libel Manual" section of the AP stylebook, outlining the current state of affairs in the field of libel law. As a working journalist, you must make it your business to keep up with court decisions and adjust your practices accordingly.

3.18   *Avoiding Libel*

There is no sure way to avoid litigation for libel. The best way to protect yourself is to practice fair and accurate journalism. Libel actions are very often more troublesome than serious. Many actions are brought as "nuisance suits" which can be costly, but not very damaging. By far the largest number of suits are won by the plaintiff at the lower court level, but overturned on appeal. Nonetheless, legal fees and other costs in a libel defense can be enormous. It is far better to avoid action where you can.

It is believed that many libel actions can be stopped early in the complaint simply by talking to the person who claims to have been defamed. It has been the traditional response in most newsrooms to take the "We stand by our story" approach. That may be the "professional" or "tough guy" stance so lovingly nurtured by certain journalists since the days of *The Front Page*, but it comes across to the public--especially a member of the public who claims to have been harmed by a journalist--as pure arrogance. I believe many a libel action can be turned aside by simply talking with the complaining person, explaining how journalistic decisions are made and why. There seems to be some evidence that people feel impotent when faced by the media. Libel actions are brought as a means of getting the media's attention. A simple conversation in a sympathetic frame of mind can, it is believed, prevent a lot of expensive grief.

Not all cases, of course, can be turned aside so easily. Some, we must admit, are legitimate. That is what we will examine here.

3.19   *Libel*

The kind of story that is likely to generate a libel action is not the great big story involving great big people. Those kinds of stories usually deal with events and people that fall outside the realm of libel action: public figures, members of Congress and so on.

The stories that generate libel actions are the simple-minded things we deal with every day. They are the wedding stories, the minor crimes, the auto wrecks--the little stories that affect only a very few people, but put those people in a compromising or embarrassing light. The best protection is careful journalism. A phoned-in kidnapping report can be a practical joke, but a terribly embarrassing one for the victim. Everything should be checked out. It is not enough that you acted in good faith with no malicious intent. If you fail to practice careful journalism, you are very likely to get stung in a libel action.

Police and court stories are frequent sources of libel actions. Many of them arise from reporting on an arrest before any charge has been made. Whenever accusations are made against a person, it is very wise to get balancing comment either from the accused or from some other person. It is also prudent to fully identify the accuser.

Simply put, libel is defamation--injury to reputation or character. Anything--words, pictures, even cartoons--that subject a person to public ridicule, hatred, shame or embarrassment, or create a negative opinion of a person, can be libels. Also libelous are stories that may be financially damaging to the subject.

There is only one sure defense against libel and that is if the facts of the story are provably true. The operative word here is *provably*. You must be able to go into a court and persuade the jury that what you published was the actual truth and that you can prove it.

3.20   *Importance of Accuracy*

Errors in facts, imprecise language or failure to double-check can be disastrous.

For example, in a group arrest such as a drug bust, it's very unlikely that all those taken into custody will be facing identical charges. Some will be charged with possession with intent to distribute, others only with possession, others only with possession of a "personal" amount and so on. It is actionable to publish an erroneous charge. There is no better protection than accuracy.

Accurate reporting is not always enough. Reporting the exact words of a person who is libeling someone else is actionable unless there is "privilege." Privilege applies to the speaker and means that whatever is said, no matter how awful, may be published with impunity.

3.21   *Privilege*

Privilege is invoked in a fair and impartial report of a legislative, judicial or other public and official proceeding. However, you must know what constitutes a "public proceeding" in your state. In some states, for example, it is not privileged to report on the filing of a summons before there has been any judicial action.

Privilege is a less comforting defense than accuracy. Absolute privilege means that utterances by certain persons cannot be held to be libelous. As stated above, that applies to legislative debate, court testimony, and public and official proceedings, such as city council meetings. And, by extension, if the person making such utterances cannot be found guilty of libel, then the publication of such utterances cannot be found to be libelous either. Do not be misled. It is the circumstance of the utterance, not the person who's doing the uttering, that's important. A member of Congress is absolutely privileged speaking on the floor of the House. For the same person speaking in a private office, however, privilege does not apply. A lawyer cannot be sued for libel for what is said in a courtroom during the course of a trial, but what is said on the courthouse steps is not protected by privilege. And neither is the publication of what is said.

The concept of "privilege" is based on the assumption that only through free, open and robust debate can the truth or the wisest course of action be determined. It is the same basis--from John Milton--that gives us the concept of freedom of speech and press. To the extent that society needs to hear legislative, judicial and public discussions, the rights of the individual who may be damaged are subordinated to the public interest.

So long as the reporting of privileged material is accurate and fair and free of malice, libel action cannot be brought for the publication of such material. The privilege of the press is considered to be "qualified"; not absolute. It is qualified by the requirement that the report be fair, accurate and free of malice. The journalist is not so fully protected against libel action as is the legislator on the floor of the House.

Generally, however, the journalist is free to report on official, legislative and judicial proceedings without fear of successful libel action.

3.22   *Privilege Laws Vary*

It is important that you know how your state defines official and public proceedings. Some states seal records in marital disputes. If you come upon or are given such a record and somehow feel impelled to publish it, you do so at your peril. You have not only published a potential libel, but you may also have broken state law.

Some occasions that look "official" and "public" are not. For example, a convention of a private organization--including a political party--is not privileged. Statements made on the floor or from the platform may not be privileged.

Publishing a story about a libel suit is a little touchy. How much detail can be safely published without repeating and extending the libel? Most of the time it is safe enough to restrict your story to details of the complaint filed with the court. However, some states do not permit the publication of contents of legal papers until there has been some judicial action.

3.23   *Fair Comment*

Comment and opinion--such as criticism of a play or book--are covered by the concept of "fair comment." Provided the criticism is fair and honest and free of malice, it is protected from libel action.

3.24   *Public Figures*

Beginning with *New York Times v. Sullivan* in 1964, the "public figure" defense has been a useful tool in defeating libel actions. That decision says public figures cannot recover damages for a report related to official duties unless they can prove actual malice. Actual malice means that at the time of the publication, those responsible for the story knew it was false or published with "reckless disregard" as to whether it was true.

This means that a publication is to be free of damages if it is honest in its treatment of a public figure, even if some of the information it published is wrong.

Determining just who is a public figure can be difficult. Clearly, elected and appointed public officials fall in the category of "public figures." That designation has been extended to include actors, professional athletes and, yes, even TV anchor persons. The difficulty emerges when a private person becomes involved in an event of public interest. That person does not, by virtue of that involvement alone, become a public figure.

The courts have said in a series of decisions through the 1970s that public figures are people who have sought public attention--have forced themselves into the limelight. A person forced unwillingly into public attention does not therefore become a public figure. Even involvement in a spectacular crime does not necessarily make the criminal or the victim a public figure.

Furthermore, a person once in the public eye, is not necessarily a public figure forever. A child prodigy, for instance, who may have drawn great attention at the age of nine, but who has lived as a recluse for the past 20 years, probably could no longer be treated as a public figure.

A number of states have enacted so-called negligence standards for libel cases. Under these standards, a plaintiff need prove only that a publication was negligent in its reporting on an individual, not necessarily reckless. That is a much narrower idea, and probably easier to prove.

Lower courts, where libel cases are very often tried before juries, have recently allowed huge damages. Libel judgments in excess of $1 million are not uncommon. Most of them are either considerably reduced or overturned on appeal, but it is still a fearsome thing to face. Not many smaller newspapers or broadcast stations could withstand the financial impact of such a judgment.

3.25 *Privacy*

There is no "right" of privacy as there is a "right" of free speech. It is an evolving concept probably begun by Justice Brandeis early in this century when he spoke of a "right to be left alone." My friend and colleague, Dr. Louis W. Hodges of Washington and Lee University, has developed a concept of "circles of intimacy"; concentric rings around ourselves, each denoting a different level of privacy, with the innermost ring that of self, where no one else gets in, to the outermost, which is the public information that is available about all of us. He says we feel "invaded" when too many people are able to enter rings we prefer to keep closed. We have found this to be a valuable way of looking at the problem of privacy.

Legally, when a person becomes involved in a news event, willingly or not, he no longer has a claim to total privacy.

Ethically, however, this is a matter of serious concern. News pictures, whether on television or in print, evoke powerful emotions and some of these pictures are guaranteed to bring protests of invasion of privacy. Is it, for instance, an invasion of privacy merely to *take* a picture of someone who doesn't want the picture taken, or does the invasion not occur until the picture is actually *published*?

There is no shortage of cases where subjects of news stories or pictures believe they have been invaded.

Generally, courts have held that a person involved in a legitimate news event, as a participant or as a spectator, has lost the right to a claim of privacy as long as the photo does not single that person out for non-news reasons.

Courts have been very sympathetic toward those who claim invasion of their privacy. Judgments are not huge as they are in some libel cases, however.

As in libel, the concept of private figure versus public figure comes into play in privacy cases. Public figures have far less claim to privacy than do private figures. The president of the United States probably has almost no claim to privacy, except in the most intimate details of his personal life. The way a president parts his hair became "news" during one recent administration. The First Lady's taste in decorating the White House is "news."

Matters of privacy are areas where a developing body of ethical thinking applies appropriately. That is, the idea that is added to all the other elements of news--timeliness, proximity, consequence and all the others—should be compassion. It is believed that journalism has evolved, technologically and professionally, beyond the days of *The Front Page*. We are now so well equipped to invade almost anyone's privacy, that we need to give compassionate thought to what we are doing to the subjects of our stories. It is the practice in most newsrooms not to reveal the names of rape victims. What does one do when the rapist is the victim's father? Do we publish the name and address of a mugging victim, giving potential muggers the rundown on an easy mark? Often, we tread on privacy in feature stories where in an effort to be entertaining we wind up inadvertently embarrassing someone taking part in what he believed was a private event. The poor person trying to learn to water-ski, for example, looks ridiculous. It makes marvelous videotape, however, and the temptation to shoot it is great. If the yet-to-be skier is identifiable, there probably is a privacy case.

It seems that the matter of privacy will continue to evolve over the remainder of this century. I believe we can expect the courts to define the issues more clearly than they so far have.

Journalists, I believe, must become more sensitive to the issue of privacy and to the feelings of the people we routinely have covered in a somewhat offhand way. Barring that increasing sensitivity, we are going to find more and more courts happily going after the media in sympathy with offended news subjects.

3.26   Free Press–Fair Trial

The problem of maintaining a free press and fair trial procedures stems from a perceived tension between the First Amendment to the U.S. Constitution and its Sixth Amendment.

3.27   First Amendment

"Congress shall make no law respecting an establishment of religion, or prohibiting the free exercise thereof; or abridging the freedom of speech, or of the press; or the right of the people peaceably to assemble, and to petition the Government for a redress of grievances."

3.28   Sixth Amendment

"In all criminal prosecutions, the accused shall enjoy the right to a speedy and public trial, by an impartial jury of the State and district wherein the crime shall have been committed, which district shall have been previously ascertained by law, and to be informed of the nature and cause of the accusation; to be confronted with the witnesses against him; to have compulsory process for obtaining witnesses in his favor, and to have the Assistance of Counsel for his defense."

If the press is to be free to inform the public of matters of public interest--that is, of matters of which the public has the right to know--then it seems to follow that all matters relating to criminal prosecutions must be open for publication.

However, also a matter of public interest is the assurance that justice is unimpaired, especially in matters of judicial fairness. Most serious journalists will agree there are times when a free press must give way to assure that an accused individual's liberty is not unfairly taken away. That is why these guidelines were developed. They are not always followed precisely by either the press or the courts. Still, Virginia journalists believe they are a valuable statement of principle and, at the very least, show there is an area in this controversy where reasonable persons can agree in the interests of both free press and fair trial.

3.29   *Virginia Voluntary Guidelines*

The following is presented as representative of similar free press—fair trial guidelines in many states--not as a model. The Virginia voluntary guidelines have been in place since 1970, with some modifications over the years. Prior to 1970, problems arose in regard to news coverage of court cases, particularly in criminal cases where the rights of the defendant to an unbiased jury were seen to be jeopardized by pretrial publicity. A ten-member committee of members of the State Bar of Virginia and the news media developed the guidelines that follow.

3.30   *Principles*

*1.   We respect the co-equal rights of a free press and a fair trial.

*2.   The public is entitled to as much information as possible about the administration of justice to the extent that such information does not impair the ends of justice or the rights of citizens as individuals.

*3.   Accused persons are entitled to be judged in an atmosphere free from passion, prejudice, and sensationalism.

*4.   The responsibility for assuring a fair trial rests primarily with the judge who has the power to preserve order in the court and the duty to use all means available to him to see that justice is done. All news media are equally responsible for objectivity and accuracy.

*5.   Decisions about handling the news rest with editors and news directors, but in the exercise of news judgments based on the public's interest the editor or news director should remember that:

   *(a)   An accused person is presumed innocent until found guilty;
   *(b)   Readers, listeners and viewers are potential jurors;
   *(c)   No person's reputation should be injured needlessly.

*6.   No lawyer should exploit any medium of public information to enhance his side of a pending case, but this should not be construed as limiting the public prosecutor's obligation to make available information to which the public is entitled.

*7.   The media, the bar, and law enforcement agencies should cooperate in assuring a free flow of information but should exercise responsibility and discretion when it appears probable that public disclosure of information in prosecutions might prevent a fair trial or jeopardize justice, especially just before trial."

3.31   *Guidelines*

"To assist in decisions on the release of information, in accord with the above principles, these guidelines are recommended:

"1.   The following information generally should be made available for publication at or immediately after an arrest:

"(a)   The accused's name, age, residence, employment, family status and other factual background information.

"(b)   The substance or text of the charge, such as a complaint, indictment, or information and, where appropriate, the identity of the complainant and/or victim.

"(c)   The identity of the investigating and arresting agency or officer and the length of the investigation.

"(d)   The circumstances of arrest, including the time and place of arrest, resistance, pursuit, possession and use of weapons, and a description of items seized.

"(e)   If appropriate, the fact that the accused denies the charge.

"2.   The release of photographs or the taking of photographs of the accused at or immediately after an arrest should not necessarily be restricted by defense attorneys.

"3.   If an arrest has not been made, it is proper to disclose such information as may be necessary to enlist public assistance in apprehending fugitives from justice. Such information may include photographs, descriptions, and other factual background information including records of prior arrests and convictions. However, care should be exercised not to publish information which might be prejudicial at a possible trial.

"4.   The release and publication of certain types of information may tend to be prejudicial without serving a significant function of law enforcement or public interest. Therefore, all concerned should weigh carefully against pertinent circumstances the pre-trial disclosure of the following information, which normally is prejudicial to the rights of the accused:

"(a)   Statements as to the character or reputation of an accused person or a prospective witness.

"(b) Admissions, confessions or the contents of a statement or alibis attributable to the accused, or his refusal to make a statement, except his denial of the charge.

"(c) The performance or results of examinations or tests or the refusal or failure of an accused to take such an examination or test.*

"(d) Statements concerning the credibility or anticipated testimony of prospective witnesses.

"(e) The possibility of a plea of guilty to the offense charged or to a lesser offense, or other disposition.

"(f) Opinions concerning evidence or argument in the case, whether or not it is anticipated that such evidence or argument will be used at trial.

"(g) Prior criminal charges and convictions although they are usually matters of public record. Their publication may be particularly prejudicial just before trial.

"5. When a trial has begun, the news media may report anything done or said in open court. The media should consider very carefully, however, publication of any matter or statements excluded from evidence outside the presence of the jury because this type of information is highly prejudicial and, if it reaches the jury, could result in a mistrial."

"6. Law enforcement and court personnel should not encourage or discourage the photographing or televising of defendants in public places outside the courtroom."

As a broadcast journalist, it is your responsibility to know the practices, laws and guidelines in your state. The guidelines above, you must realize, apply only to Virginia. Furthermore, they are guidelines only, and do not have the force of law.

---

*It has become routine to report that a person accused of drunken driving refused to submit to a blood-alcohol test.

**Many jurisdictions now permit cameras in certain courts. This same prohibition, or something similar, applies to live or recorded in-court television.

PART FOUR

USAGE GUIDE

Introduction

There is no excuse for a professional writer to use the language in a sloppy or plainly incorrect manner.

Misuse of the language is malpractice.

Words are the tools of the journalist. As with any craft or art, the tools must be of the highest quality, kept in good condition and used with care and precision.

There are honest disagreements among excellent writers on matters of usage, but most would not forgive careless misuse.

So many misuses and careless uses have crept into our daily speech it's not possible to catalogue them all. Those included here are frequently heard and constitute what I think of as some of the worst of the linguistic pollution.

We are not talking about slang here--most slang has no place in serious newswriting. What we are about to examine are examples of the common misuse of ordinary words. I suppose every writer has favorite linguistic horrors heard or seen with distressing frequency. I suppose that's what leads us to compile usage guides.

This guide is intended to be especially for broadcast writers, but one will find many entries that would apply to all good writing. All of these I have collected listening and reading. Some are included because they are frequently mispronounced, not necessarily misused. Some of the entries would not be considered "good" words for broadcast news. Use words that are comfortable for you--that fit easily on your tongue. If you are uncomfortable, your audience will sense that discomfort and this will get in the way of efficient communication.

Many words have many meanings. For the most part we will look at the primary or most common meanings and usages. After all, we are trying to communicate--so we should do it in the least complicated and most readily understood way we can.

The Usage Guide A-Z

A/An The rule of thumb (or tongue) here is if the first sound of the following word is a vowel use *AN*, if the sound is a consonant you want *A*. It's the sound that's important, not the spelling. I still cling to *an* historic . . .," even though many experts now claim because the *h* in history is sounded (aspirated) the word should be preceded by *A*. I would say "*A* history book." Note the *h* in history is sounded (aspirated) and therefore takes *A*. The *h* in historic is almost not sounded, so *AN* is preferable. Many words change their pronunciation and syllabic emphasis from their noun to adjective forms. A problem with *A/AN* arises when we use them preceding abbreviations and acronyms. Do we use *A* or *AN* before RTNDA? It should be "*A* Radio and Television News Directors Association committee," but "*An* RTNDA committee," because we're dealing with the sound of the following word. That's the way to handle it for broadcast. In print, I have seen well-written and well-edited pieces using both methods.

Ability/Capacity *ABILITY* is simply the power to do something. *CAPACITY* has to do with the power to hold or contain.

About/Almost/Around These words are frequently used interchangeably, but there is a distinction. *ABOUT* and *AROUND* are references to place, while *ALMOST* refers to number or quantity.

Above When used as a back-reference, as in "as mentioned *ABOVE*," the word only sends listeners racing through their memories to try to recall what you're talking about--thereby missing the rest of the story. Avoid such use. The same can be said for other such back-references as "former" and "latter."

Abysmal/Abyssal Closely related words both having to do with great depth. *ABYSMAL* is the broader of the two terms, meaning immeasurably low condition or huge extension downward. We speak of *abysmal* poverty. *ABYSSAL* refers to the greatest depths of the ocean, unfathomably deep. An *abyss* does not necessarily have to be in the ocean--it can be any deep chasm.

Accelerate Is pronounced ak-CELL-ur-ayt.

Accessory Is pronounced ak-SESS-ur-ee. There is no such word as *assessory*. An *ACCESSORY* is a person indirectly involved in a crime: *accessory* before or after the fact. The word is also used to describe an article that may be enhancing, such as a purse, necktie or whitewall tires.

Accident/Mishap Some newswriters try to avoid the word *ACCIDENT* in highway crash stories, contending they are seldom truly *accidents*, but caused by carelessness or stupidity. That may be a bit extreme, but it does point up the real meaning of the word. An *accident* is an event that occurs without planning or direct cause. A *MISHAP* is a minor accident, so a serious auto crash should not be termed a *mishap*. Usage has it, by the way, that accidents "occur," they do not "happen."

Accused/Alleged/Suspected *ACCUSED* carries the connotation of a formal charge. *ALLEGED* is an assertion of truth--or questionable truth--but does not indicate a charge has been made. *SUSPECTED* is about the same as *alleged*. *Alleged* and *suspected* should be used with great care in crime stories. Make sure someone you can quote has made the allegation.

Acme/Epitome *ACME* is pronounced AK-mee, *EPITOME* is pronounced ee-PIT-oh-mee. *Acme* means the summit--the top--the best. *Epitome* means the best example--a typical representation--ideal form. There is another, uncommonly used, meaning of *epitome* which is to represent in brief or summary form. Neither is a great broadcast word.

Acre/Tract *ACRE* and *TRACT* both refer to land. It is redundant to write "An *acre* of land." You can't have an *acre* of anything else. Actually, you can--we speak of *acres* of sailcloth, for example. But that's simply a metaphor, meaning enough sailcloth to cover acres of land. *Tract*, however, does have other meanings--as in political or religious tracts--pamphlets, theses. However, when the context of the story clearly relates to land, *tract* standing alone is to be preferred.

A.D./B.C. *A.D.* is the abbreviation of anno Domini; in the year of the Lord. The reference is to years in the Christian era, since the birth of Jesus of Nazareth. *B.C.* is the abbreviation of before Christ. The usage is 463 *B.C.*, but *A.D.* 1776. In broadcast copy the form would be "B-C" and "A-D."

Adapt/Adopt These are somewhat related words that are often confused. *ADAPT* means to adjust or to accommodate, to make suitable to the situation. Earlier it was pointed out that newswriters must *adapt* to the style in use in the newsroom where they find themselves. *ADOPT* means to take on a change or relationship. In the above sentence, we could have said newswriters must *adopt* the style of their newsroom. *See also* **Adopted**.

Addict An *ADDICT* is a person physically habituated to a substance or some other addictive thing. It should not be used in the sense of having the practice of or being a devotee. A person may be devoted to classical music--but would not be called an *addict*.

Ade/Aid/Aide/AIDS *ADE* is a kind of soft drink made with sweetened fruit juice and water--lemonade. To *AID* is to give help or support. An *AIDE* is a person whose job is to provide help or support for a person of rank. Originally it was "*aide*-de-camp," meaning an assistant to a military officer, now shortened to *aide* and broadened in meaning to refer to virtually anyone who is hired to serve in a support or advisory position. *AIDS* is the acronym for *a*cquired *i*mmuno*d*eficiency *s*yndrome. It is well-enough known to stand alone in broadcast news stories. Take care not to write "*AIDS* syndrome," thereby saying "syndrome" twice. *See also* **HIV**.

Adjacent/Contiguous *ADJACENT* in most common use means to be nearby, but not touching. *CONTIGUOUS* means to be touching along boundaries. Virginia and North Carolina are *contiguous* states. The West Indies is a group of *adjacent* islands.

Admit/Confess *ADMIT* has a number of meanings, probably the most common of which is to allow to enter. Another common use has to do with acknowledging fact--the witness *admits* to having seen the crime. However, it does not have the sense of *CONFESS*, in the acknowledgment of one's guilt, either in court or as a penitent before a priest, although it is frequently used that way. In your copy, use *confess* when you're talking about criminals telling what they did. Not only is that usage more precise, it also avoids a possible confusion. In court, judges are said to *admit* evidence when they allow it to be placed in the record.

Adopted/Adoptive The child is *ADOPTED*, the parents and siblings are said to be *ADOPTIVE*.

Adult/Explicit Both have come to have the meaning of pornographic, obscene, fit only for grown-ups. Euphemisms to be avoided. *EXPLICIT* means unmistakably clear--leaving nothing in doubt.

Adverse/Averse *ADVERSE* means opposing, acting against. *AVERSE* means to have a feeling of dislike or distaste.

Advice/Advise *ADVICE* is the noun, *ADVISE* is the verb form. *Advice* is what an *advisor* gives. *Advise* is pronounced ad-VYZ.

Aerial/Antenna There was a time when *ANTENNAS* were called *AERIALS*, but now the accepted term is *antenna*. In AM radio, the entire tower is the radiating or receiving element, and they get shorter as frequency increases. In television and FM, the tower supports a radiating element, so the towers can be of any height. The higher the better, in fact.

Affect/Effect The confusion with this pair will probably be with us forever. *AFFECT* means to influence or to have a bearing upon someone or something. *EFFECT* means to bring about, to accomplish. That is the verb form. As a noun, you almost always want *effect*. "She was deeply *affected* by his presence." "That was the exact *effect* he wanted."

Affidavit A document, usually legal, containing a statement made under oath. A deposition in which testimony is sworn. Note especially the spelling--it is *affiDAVIT*, not *david*.

Affinity Except in some scientific applications such as partical physics, only people feel an *AFFINITY* toward one another. The word originally had to do with marriage, but now means a general attraction. It does not mean a liking for something other than another human. A person might have a deep liking for reading, for example, but would not be said to have an *affinity* for it. Again, we're up against common usage which is probably going to broaden the definition.

Affluent/Effluent *AFFLUENT* is an adjective usually indicating wealth-- "our *affluent* society." It has the sense of a strong flow. *EFFLUENT* also has the sense of flowing, but usually refers to an environmental pollutant such as sewage.

Aftermath An *AFTERMATH* always follows something bad--such as a flood or fire. It is the resulting wreckage or devastation. It is not correct to refer to the *aftermath* of an election or a party. Unless it was one stupendous party!

Afterward/Toward/Forward These and other words such as anyway, anywhere, and so on, do not have a final *s*. This leads to some strange pronunciations. *TOWARD* seems to demand the final *s* but it is chiefly British. We often hear (this may be a regionalism) something close to "TORGE." The preferred pronunciation for broadcasting is T'WARD.

Aggravate *AGGRAVATE* means to make worse in degree. "His cold was *aggravated* by the wet weather." It does not have a meaning of pester or tease, except in the most informal use.

Alibi/Excuse An *ALIBI* is a specific rebuttal of evidence based on place. That is, the accused person can prove he was somewhere other than at the scene of the crime when the crime was committed. It is not a general *EXCUSE*, although some dictionaries cite such a secondary usage.

All . . . Is Not . . . Be very cautious of this construction. It will very often say just exactly the opposite of what you want. "*ALL* that glitters *IS NOT* gold." Think about it. That really says that nothing that glitters is gold, which we know is not true. (The Shakespeare quotation actually uses the word *glisters*, but that's too odd.) The construction has a touch of class about it, but it can be very tricky. During one summer Olympics we were told "All the marathon runners will not finish." Think about it. It's a case of misplacing *not*. *See also* **Only**.

All Present . . . The phrase is *"ALL PRESENT* or accounted for." We usually hear it as *"all present* AND accounted for." What it means is the contingent of troops or whatever is either present OR otherwise accounted for.

Allergic The primary (and I would suggest only) meaning of *ALLERGIC* has to do with disease--to be *allergic* to some food or other substance that makes one ill. It is possible to say one is *allergic* to another person--offended or put off by him--but I would consider that to be non-standard. Webster's accepts it as a secondary usage.

All Right/Alright *ALL RIGHT* means satisfactory, acceptable, suitable and so on. Everything's OK. *ALRIGHT* means exactly the same thing, but is considered non-standard, even though it is used by excellent writers.

All Together/Altogether *ALL TOGETHER* and *ALTOGETHER* express altogether different ideas. *All together* means just that--we are all together, a group. *Altogether* means in the entirety: "there are 510 books, *altogether.*"

Allude/Elude To *ALLUDE* to something is to make an indirect reference. To *ELUDE* is to evade cleverly. Both words come from the Latin *ludere*, which means to "play."

Allusion/Illusion An *ALLUSION* is an indirect reference, a hint. An *ILLUSION* is a misleading image or idea--an "optical *illusion*," for instance.

Almond/Salmon The nut and the fish are pronounced without the sound of the *l*, preferably. It is AW-mund and SAM-un. Both are also family names; in which cases the *l* is sounded. Oddly, both have been state governors: *Almond* in Virginia and *Salmon* in Vermont.

Almost/Most Do not use *MOST* in the sense of nearly, not quite. "*Most* all of us were there" is unacceptable, while "*Most* of us were there" is OK. Test each usage to see if *ALMOST* may be what you want.

A Lot This is a two-word phrase. A few years ago the "word" *A LOT* started showing up in students' work. It persists. The colloquial "quite *a lot*" or "I feel *a lot* better" are not acceptable as standard English, although the expressions are certainly widely used and readily understood to mean "a great deal" or "considerably." They are imprecise and probably should not be used in broadcast news copy.

Altar/Alter An *ALTAR* is a raised platform on which religious rituals are performed. Originally it was a place of sacrifice. *ALTER* means to change. *Altar* is also used metaphorically: "He was sacrificed on the *altar* of greed."

Alter Ego Literally, "another I." Correctly used, *ALTER EGO* refers to someone very close with whom intimate things are shared--another self. It does not mean, except in psychological circles, a second personality or another phase of one's personality.

Alternate/Vacillate/Oscillate Many words in our language have a sense of number built in. *ALTERNATE* is one of them. It means first one, then the other--between two (and only two) points. You should not confuse it with *VACILLATE* which means to waver, be uncertain; or with *OSCILLATE* which means to swing back and forth or up and down, like a pendulum or a sine wave.

Alternative Knowing that *alternate* has the built-in sense of two, then the number of choices we face when we have *ALTERNATIVES* cannot exceed two. It is possible to have more than two courses of action, but in that case you have choices, not *alternatives*. Admittedly, *alternative* is used in a casual way to mean two or more choices, but that's not strictly precise.

Alumna/Alumnae/Alumni/Alumnus Girls and boys together. One does not have to be a graduate of a school to be considered an "alum(na)/(nus)," one merely has to have been enrolled at some point. *ALUMNA* is a feminine alum, *ALUMNAE* (pronounced uh-LUM-nee) is the plural, but *alumna* is also accepted; an *ALUMNUS* is the male counterpart, and *ALUMNI* (pronounced uh-LUM-neye) is the masculine plural. *Alumni* is also used as a collective to refer to all who have attended a coeducational institution.

Amateur An *AMATEUR* is one who pursues a hobby, sport or other activity just for the fun of it. An *amateur* is not necessarily clumsy or new to the activity. Therefore, to refer to someone who is inept as acting in an "amateurish fashion" is not necessarily correct. Words you may want are *neophyte*, *novice* or *tyro*, all of which mean "new to the activity" or "inexperienced, unskilled."

Ambivalence/Indecision Like *alternative*, *AMBIVALENCE* suggests two and only two positions or attitudes: love-hate, for example. The two sides are very often seen as being in conflict. It goes beyond mere *INDECISION*, which is a broader term.

America/Canada *AMERICA* usually refers to the United States. However, in a story in which both the United States and *CANADA* are mentioned, it is best to recognize that *Canada*, in fact, is also part of North America and make your reference to "*Canada* and the United States," and not to "*Canada* and *America*." The same can be said for any nation of the Americas--North, Central or South. *See also* **North America**.

America's Cup The sailing trophy awarded following an elimination race between two vessels approximately every four years is named for the yacht *America*, which won the first cup in competition off the English coast in 1851. It is always written as a possessive--with an apostrophe. There is also the *Americas Cup*, in golf, without the apostrophe. Confusing? Certainly!

Amerind A sometimes seen but very uncommon shortening of *Amerindian*, which, in itself, is an uncommon word. It is a short way of saying American Indian. I would suggest neither word be used for broadcast, unless in an area where there may be a population of Native Americans (the preferred reference) and the word is locally familiar. Take care the word is not looked upon as a racial slur.

Amiss/Remiss Not a common error, but one heard occasionally. *AMISS* means there's something wrong--something's gone awry. *REMISS* means we have neglected something. We have been *remiss* in our duties. The error I hear is using *amiss* when *remiss* is wanted.

Amok/Amuck The correct spelling is *AMOK* and refers to an uncontrollable frenzy. The term originated in Malaysia, but has now entered English with exactly the same meaning. *AMUCK* is a common English spelling, but is considered non-standard. The formation is almost always "run *amok*."

Among/Between Do we need to even discuss this after all these years? I think so, because the misuse continues. Use *AMONG* when three or more persons or things are involved. Use *BETWEEN* when there are only two. A team does not share its prize *between* its members, unless there are only two.

Amoral/Immoral *AMORAL* means non-moral, neither moral nor immoral. *IMMORAL* means not moral, inconsistent with good behavior.

Amphitheater Look at the word. It is not related to amplifier. It is pronounced AM-fuh-theater, NOT AMP-lih-theater. Thank you.

Amputations Many people who have suffered amputated limbs dislike the phrase "he lost his leg (or whatever)." They say, quite correctly, the leg is not lost at all, they know exactly where they left it. The usage is so common, however, that it is probably acceptable.

Amuse/Bemuse The most common usage of *AMUSE* is to mean to entertain or engage in a pleasurable pastime. *BEMUSE*, on the other hand, means to confuse or bewilder. A less-used meaning is to cause to dream.

Ancestor/Descendant It's a mystery why these two are confused, but confused they are with distressing frequency. Your *ANCESTOR* is your forebear, the one who has gone before, an earlier generation. Your *DESCENDANT* is one of a generation later than yours; a child, grandchild, and so on. An *ancestor* comes before, a *descendant* comes after. Perhaps the confusion comes from the fact that you are descended from your ancestors.

Anecdote/Antidote Often confused, sometimes with hilarious results. An *ANECDOTE* is a brief story illustrating a point, often humorously. An *ANTIDOTE* is a medicine given to counteract a poison, or metaphorically, to counter a bad idea. *See* **Antivenin.**

And Et Cetera A redundancy. *ET* means *AND*. You shouldn't use *et cetera* in broadcast copy, anyhow. If there's more that people should know, tell them.

Angina Usually used to denote intense chest, arm or jaw pain resulting from poorly circulating blood in the heart muscle. Medical people often pronounce it AN-jih-nuh. Most other people say an-JY-nuh.

Angry/Mad Don't say *MAD* when you mean *ANGRY*. *Mad* means insane and some folks might just think *LIBEL* if you suggested they were *mad*.

Anile/Senile *ANILE* refers to an old woman. *SENILE* (pronounced SEE-nyl) refers to an old man, but has come to be genderless. It refers to the effects of old age. Neither has the primary meaning of mental erosion, although *senile* is commonly used that way and has taken on the sense of mental incompetency. *Anile* is almost never used, and I'd suggest it be avoided as too obscure. The correct term for the effects of old age on one's mental ability is "*senile* dementia." Similar effects are caused by Alzheimer's disease, which ordinarily exhibits itself before old age sets in.

Ante/Anti *ANTE* means to come before--antebellum, before the war, antediluvian, before the flood. Poker players *ante* up--place their money in the pot--before play begins. *ANTI* means acting against. "*Anti*freeze."

Antique/Antiques Something that is very old is said to be *ANTIQUE*. There is considerable debate over when *antique* status occurs. The establishment where *antiques* are sold is called an *ANTIQUES* shop. It is the merchandise, not the shop, that are *antiques*, so it is not an *antique* shop.

Antiseptic/Aseptic/Septic *ANTISEPTIC* (in its usual usage) refers to a substance that arrests or prevents the growth of bacteria. *ASEPTIC* means that the subject in question is free of bacteria. *SEPTIC* means it is contaminated.

Antivenin/Venom Note the spelling. *ANTIVENIN* is the antidote to *VENOM*, as from a snakebite.

Anybody/Anyone They mean the same thing, but prefer *ANYONE* for broadcast copy.

Anymore *ANYMORE* should be used only as a negative: "Sally doesn't live here *anymore*." The sense of nowadays is non-standard, as in "We keep seeing the same birds *anymore*." The positive construction is common in some regions of the country.

Anxious/Eager Only in a minor way does *ANXIOUS* mean anything close to *EAGER*. *Anxious* indicates an element of worry or suspense--brooding fear. *Eager* means happy anticipation.

Apiece/Each *APIECE* is unsophisticated in most constructions. "The team members were paid five-hundred dollars *apiece*," is not good form. "The apples cost 50-cents *apiece*," is probably OK. *EACH* is almost always preferable.

Appalachia That region of the Eastern U.S. mountains that is viewed by some as severely affected by poverty, particularly in parts of West Virginia, Kentucky and Tennessee. In that portion of these mountains the word is pronounced AP-uh-LATCH-uh, not AP-uh-LAY-chuh. Early dictionaries recognize only AP-uh-LATCH-uh. The entire *Appalachian* mountain chain runs from Quebec to Alabama.

Appraise/Apprise *APPRAISE* usually means to set a value on something--real estate, auto damage. *APPRISE* also carries that notion in a rare usage. Most often, however, it means to inform.

Arbitrate/Mediate A person who *ARBITRATES* listens to arguments on both sides of an issue, then makes a decision. A *MEDIATOR* listens to both sides, then through persuasion attempts to reconcile differences and get the sides to come to terms. *Arbitration* is sometimes said to be "binding," meaning the two sides at the beginning of the process agree to abide by the arbitrator's decision.

Arctic/Antarctic These refer to the north and south polar regions of the earth. Mostly, I want you to note the spellings and pronunciations. It is ARK-tik and ant-ARK-tik. Not AR-tik.

Arthritis It is a painful disease that is pronounced arth-RYE-tiss. Only three syllables, note--it is not arth-ur-EYE-tiss.

Artesian ar-TEE-zhun. A well; usually a deep-drilled well from which water flows on its own--no pump needed. *ARTESIAN* has nothing to do with art. The word comes from a town in France.

Artisan/Artist An *ARTISAN* is not necessarily an *ARTIST*. An *artisan* is one who engages in skilled manual work, a cabinetmaker or jeweler, for example. An *artist* is one who engages in creative activity that may or may not involve the use of the hands. I think a person who hires out as a sculptor, for example, would be considered an *artisan*, while a person who works alone as a sculptor would be seen as an *artist*.

Asian/Asiatic Use *ASIAN* when referring to the people of the continent; use *ASIATIC* when referring to something to do with the Asian continent. There is some disagreement about this distinction--but most authorities say *Asiatic* is derogatory when applied to people.

As If/As Though/Like In most broadcast usage *AS IF* or *AS THOUGH* are equally acceptable. Do not use *LIKE* as a substitute.

Ascent/Assent *ASCENT* refers to rising upward, climbing. *ASSENT* means to agree to something. They are pronounced identically.

Ascertain/Inquire To *ASCERTAIN* is to make certain of--to learn something. To *INQUIRE* is simply to ask about. One *inquires* in order to *ascertain*.

Assemble *See* **Dissemble.**

Assume/Presume *ASSUME* has many meanings; refer to a dictionary for a full discussion. Most often it is used to mean to take on--as an office--or to take for granted. *PRESUME* is very similar. It means to take upon one's self without authority, to expect or to accept as true without proof.

Astonish/Surprise The sense of *SURPRISE* in which we often use *ASTONISH* is one of its lesser meanings. *Astonish* has as its first meaning to stun as with a blow. It also means to bewilder, which is the most common usage.

Attorney/Counsel/Lawyer There's a good deal of disagreement about the distinctions among these three words. I have found it useful to draw them, however. Use *ATTORNEY* as a generic term for all persons who have been graduated from a law school. Use *COUNSEL* or *LAWYER* when referring to an attorney who is involved in a case. Use *COUNSEL* when the attorney is employed in some form other than general practice--such as a corporate counsel. Again, there's disagreement on this.

Audience/Spectators The crowd at a football game is not an *AUDIENCE*, nor are the folks at a concert *SPECTATORS*. Look at the words. *Audience* has to do with hearing, doesn't it? And *spectators* with seeing. The primary role of the football fans is to see and the music lovers to listen, except some concerts today certainly have become spectacles. There are exceptions to these observations in common usage. TV *audience* for example, refers to TV viewers. That is a borrowing from "radio *audience*," which came first and refers to listeners. Indeed, TV viewers are also listening, but that's not their primary attraction to the medium.

Aught/Ought Sound-alikes that have no similarity of meaning. *AUGHT* is an old word rarely used today. It means of little or no value, worthless, futile. It also means zero, cipher. Sometimes spelled *naught*. *OUGHT* is an archaic past tense of the verb "to owe." Today it is used to refer to an obligation. "A journalist *ought* to act responsibly."

Aunt Depending on where you are, this female relative is pronounced either ANT or AHNT. It's a regional variation.

Author/Host PLEASE, PLEASE, PLEASE, Don't use these or similar nouns as verbs. Some language authorities are beginning to bend on this. Don't let them! Webster's cites *author* as a verb, as in one authoring something, as being first used in 1596, but most serious writers would not use it that way.

Automatic/Pistol/Revolver There are two types of handguns--*AUTOMATICS* and *REVOLVERS*. They are both *PISTOLS* but they are not the same. A *revolver* has a cylinder that contains the *CARTRIDGES*, an *automatic* carries its ammunition in a clip, usually in the handle. The ammunition is referred to as *ROUNDS*. The *BULLET* is the projectile, the *cartridge* is the case that holds the bullet and powder. Handguns and rifles are measured in *CALIBERS*--an expression of the diameter of the barrel in inches. A .25 caliber pistol's barrel is a quarter-inch across. In copy write it "25-caliber." Some calibers are a combination of size and other information about the weapon. A 30-06 rifle, for example, is a 30-caliber weapon designed in 1906. Shotguns are measured by *GAUGE*. The larger the gauge, the smaller the diameter of the barrel, except a .410, which is an expression of diameter in inches. Standard-issue police weapons today are often nine-millimeter, again referring to the diameter of the barrel. Anyone who has served in the army will tell you--perhaps in colorful terms--that a rifle is not a gun, it is a weapon.

Autopsy/Post-Mortem An *AUTOPSY* is a procedure performed on a dead person (or animal), most often to determine the cause of death. It is therefore usually redundant to say "An *autopsy* will be performed to determine the cause of death." Avoid referring to an *autopsy* as a *POST-MORTEM* even though it is performed after life ends. *Post-mortem* is not a noun, it is an adjective describing when the procedure takes place. *AUTOPSY*, by the way, is pronounced AW-tup-see.

Avocation Usually refers to a hobby, something outside one's occupation. There's a strong tie to *vocation*, a calling.

Baby, Don't Throw ... The cliché is: *DON'T THROW THE BABY OUT WITH THE BATHWATER*. It's a useful thought in the sense that one's reforms or changes should not destroy that which is to be reformed. The problem is, many people say *Don't throw the baby out with the dishwater*. That's pretty funny, but makes no sense. Recently a cartoon had it *Don't throw the baby out with the dishes*. Now, that's really off the wall. And I have heard, and I'm not certain that the speaker was trying to be funny, *Don't throw the baby out with the dishwasher*.

Baby/Infant/Toddler Here we encounter a similar problem to that we have with older children--what is the distinction we draw when we call a child a *BABY*, *INFANT* or *TODDLER?* I believe a *baby* to be a newborn up to about three months, then the child becomes an *infant* until it begins to talk and walk; it then becomes a *toddler* until about age three or four. *Infant* means not yet speaking. *Baby* and *toddler* have no complex meanings. This is strictly my opinion and is subject to challenge and change.

Badly In the mistaken notion that it sounds "better," many people say they feel *BADLY* when they feel sick. That usage is British and is not considered standard American English. In the United States, we feel *BAD* when we're sick and feel *badly* when there's something wrong with our sense of touch. On the other hand, when we want something deeply, we colloquially but correctly say "I want that *badly*."

Bail/Bale/Bond *BAIL* and *BOND* differ in the source of the security. The distinction is unsupported by Webster's. *Bail* is usually a sum of money or property posted by the accused privately, while *bond* is put up by a bondsman or some other institution. Both allow a prisoner to go free while awaiting trial or other legal procedure. *Bond* is a much broader term than *bail*, having many additional meanings. In our current sense, both are intended to assure the re-appearance of the person in question. A *BALE* is a large bound bundle--among other things. One is not released "in lieu of *bail*." One is held in jail in lieu of bail. In lieu of means instead of, in the absence of.

Bait/Bate A *BAIT* is something that might entice someone or some animal into a trap or onto a hook. *BATE* is related to *abated* and means to restrain. The most common use is in the cliché "with bated breath," meaning anxious. To wait with bated breath means to be so anxious that one's breathing is in short, shallow gasps.

Balkan/Baltic The countries that make up the *BALKAN* Peninsula are Albania, Bulgaria, Greece, Rumania (Romania) and what used to be Yugoslavia. The countries that are on the Baltic Sea and make up the *BALTIC* States are Estonia, Latvia and Lithuania. The *Baltic* States are now independent, but for many years were part of the Soviet Union. The *Balkans*, except Greece, were part of the Soviet "sphere," but not part of the USSR. Political, economic and ethnic instability within many of the Balkan countries promises to change the map of Europe.

Balloon/Blimp/Dirigible/Zeppelin All are airships. A *BALLOON* is usually more or less round in shape and carries a suspended basket in which passengers ride. A *balloon* is filled with hot air or a lighter-than-air gas to provide lift. It is capable of being controlled vertically, but not horizontally. A *BLIMP* is an elongated balloon that has engines and an enclosed "gondola" for passengers and crew. It can be controlled on all axes. We are most familiar with the Goodyear Blimp at sporting events. A *DIRIGIBLE* (pronounced DEER-idg-uh-bul) differs from a blimp in that it has a rigid frame inside a fabric covering and carries lighter-than-air gas in several bags within the covering. *Dirigible* literally means "steerable," and originally was an adjective describing a steerable balloon. The name has nothing to do with the fact that the airship is rigid. A *ZEPPELIN* is a dirigible named for Count Ferdinand von Zeppelin, a German aeronaut who pioneered such airships. *Aeronaut* is a nifty old word that might be used in a facetious way these days, but not in serious newswriting, I think. To my knowledge there are no dirigibles flying today, following a series of disastrous crashes in the 1930s.

Balogna/Baloney/Bologna *BALOGNA* is a common cold meat, while *BOLOGNA* is a city in Italy from which the cold meat takes its name. The city is pronounced buh-LOHN-yah. The meat is pronounced just like *BALONEY*, which is a slang expression denoting disbelief.

Banded/Banned When a group has come together for some common cause it is said to have *BANDED* together. Something that is *BANNED* is forbidden. A recent report told me that a group of governments had *banned* together for industrial development. You don't get very far that way!

Bank/Coast/Shore Rivers and streams have *BANKS*; seas and oceans have *COASTS*; seas, oceans, lakes and ponds have *SHORES*. *Bank* implies a steep slope, so it is possible for some lakes and ponds to have *banks*. However, when used as a general referent, use *shore* for lakes and ponds.

Base/Bass/Bass A *BASE* is a footing, a foundation, as well as a number of other things. In music, a *BASS* is pronounced BAYS (just like base) and means an instrument or voice of the low range. The fish, on the other hand, is pronounced BASS.

Basic/Bottom/Fundamental *BASIC* and *FUNDAMENTAL* are essentially synonyms referring to foundations or underlying principles. *BOTTOM* has some similar meanings, but most connote the underside of something and do not carry the idea of a foundation.

Bathing Suit The preferred reference (perhaps thanks to the Miss America folks) is *SWIMSUIT*.

Bazaar/Bizarre We all know this, don't we? A *BAZAAR* is a fair or marketplace where a wide variety of goods are for sale. *BIZARRE* refers to erratic behavior or something or someone eccentric in style. There is a slight difference in pronunciation based on the initial vowel--buh-ZAHR and bih-ZAHR.

Beak/Bill Both are found on birds. *BILL* is the broader term. A *BEAK* is associated with birds of prey, such as an eagle--sharp and hooked. However, *beak* can apply to the pointed mouthpart of most other birds. A *bill* is usually the mouthpart of certain waterbirds, such as ducks. It's also a kind of cap, the visor of which is shaped like a duck's bill.

Beaufort Variously pronounced BOH-furt or BYOO-furt. Go with the flow--whatever the local pronunciation is, use it. The *"Beaufort* Scale" (pronounced BOH-furt) is a measure of wind velocity expressed as *"Beaufort* Force 0-12," with 0 being dead calm and 12 being hurricane force and above (more than 74 miles an hour).

Because/Since/Due To In broadcast copy prefer *BECAUSE*. *SINCE* used in this sense can be confusing and *DUE TO* is pretentious.

Before/In Front Of In one sense, *BEFORE* means *IN FRONT OF* as in "this program was taped *before (in front of)* a live audience." However, it is jarring to hear it reported that a witness appeared *in front of* a committee of Congress. To my ear, at least, the usage is substandard.

Believe/Feel/Think These words are not interchangeable, although one would think so reading and listening to current American journalism. Did it come from the awareness days of the '60s and '70s, when a lot of people were *feeling* instead of *thinking?* Perhaps. *FEEL* means to internalize an emotion or stimulus. You can *feel* ill or cold or sad. You do not *feel* a thought. You *THINK* a thought or an opinion. You *BELIEVE* something that depends on faith or trust. Please be very careful with these distinctions. Fine points such as these are the mark of a careful writer.

Bellwether Here's a word we hear often in political years when we speak of *BELLWETHER* precincts--ones that indicate a trend or are predictive of the way an election might go. Note the spelling; it has nothing to do with weather. Originally, it referred to the practice of putting a bell on the leader of a flock of animals, usually sheep or goats. That animal would then lead the others to pasture or to slaughter (Judas goat). The *wether* part comes from the Middle English for *ram* and refers to a male sheep that has been castrated.

Bemuse *See* **Amuse.**

Be Sure To (And) Prefer *BE SURE TO. Be sure and* implies two actions. *See also* **Try And.**

Between *See* **Among.**

Biannual/Biennial *BIANNUAL See* **Prefixes.** *BI-ENNIAL* means occurring every two years. It's best to hyphenate in scripts: *bi-annual* and *bi-ennial.*

Billion A thousand million. The British sometimes call it a *milliard.* Their original *BILLION* was a thousand milliards, what Americans call a *trillion.* When dealing with foreign news, be sure what sort of *billion* is being referred to.

Bisect/Dissect *BISECT* means to divide into two parts--usually equal. *DISSECT* (note spelling) can be pronounced either DY-sect or dih-SECT depending on the construction of the sentence. It means--among other things--to divide into parts for study.

Bite/Sting Generally, it's understood that animals *BITE,* and insects *STING.* But, isn't it almost universal to refer to a mosquito *bite?* And a spider *bite?* Yep. There's wonderful English usage again. Actually, insects with pincers, such as spiders and ants for example, do *bite.* Insects with a stinger or proboscis, such as bees and hornets, as well as mosquitoes, *sting*. *Sting* may carry the sense of injecting a poison.

Bitter/Bitterly *See* **Weather Words**.

Biweekly/Semiweekly   There's a bunch of confusion here. Webster's says *BIWEEKLY* means every two weeks, but has a secondary meaning of twice a week. *SEMIWEEKLY*, however, means only twice a week. So, let's let *biweekly* mean every other week. In any case, hyphenate in scripts: *bi-weekly* and *semi-weekly*. *See* **Prefixes**.

Blatant/Flagrant   A *BLATANT* action would be one carried out in a noisy, offensive manner. A *FLAGRANT* action would be an evil or distasteful one carried out in a conspicuous manner. *Blatant* is frequently misused when *flagrant* is wanted. There are *"flagrant* fouls" in basketball. I always found that amusing, for some reason.

Blazed The Trail   A mark on a tree, made with an ax or a spray paint can, is called a *BLAZE*, and a series of them is used to mark trails through woods. The phrase does not have the sense of speed or intense activity. During a recent political campaign we saw this headline: "CANDIDATE *BLAZES* CAMPAIGN TRAIL." The story had to do with a day of frantic dashing from one appearance to another. Wrong. The phrase may be used in the sense of breaking new ground, leading the way. A *blaze* is also a fire, of course, and a streak of white hair on the forehead of a horse or other animal, or on the head of a human.

Blimp *See* **Balloon**.

Blindman's Buff   Note: it is *BUFF*, not *BLUFF*. This is a child's game in which one player is blindfolded and attempts to find and name other players who are not blindfolded. It is used metaphorically to describe some activity in which the key player is operating without all the facts. It is very often mis-spoken as *bluff*. Most recently I heard a space engineer mention *blindman's bluff* on a network news program.

Blizzard *See* **Weather Words**.

Bloc/Block   A *BLOC* is a group of individuals or nations that have banded together to pursue a common purpose. The term is frequently (and almost exclusively) used to refer to political divisions. ("The Eastern Bloc nations" is the most common, but probably no longer exists.) We all know the many meanings of *BLOCK*, don't we?

Blowtorch A *BLOWTORCH* is becoming a rarity with the increasing use of propane and other highly portable torches. It was recently reported that divers were cutting victims from a submerged railcar with *blowtorches*. Nope. A blowtorch cannot operate under water; it requires oxygen to keep its flame burning. The rescuers were using "cutting torches." Besides, a *blowtorch* cannot be used to cut metal, only to heat it.

Boarder/Border A *BOARDER* is a person who takes his meals regularly at a place away from his own home. He is not necessarily also lodging there. A *BORDER* is a boundary, usually between nations, among other things.

Boat/Ship A *BOAT* is a vessel small enough to be carried on a *SHIP*, but there are numerous exceptions--tugboat, for example, and "Love *Boat*." *Boat* is the broader term. A *ship* is always big.

Boor/Bore A *BOOR* is a lout, someone uncouth in manners or insensitive. A *BORE* (when referring to persons or situations) is someone or something that is uninteresting, dull. *Bore*, of course, has many other meanings.

Bouillon/Bullion *BOUILLON* is a thin, clear soup usually made from chicken or beef stock. *BULLION* is metal in a mass. It can be any metal, but usually refers to gold or silver in ingots, most often gold. It is not redundant to refer to "gold *bullion*." The pronunciations differ. *Bouillon* is BOOL-yahn, *bullion* is BULL-yuhn.

Boyfriend/Girlfriend Neither of these phrases should be applied to adults, except in a facetious manner, or in a gossip column.

Boy/Man Somewhere back in the 1960s we lost track of when a *BOY* becomes a *MAN*. It probably had to do with the lowering of the voting and drinking ages. We have since seen such absurdities as a lead saying "Two county men drowned today in Smith Pond," only to read that one was 19 and the other 14! Let's settle on 18 as the age when man- and womanhood occurs. A preteen male is referred to as a *Boy*; 13–17 he is a *youth*; after that he becomes a *MAN*. We don't have an equivalent word to *youth* for teen-age girls, so use *girl* until age 18, then *woman*. If married, no matter how young, use *Man* and *Woman*. Some authorities say *youth* is a genderless word and applies to both teen-age boys and girls. I have always thought of it as a masculine term. Some say get rid of *youth* altogether and call them all *teens* or *teen-agers*.

Brackish Maybe I'm the only person who reached midlife believing that *BRACKISH* meant muddy, dirty or polluted water. It doesn't, of course. It means somewhat salty--less so than seawater--but still undrinkable. The word has been used to mean unpalatable. *Brackish* water occurs where the sea enters a river or bay and meets fresh water flowing out. Certain marine life, such as the blue crab, need brackish water at certain times of year. See how much you can learn just by reading a word guide?

Brassiere/Brazier You can get yourself terribly embarrassed by confusing these two. The women's undergarment is correctly pronounced bra-zhee-AIR. However, it is usually pronounced bruh-ZEER and ordinarily shortened to BRA. A *BRAZIER* on the other hand, is a fire pit, such as an outdoor barbecue grill. It is pronounced BRAY-zhur.

Breach/Breech/Broach/Brook Here we have a group of almost-sound- alikes that are easily confused. A *BREACH* is a violation--*breach* of contract, or a gap such as a *breach* in a dam. *BREECH* is the lower part of the human torso, hence *breeches* (pronounced BRITCH-ez); it is also that part of a rifle or cannon that receives the ammunition, which is pronounced BREECH. *Breech* is also the term to describe the action of whales and other marine mammals when they leap from the water. *BROACH* most often means to bring up a subject; it is also a nautical term for a very dangerous situation in which a sailing vessel veers broadside to the wind and waves. *BROOK*, aside from being a small stream, means to tolerate--to put up with. It is usually used in the negative sense: "The Governor will brook no criticism."

Bring/Take One *BRINGS* something here and *TAKES* something there. That's pretty simple. Why do we keep hearing "*Bring* this to Uncle Charlie in Baltimore?"

Broad/Wide Yes, there's a difference. *WIDE* generally refers to the distance that separates two implied boundaries--a wide river. *BROAD* is a reference to what lies between the limits--a broad field. The words are often used interchangeably, especially in colloquial expressions such as "*wide*-eyed" or "*broad* daylight."

Broken Bones Don't write "The man *broke* his arm." That implies he somehow deliberately broke the bone. It would be a very unusual story indeed if someone purposely broke a bone. Say "The man suffered a *broken* arm."

Bullet *See* **Automatic.**

Bulletin *See* **Wire Services.**

Burgeon To sprout or flourish. There is the sense of sudden and widespread growth. We speak of a *BURGEONING* city.

Burglary/Robbery A *ROBBERY* is the taking of another's property through threat or violence. Thus, an empty house is not *robbed*, but *BURGLARIZED*, which has the sense of breaking in and stealing built in.

Bury Watch the pronunciation. It is BURR-ee, not BAIR-ee.

Bus/Buss A *BUS* is a vehicle. The word is derived from *omnibus*, which is what the British call their public transport. The plural is *buses*. A *BUSS* is a kiss, usually with the sense of a sudden, impulsive show of affection. *Buss* also refers to a number of other things, such as a row of buttons on a TV switcher, or the common ground in an electrical fuse box.

Bust I suppose the use is sufficiently widespread that we can accept the slang "drug *BUST*." I still find it a bit jarring. Some dictionaries ignore it, others dismiss it as slang.

Cache/Cash Yes, you can have a *CACHE* of *CASH*. A *cache* is a hiding place and, by extension, what is hidden there. It is pronounced just like *cash*.

Cahoots kuh-HOOTS. To be involved in a conspiratorial partnership. Always expressed as a plural. Usually, but not always, jocular. One is said to be "in *cahoots*," as "in *cahoots* with the devil." I would use the word with great caution. It has a pejorative connotation, suggesting stealth or conspiracy.

Caliber/Gauge *See* **Automatic.**

Callous/Callus Both words have the meaning of hardened or thickened skin, but *CALLOUS* also means to be insensitive and unsympathetic. They are both pronounced the same: KAL-us.

Calvary/Cavalry Some people seem to be incapable of uttering *CAVALRY* and will almost always say *CALVARY* instead. Even respected network correspondents make the error. *Calvary* is a hill near Jerusalem where Jesus of Nazareth is believed to have been crucified. The *cavalry* used to be horse-mounted troops, and today the word is used to refer to some motorized military units; armored *cavalry*, for example, much in evidence during the Persian Gulf War.

Can/May Easily and often misused. Use *CAN* when your sense is "is able to," use *MAY* when the sense is "has permission to." Both words have other uses and senses, but the mixup occurs between ability and permission.

Canada *See* **America.**

Canada Goose The bird is a *CANADA GOOSE*, not a "Canadian Goose."

Cancel Out *OUT* is unnecessary. The idea is built into *CANCEL*.

Cannon/Canon A *CANNON* is a field weapon, as we all know. A *CANON* is a law or rule, usually having to do with the practice of religion. However, some secular organizations have codified their rules of conduct into what they call *canons*.

Canuck A disparaging term for a Canadian, especially a French Canadian. Even though they themselves may use the term--even naming a hockey team the *Canucks*--it is still a term many Canadians find offensive.

Canvas/Canvass Both pronounced the same--KAN-vus. *CANVAS* is a heavy cloth, usually cotton, used to make tents, tarpaulins and, in the old days, sails. A *CANVASS* is a poll or survey. A few days following an election, there is conducted what is known as the official *canvass* in which election officials examine and certify the results.

Capacity *See* **Ability**.

Cape A point of land or peninsula that juts out into water. Note: The *CAPE* is the land, not the water. Massachusetts' Cape Cod, for example, separates Cape Cod Bay from Nantucket Sound.

Capital/Capitol The city and the money are the *CAPITAL*. The building is the *CAPITOL*, both national and state. In Washington, D.C., and Richmond, Virginia, and no doubt elsewhere, the site of the capitol building is known as "*Capitol* Hill." *Capital* used in the sense of a crime punishable by death comes from the Latin for head. *Capital* has other uses as well, most having to do with the head or top of something.

Carat/Caret/Carrot/Karat Here we have another group of sound-alikes. A *CARAT* is a measure of weight of precious stones or metals. *KARAT* means about the same thing, but is usually reserved for gold. A *CARET* is a proofreader's pointed mark indicating where material is to be inserted in a page of copy, like this ^. Of course you know what a *CARROT* is.

Careen/Career *CAREEN* and *CAREER* share one meaning--that of lurching, usually out of control. But they both have more common use. *CAREEN* is the act of beaching a boat so it will tilt to one side at low tide so work can be done on the bottom below the waterline. The most common use of *CAREER* is to refer to one's employment or course through life. It has several other meanings as well, most having to do with short bursts of speed, as in a horse race.

Caribbean The sea is pronounced kahr-uh-BEE-un or kuh-RIH-bee-un. Some dictionaries prefer the latter, I prefer the former. Other dictionaries agree with me, as does Elster, who says kahr-uh-BEE-un is to be preferred, although kah-RIB-ean has been included in dictionaries for more than half a century. The *Caribbean* Sea, by the way, lies to the south of Cuba and north of South America. It is bounded on the east by the Leeward and Windward islands, and on the west by the Yucatán Peninsula. The Gulf of Mexico is not included.

Carpet/Rug Modern usage, unsupported by Webster's, has *CARPET* meaning wall-to-wall floor covering, and other floor coverings referred to as *RUGS*. This is an area of disagreement. After all, the legendary Magic Carpet was a rug.

Cartridge *See* **Automatic**.

Caster/Castor In the usual sense, *CASTER* refers to a swiveling wheel on furniture, but it does have other meanings. *CASTOR* is most familiar as "*castor* oil." It, too, has other meanings, including the name of one of two bright stars in the constellation Gemini. The other is Pollux. They were twins in Greek mythology. Hence the NASA program Gemini, in which the orbiting capsules carried two astronauts.

Casual/Causal Mostly, be careful with the spellings and be sure to clearly mark your copy if you expect to have *CAUSAL* pronounced correctly on the air. A *casual* relationship and a *causal* relationship are two very different things! It is best to avoid *causal*.

Casualty *CASUALTY* should be reserved for the victims of war or disaster. Not all casualties are dead--they include injured, wounded, missing and any others who may be lost to a military command for whatever reason other than leave. It may be clever to refer to a former office-holder as a *casualty* of an election, but it is not accurate and can mislead an audience that may not be listening closely.

Catsup/Ketchup They are both pronounced KEH-chup and so is *catchup*, which we sometimes see. For broadcast scripts, use the spelling *KETCHUP*.

Celebrant/Celebrator It is good to draw the distinction. *CELEBRANT* usually refers to a person performing a public religious ceremony, especially in the Catholic churches. A *CELEBRATOR* is simply one taking part in a celebration of whatever nature.

Celt The preferred pronunciation is KELT, although the Boston basketball team calls itself the SEL-tiks. The Celts were a major division of early man, spreading over western Europe and Asia Minor. The modern reference is to the people of the northern British Isles--Highland Scots, Northern Irish, Welsh--the Gaels. The distinction today has more to do with language than with race. However, many Celts will be quick to point out they are not Anglo-Saxon. *See also* **Wasp.**

Cement/Concrete *CEMENT* (pronounced suh-MENT; the common mispronunciation is SEE-ment) is only one ingredient in *CONCRETE*, which also contains water, sand, gravel or some other aggregate. Once mixed, it is *concrete.* Therefore, that big mixer truck is a *concrete* truck, not a *cement* truck. The same is true of the mixer at a construction site--it is a *concrete* mixer, not a *cement* mixer.

Censer/Censor/Censure/Sensor A *CENSER* is an incense burner such as is used in certain religious ceremonies. We all know what a *CENSOR* is, don't we? The person who, sometimes officially but often not, checks various forms of communication for materials deemed unfit for the public. To *CENSURE* is to officially reprimand or disapprove. A *SENSOR* is a device, today usually electronic, that senses operating conditions of various machines and other things and sends impulses to control units or alarms.

Center On/Revolve Around Think about it. You cannot *CENTER* around something.

Centers For Disease Control In Atlanta. Note it is expressed as a plural. The CDC includes a number of agencies within the National Health Service for control of contagious, infectious and preventable diseases. *See also* **National Institutes Of Health.**

Chair A *CHAIR* is a piece of furniture intended for sitting upon. The word should not be used to indicate the person who presides at a meeting, the head of a committee or any other such thing. It has come into use to avoid what some perceive to be the sexist *chairman.* If the honcho happens to be a woman, call her a *chairwoman.* Yes, Webster's almost says *chair* is an adjective for a person presiding over a meeting. Here's one place we diverge. I think its use in that sense is confusing.

Chaise Longue Note the spelling. It is NOT a *lounge.* We can get fairly close to the French pronunciation with SHAYZ LAWNG. Literally, it means "long chair." Webster's accepts *chaise lounge* as a secondary spelling. It's another of those foreign terms that has been halfway absorbed into English. Petit fours--the confection pronounced "petty fours"--is another, as is papier-mâché, which retains the French spelling, but is pronounced "paper muh-SHAY."

Champagne/Champaign/Champlain *CHAMPAGNE* is the sparkling white wine originally from the Champagne region of France. A *CHAMPAIGN* is a broad open field, hence the name of the Illinois city. Both are pronounced sham-PAIN, in English. *CHAMPLAIN* is the lake that forms about a third of the boundary between Vermont and New York State, named for French explorer Samuel de Champlain who discovered it in 1609.

Chargé D'affaires A member of a diplomatic mission or embassy who ranks below the person in charge, but acts in his behalf in his absence or at certain ceremonies. The French term is pronounced shar-ZHAY duh-FAIR.

Chauvinist A *CHAUVINIST* is one given to excessive nationalism or patriotism. With the feminist movement it has taken on the additional meaning of one who takes a superior attitude toward the opposite sex, generally meaning males toward females.

Chic Pronounced SHEEK, regardless of what the jeans-maker tells us. It's French and means elegant, stylish and attractive. Applied mainly to women.

Chicano An American of Mexican origin, also applied to illegal aliens from south of the border. It does not apply to all people with Spanish surnames. Pronounce it shih-KAHN-oh.

Chief Justice The correct reference is to the *CHIEF JUSTICE* of the United States, not of the Supreme Court. The other eight are referred to as "associate justices," but Justice alone will usually do.

Childish/Childlike *CHILDISH* behavior is immature. The term is usually used as a criticism. *CHILDLIKE* is used, on the other hand, to imply innocence or playfulness and is most often used as a compliment.

Chile/Chili/Chilly All are usually pronounced *CHILLY*. *CHILE* is a country in South America, the pronunciation of which sometimes is given a Spanish try with CHEE-lay. *CHILI* is a spicy bean dish. When meat is added, it becomes "chili con carne." Pronounced kohn-KAR-nay.

China There once were two: The People's Republic of *China* on the Mainland, and the Republic of *China* established following World War II on the island of Taiwan (ty-WAHN). Today, only the mainland People's Republic is recognized as being *China*.

Choral/Chorale/Coral/Corral *CHORAL* and *CHORALE* both refer to music. *Choral* is a kind of music written to be sung by a chorus or choir. A *chorale* is the performance of a chorus. *Choral* and *CORAL*--the residue of tiny marine animals--are both pronounced KOH-rul. *Chorale* is pronounced koh-RALL, just like the horse pen, *CORRAL*.

Chord/Cord *CHORD* is chiefly a reference to a musical sound, but the word also has meanings in geometry and construction. A *CORD* is either a length of line somewhere between a string and a rope in diameter, or a stack of firewood four feet wide, four feet high and eight feet long. It has many other meanings as well, including a kind of fabric and the nerve bundle in the spine.

Christmas Eve It used to be that *CHRISTMAS EVE* was the night before Christmas. It seems now, however, that all of December 24th is referred to as *Christmas Eve*. Maybe the same applies to New Year's Eve as well.

Cipher There are two completely unrelated meanings for this word, as far as I can tell. *CIPHER* means zero, nothing. *Cipher* also means to write in code, hence *decipher*, which is a much more common word, meaning to interpret or decode. The British spell it *cypher*, as it is pronounced.

Citation Here we encounter another of those words that has two distinct uses and seems to contradict itself. A *CITATION* can be a summons to court--such as a parking *citation*, a ticket. Or it can be the bestowing of an honor or prize. It's all in the context. See the next entry for another meaning.

Cite/Sight/Site To *CITE* is to call attention to, especially some quoted material brought out as evidence. *SIGHT*, of course, has to do with vision or seeing. A *SITE* is a location; we speak of a building *site*.

Clambered/Clamored Both pronounced CLAM-urd. *CLAMBERED* refers to climbing, usually in an awkward or hurried fashion. *CLAMORED* has to do with insistently making noise--the cat *clamored* for its food.

Clandestine Something kept secret, surreptitious, often illegal. Pronounced klan-DESS-tin.

Clapboard A type of building siding. The preferred pronunciation is KLA-burd, just like curdled sour milk: clabbered.

Clean/Cleanse Perhaps soap commercials have caused this problem. Both *CLEAN* and *CLEANSE* (pronounced KLENZ) mean to rid of soil, but in different ways. *Clean* has to do with removing physical dirt. *Cleanse* has to do with spiritual matters--*cleansing* oneself of guilt, for example. Wouldn't it be wonderful if we really could buy a *cleanser* in a box at the grocery store? Webster's accepts the soap powder idea as a secondary meaning of *cleanser*.

Cleave Here's another of the little tricks English plays on us from time to time. *CLEAVE* has two directly opposing meanings. In one sense it means to split apart--hence meat cleaver. Its other sense is to cling together--to be loyal. Some marriage rites use the term to describe the bond between husband and wife. I guess it's fortunate the word is not commonly used. I would not suggest it as a good broadcast word.

Clench/Clinch *CLENCH* is to close tightly, as your fist or jaw. *CLINCH* means to secure firmly--we speak of clinching the end of a nail by bending it over so it cannot pull out. It is used quite correctly in saying "the team clinched the title," but in that use it is a cliché.

Client/Customer/Patron We generally think of a *CLIENT* as one who seeks personal help from a professional, such as a lawyer, although the word does have broader meaning, including persons who are served by social agencies. *CUSTOMERS* are found in stores and other businesses and the word is also used to describe those who purchase various services. *PATRON*, on the other hand, is a confused word. It means one who supports, usually financially--a *patron* of the arts, for example--and is also used to denote one who is served. Restaurants often refer to their *customers* as *patrons*. (Literally, those who bring financial support in the form of *patronage*.) It is best not to use *patron* when you mean *client* or *customer*.

Climactic/Climatic *CLIMACTIC* refers to the climax, usually accompanied by *moment*, of a novel, play or any other activity that builds toward a high point. *CLIMATIC* refers to climate--the weather.

Clique Pronounced KLEEK. It means a close (often closed) group.

Close Proximity A redundancy. If something is proximate, it is close.

Clue/Cue A *CLUE* is a hint, a tip, a bit of evidence. The word has other meanings as well, most having to do with sailing rigs, in which case it is often spelled *clew*. A *CUE* is most often a signal, such as an actor's *cue* line or a TV floor director pointing at the anchor whose camera is about to be switched on. It, too, has other meanings. Be careful; we frequently hear *cue* when the speaker means *clue*, as in "*Cue* me in."

Coast *See* **Bank.**

Coincident/Simultaneous Both words mean occurring or existing at the same time, but *COINCIDENT* is a much broader term. *SIMULTANEOUS* has to do only with time. When two things arrive at exactly the same moment they are said to be *simultaneous*. A *coincidence* can involve things that take place at the same time, or in the same place or under the same circumstances.

Cole Slaw And The Rest Of The Menu How many menus have you seen--usually hand-lettered but sometimes elaborately printed--that say you may have "*COLD* slaw, *ICE* tea, *TOSS* salad, *CORN* beef, *GRILL* cheese, all done up in *WAXED* paper"? They are all wrong, of course. It is *COLE, ICED, TOSSED, CORNED, GRILLED* and *WAX*. Menu editing can be a great pastime while waiting for service.

College/University The most common usage in the United States has *COLLEGE* meaning an institution of higher learning that offers courses leading to the bachelor's degree. A *UNIVERSITY* is often made up of *colleges* and offers educational programs at the master's or doctoral level.

Collision There is some shifting from the original usage of *COLLISION*. Purists (myself included on this one) insist that a *collision* is the violent coming together of two moving objects. Therefore, an automobile cannot *collide* with a tree. Recently, some wordsmiths have been saying that sticking to that narrow meaning of the word is sophistry.

Collusion/Connivance *COLLUSION* is a secret agreement formed for the purpose of deceiving someone not in on the secret. *CONNIVANCE* is the intentional ignoring of wrongdoing, or the condoning of wrongdoing.

Commitment/Committal *COMMITMENT* and *COMMITTAL* (note spellings) have numerous meanings, but they are quite distinct in their most common uses: *commitment* has to do with emotional or moral attachment, being pledged; *committal* is the act (usually legal) of consigning one to prison or a mental institution. The hearing in such cases is called a *committal* hearing, not a *commitment* hearing. We also speak of a *committal* service when burying the dead.

Comparable Often mispronounced. It is KAHM-pur-uh-buhl.

Complacent/Complaisant *COMPLACENT* means self-satisfied, even smug, about one's accomplishments or place. It is not always a complimentary term. *COMPLAISANT* has to do with a willingness to be pleasant or to serve, sometimes in a fawning manner. Again, not always complimentary.

Complected/Complexioned Use *COMPLEXIONED* when referring to skin color. *COMPLECTED* is not accepted as standard usage, although Webster's finds it as early as 1806.

Complement/Compliment There is a tiny difference in the pronunciation of these two, as well as huge differences in meaning. *COMPLEMENT* (pronounced KOM-pleh-ment) means to make complete, but in common usage it has come to mean something that enhances, such as "her makeup complements her dress." A *COMPLIMENT* (pronounced KOM-plih-ment) is an expression of approval or praise.

Compose/Comprise These are frequently confused, and often are used interchangeably. But they are distinct. *COMPOSE* means to combine things, "Ninety-eight counties compose Virginia." *COMPRISE* means to be made up of: "Virginia comprises ninety-eight counties." It might help to think of it this way: *compose* starts with the parts and makes up the whole, while *comprise* starts with the whole and discusses the parts. Another point is that *comprise* should never be used with *of*, but *composed of* is entirely correct.

Comprehensible/Comprehensive It's surprising these two almost identical words have completely different meanings. They are, however, related. *COMPREHENSIBLE* means to be capable of being understood. It comes from a Latin root meaning "to grasp," and is the adjective form of the verb *comprehend*. *COMPREHENSIVE* means to be inclusive, complete, all-encompassing. It comes from the Latin, as well, the root also meaning "to understand," but is the adjective form of the noun *comprehension*.

Compress There are two meanings and two pronunciations here. The verb *COMPRESS* is pronounced kum-PRESS and means to apply pressure. The noun *compress* is pronounced KAHM-press and refers to a folded pad, usually of cloth, applied to a wound to stop bleeding. It also refers to a machine designed to apply pressure.

Comptroller No matter how it's spelled, it's pronounced *controller*. *COMPTROLLERS* are found in business, industry and government. They are the keepers of accounts--superaccountants, if you will--who often have the authority to determine whether expenditures are appropriate.

Communiqué The French word is frequently used to describe a statement issued following diplomatic talks. It can mean any formal message. It is pronounced kuh-myoon-ih-KAY.

Conclave Originally, a term for secret meetings of religious organizations. The meeting of cardinals to select a new Roman Catholic pope is still called a *CONCLAVE*. It has also come to mean any secret or closed assembly.

Concrete *See* **Cement.**

Confess *See* **Admit.**

Confidant/Confident A *CONFIDANT* (pronounced KAHN-fih-DAHNT) is a person in whom secrets are confided and entrusted. To be *CONFIDENT* (pronounced KAHN-fih-dent) is to be self-assured and free of worry.

Confluence A coming together of streams, ideas or events. But not roadways; that's an intersection. *CONFLUENCE* carries a sense of flowing.

Congress When we say *CONGRESS* we are usually referring to the U. S. House and Senate. It is an inclusive term, involving both houses. It is frequently used to mean just the House of Representatives. "He is running for Congress; she is running for the Senate." And the region a member of the House represents is correctly called a "congressional district."

Consecutive/Successive *CONSECUTIVE* means one after another, a continuous progression. *SUCCESSIVE* has a similar meaning, but also a number of others having to do with lines of inheritance. Be careful which you use, to avoid confusion.

Consensus A general agreement. The phrase "*CONSENSUS* of opinion" is widely believed to be redundant because a *consensus* is an agreed-upon opinion. Avoid the phrase. *Consensus* standing alone will usually do. I have seen "General *consensus* of public opinion." There are at least three redundancies in that.

Consequent/Subsequent *CONSEQUENT* means to follow as the result of some prior happening. *SUBSEQUENT* is a broader word, meaning to follow at a later time, but not necessarily as the result of something earlier.

Console To *CONSOLE* (kuhn-SOAL) someone is to offer sympathy or comfort, usually emotional support. A *CONSOLE* (KAWN-sohl) is a variety of things, but to broadcasters it generally refers to audio and video control panels in the (where else?) control room.

Consortium A group of businesses or other enterprises collaborating for the common good. Pronounced kuhn-SOR-tee-um most recently, but also frequently heard as kuhn-SORSH-um. Elster disagrees with both. He says kuhn-SOR-tee-um is simply wrong and kuhn-SORSH-um is non-standard. Four syllables: kuhn-SOR-shee-um.

Contagious/Infectious *CONTAGIOUS* means communicable by contact-- catching. It can also have a subtler meaning, as in "her happiness was *contagious.*" *INFECTIOUS* (note spelling) means capable of causing infection. It also has the similar metaphorical use: "His laugh was *infectious.*"

Contemporary *CONTEMPORARY* is not a synonym for "modern" in its primary sense. *Contemporary* means living or existing at the same time. Jefferson and Washington were *contemporaries.* The word is used to describe modern--often unconventional--styles of homes or furnishings. The usage is confusing and should be avoided.

Contentious/Controversial A *CONTENTIOUS* person is one given to quarrels. It is proper to refer to a person as being *CONTROVERSIAL*, but that means the person is an object of controversy. The usual sense has to do with issues.

Contiguous *See* **Adjacent.**

Continual/Continuous The ticking of a clock is a *CONTINUAL* sound; so is the fall of a trip-hammer. The flow of a river is *CONTINUOUS*--going on without interruption.

Convict/Inmate/Prisoner Be careful here. The key point is that not everyone in jail is a *CONVICT*; many are being held for trial or other action and have not been convicted of anything. You can be assured that everyone in a state or federal penitentiary is a *convict.* It is best to refer to all folks in a local jail as *PRISONERS.* They are all *INMATES*, no matter where they are locked up.

Cooperate It is a common redundancy to say "*COOPERATE* together." *Cooperate* means just that--operate together.

Cop When Joe Friday on Dragnet introduced himself at the beginning of the program he said: "I'm a *cop.*" *COP*, to my way of thinking, is not a good way to refer to a police officer. It is informal at best and probably substandard for broadcast journalists. The word is frequently heard and I always find it jarring. Most policemen consider the term offensive.

Copter Do not use as a verb: "He *coptered* to New York." In fact, it is an unfamiliar reference to *helicopter*; let's avoid *copter* altogether. For broadcasting, I think *chopper* is acceptably familiar.

Copy/Replica This may be a lost cause. A *COPY* of the *Mayflower* is not a *REPLICA*. To be a true *replica* an object must be a copy of an original done by or under the supervision of the original artist.

Coronary/Heart Attack Informally, a *HEART ATTACK* is often referred to as a *CORONARY*. Technically--and correctly--*coronary* refers to the arteries of the heart which might become obstructed resulting in a *heart attack*. One should not refer to a heart attack as a *coronary*. It might be a "*coronary* occlusion" or a "*coronary* thrombosis," which are specific kinds of heart artery problems. Please do not refer to a "massive heart attack" unless you are quoting medical authority. From the standpoint of the victim, most heart attacks are massive.

Coroner/Medical Examiner/Pathologist A *CORONER* is not necessarily a medical doctor. A *coroner* is a public official--often elected--whose duty it is to investigate any death deemed to be of other than natural causes. A *MEDICAL EXAMINER*, on the other hand, usually is a medical doctor, usually appointed, whose duties are similar to those of a *coroner*. The title varies by locality or state. *Autopsies* (which see) are conducted by *PATHOLOGISTS*, who are medical doctors and may or may not be appointed *medical examiners*. A *medical examiner* or a *coroner* may call an "inquest" to investigate a suspicious death. A special "*coroner's* jury" is impaneled to carry out the investigation. The jury recommends whether a police investigation should be conducted.

Corporation/Incorporated Do not use *incorporation* as part of the name of a company. It is either *CORPORATION* or *INCORPORATED*. *Incorporation* is the act of incorporating.

Corps Pronounce it KOR. It's one of those rarities where two consonants are silent.

Couch/Davenport/Divan/Sofa As nouns, these are all about the same thing: something to sit or lie on. *DAVENPORT* probably comes from the family name. A *DIVAN* very often has no back or arms. It's probably a good idea to use *SOFA* in most references. I believe it is the most familiar.

Could Not Have Cared Less The phrase *I could have cared less* came into the idiom (or at least came to my attention) in the early 1960s. What is meant, of course, is *I COULD NOT HAVE CARED LESS*. The origin of this nonsense is a mystery to me. I thought it may have been passing out of use, but I keep hearing it--most recently in a formal speech before a distinguished university audience from the lips of an undeservedly revered newspaper executive.

Counsel *See* **Attorney.**

Countless This and other superlatives should be watched closely. The latest story had to do with massive labor unrest. *COUNTLESS* factories were closed. Hardly. Someone knew exactly how many factories were involved, and how many workers. It was the reporter who didn't know. *Bottomless, unfathomed, immeasurable*, are other examples.

Country/Nation *COUNTRY* is a much broader concept than *NATION*. *Nation* usually refers to an independent state, while *country* can be a regional concept. Generally the words are considered synonymous.

Coup D'État Pronounced KOO-day-TAH. It is the violent overthrow of a government, usually by the military. *Coup* means "stroke," so a *coup d'état* is a stroke against the state.

Coup De Grâce Pronounced KOO-duh-GRAHS. A death blow, usually meant to end the suffering of a wounded enemy or animal. It also is used symbolically to refer to the final act that ends a regime or idea of long standing.

Couple A collective noun that is to be treated as a singular in most cases. However, see an earlier discussion (item 2.40 in Part Two) of collectives where you will find advice not to drag the singular treatment on to nonsense.

Coyote A wild canine usually associated with the North American West, but which is found as far east as the Appalachians in increasing numbers. It is pronounced ky-OH-tee.

Crane/Derrick These terms are used interchangeably and that probably leads to little misunderstanding. But there is a difference. A *CRANE* and a *DERRICK* are both devices for lifting heavy objects. A *crane*, however, involves a vertical mast and a boom that rotates on the mast's vertical axis. A *derrick* can be something similar, but also is the term used for a tower or framework that supports a lifting or drilling device, such as an oil *derrick*.

Craps The game played with dice is *CRAPS*. Always expressed as a plural. *Crap* is something else entirely, except in a game of *craps* when a player throws a 2, 3, or 12; then the player is said to have rolled a *crap* or *craps*.

Credible/Creditable/Credulous Very closely similar and easily confused are *CREDIBLE, CREDITABLE* and *CREDULOUS*. Journalists place great value on being *credible*, as in to be *creditable* and hope to heaven they are not *credulous*. *Credible* means believable--reliable; *creditable* has a similar meaning in an older, rarely used and mostly obsolete sense in which credit means to believe, but in modern use it means commendable, trustworthy. *Credulous* means to be easily fooled--gullible, ready to believe without proof.

Creditor/Debtor A *CREDITOR* is someone to whom something, usually money, is owed. A *DEBTOR* is someone who owes--again, usually money.

Cry/Weep *CRY* carries the notion of sound and goes far beyond just the shedding of tears. We speak of a pack of hounds being "in *full* cry." It is a much broader term than *WEEP*, which means only to shed tears, or in other restricted senses, to ooze some sort of fluid. Many brick walls have "*weep* holes" to allow water to drain away.

Cryptic Why do so many people seem to think *CRYPTIC* means terse, brief, to the point? *Cryptic* means secret, coded, intentionally obscure. Coded messages are said to be *encrypted*.

Cue/Queue Both pronounced KEW. A *CUE* can be a number of things: a pool cue, an actor's entrance line and so on. A *QUEUE* is usually one thing only--a waiting line--but it can also refer to a braid of hair hanging down the back.

Currently/Presently *CURRENTLY* and *PRESENTLY* are not synonymous. "The temperature is *presently* 60 degrees" is not literate. *Currently* means right now, *presently* means soon, in a short time. "He will arrive *presently*." I think the problem here stems from *present* meaning right now. The *-ly* gets tacked on because it "sounds better." But it's wrong.

Cyclone/Hurricane/Tornado/Typhoon A *CYCLONE* is a circular motion of wind around an atmospheric low pressure area. It is usually characterized by moderate winds and precipitation. Weatherpeople refer to *cyclonic* air circulation. Around a high pressure area it is called a *cyclone*, around a low, an *anticyclone*. In the Western Hemisphere it is not necessarily a damaging storm and it is not a synonym for *TORNADO*. A *HURRICANE* is a widespread intense cyclone in which sustained winds have exceeded 74 miles an hour. A *TORNADO* is an intense cyclone over land (over water it is called a *water spout*) characterized by a funnel-shaped cloud and accompanied by heavy rain--a very dangerous storm. A *TYPHOON* is an intense cyclone occurring in the area of the China Sea. *CYCLONE* is the term used for a similar storm in the Indian Ocean. Both are what we call a *hurricane*.

Cynic/Skeptic Both words derive from ancient schools of philosophy. A *CYNIC* is a person who believes or expresses the opinion that human conduct is motivated primarily by self-interest. A *SKEPTIC* is a doubtful person, one who believes that some knowledge is unknowable.

Dairy/Diary Be careful with the spellings. If the construction of your sentence could cause confusion for your anchor, then mark your copy to make sure the right word is used.

Dais/Lectern/Podium *DAIS* and *PODIUM* are the same thing. Either is a proper name for a raised platform on which a speaker, for example, stands before an audience. Take your pick, but I think *podium* is the more familiar. A *LECTERN* (note spelling) is a stand or box with a sloping top on which a speaker places his script.

Damaged/Injured/Wounded *DAMAGE* occurs only to inanimate objects. You are *INJURED* in an accident, but *WOUNDED* by a weapon. A *wound* must penetrate the skin, ordinarily, but we do speak of *emotional wounds.* In medical circles penetrating injuries, including surgical incisions, are referred to as *wounds.*

Damper/Draft The *DAMPER* on a woodstove or fireplace is the device used to control the *DRAFT.* A favorite "fool's errand" in the old days was to send an apprentice boilermaker back to the shop to get the *draft* for the furnace. The *draft* is the airflow through the firebox, controlled by the *damper.*

Data/Datum We may be witnessing the death of a word. *DATA* is plural, the singular is *DATUM.* Correct usage is "Data are . . . ." It sounds awkward to many people and we hear *data* used as a singular more and more frequently. I still treat it as a plural, and I think you should too.

Dating (Back) To . . . The *BACK* is unnecessary; *DATING TO* gives the same information.

Davenport *See* **Couch.**

Davit *DAVITS* usually appear in pairs. A *davit* is a small crane on the deck of a boat that is used to raise and lower lifeboats or other small craft. Note it is not pronounced DAVID.

Deaf-Mute A *DEAF-MUTE* is a person who lacks both a full sense of hearing and the ability to speak. Not all deaf people are mutes. Avoid *deaf and dumb,* which in the insensitive days of the past was used for *deaf-mute.* It is now considered derogatory. Technically, a person or animal that is said to be *mute* cannot utter sound of any sort. *Deaf-mutes* usually can make sounds, but cannot form words well. Today the term *hearing impaired* is used instead of *deaf.* Why use two words, four syllables and fifteen letters when one word, one syllable and four letters will say the same thing?

Death *See* **Casualty.**

Deaths Be careful of the pronunciation of the plural. There is no really good way to write a phonetic for the *th* sound, which differs from the sound of SMITH and that of ALTHOUGH. The plural of *DEATH* should sound like SMITH'S.

Debtor *See* **Creditor.**

Debut/Debuted A *DEBUT* (pronounced day-BYOO) once meant specifically the introduction to society, or the introduction of a new performer or performance. It has come into much broader use in recent times, but still carries the idea of an introduction to the public. There is no such word as *DEBUTED*, which we often see as the past tense of *debut* erroneously converted into a verb. If you write that in broadcast copy, you may get *de-butted. Debut* is a noun. It has no past tense.

Decade/Decayed The difference in pronunciation here is the problem. *DECADE* is pronounced DECK-aid, ten years. *DECAYED* is pronounced duh-KAYED, rotted. Many words that begin with *de-* have the initial syllable pronounced as duh. Avoid hitting a stressed DEE sound is a good all-around broadcast rule.

Decimate In the bad old days, Roman soldiers followed the quaint practice of *DECIMATING* a defeated army. That meant to go through the ranks and kill every tenth man. *Decimate* means to reduce by one-tenth. However, the word has come to mean the destruction of a considerable part of something. Be careful in its use. I would avoid saying "The Yankees *decimated* the Red Sox," particularly if you live in Boston.

Declaim/Disclaim *DECLAIM* means to speak pompously or rhetorically as one might in an elocution exercise. *DISCLAIM* means to deny a connection with something. A *disclaimer* is often used in broadcasting to notify the listener that an opinion expressed on the air is not necessarily shared by the station or its employees.

Decorum *DECORUM,* by definition, refers to good behavior. Proper *decorum* is a redundancy. Pronounce it deh-KOR-um.

Defuse/Diffuse How do these get confused? In several recent articles by writers who should know better, I have seen *DIFFUSE* when the context clearly indicated the word wanted was *DEFUSE. Defuse* means to render harmless--as in "defuse the bomb." *Diffuse* means to scatter, spread around. In television we used *diffusers* on studio lights to soften harsh shadows and "hot spots." *Defuse* breaks the rule about avoiding stressed DEE sounds. Pronounce it dee-FYOOZ.

Degree/Diploma   You earn a *DEGREE* and it is conferred upon you by an institution of higher learning (high schools do not confer degrees). Usually, you are handed a *DIPLOMA* to hang on your wall to proclaim to the world that you earned the *degree*. A *degree* is a rank; a *diploma* is a document.

Delve/Dive   It's difficult to understand how these two completely different words get confused, but they do, in that DIVE is often used where DELVE is wanted. *Delve* means to dig and is usually used figuratively, as in "*delve* more deeply into the subject." *Dive* has several meanings, most having to do with a sudden descent or plunge. A *dive* is also a disreputable saloon.

Demur/Demure   *DEMUR* is a term used chiefly in legal matters, the action being known as a *demurrer*. It means to object to something, to take exception to. *DEMURE* means to be modest, perhaps even being affectedly reserved. To me it has always also had the connotation of referring to a small, apparently shy young woman.

Derrick   *See* **Crane.**

Descendant   *See* **Ancestor.**

Despite/In Spite Of   Both are used to mean "notwithstanding." *DESPITE*, however, has a number of other meanings, all having to do with spiteful behavior. Use *IN SPITE OF*.

Destroyed   To say something is "totally *destroyed*" is a redundancy. Destruction is, by definition, complete. We, of course, frequently hear the expression "partially destroyed." What is meant is *damaged*. "Demolition" and "annihilation" are also, by definition, complete.

Detroit/Tennessee/Vermont   All frequently mispronounced by stressing the first syllable. It is dih-TROIT, ten-uh-SEE (with light stress on the ten) and ver-MAHNT.

Diagnosis/Prognosis   *DIAGNOSIS* in medical usage is the process of identifying a disease by its signs and symptoms. The word has come into use by auto mechanics and computer operators, among others--but still means about the same thing. A *PROGNOSIS* is a prediction of the course of and result of an illness. It, too, is used in other contexts. Weatherpeople speak of "progging" the weather--forecasting. Please, let us not. It is Weather Service jargon.

Die From/Die Of   We *DIE OF* a disease or accident; we do not *DIE FROM* such causes, or any others for that matter.

Die/Perish In *Euphemisms & Other Doubletalk*, Hugh Rawson offers an excellent catalogue of the many ways English-speakers refer to death without actually saying it. There seem to be scores (maybe hundreds) of such euphemisms, but *PERISH* is not one of them. In common use, *perish* carries the sense of slow death, such as from freezing. Vegetables are said to be *perishable* because they will slowly decay. I don't think it would be advisable to refer to a traffic fatality as having *perished*. I think, perhaps, people *perish* in fires. *Perish* sounds quaint. Some, but not all, authorities say *perish* involves violent or untimely death. I'd not use it that way.

Different From/Different Than It is *DIFFERENT FROM*, no matter how many extra words it takes to use that form. *DIFFERENT THAN* is nonstandard, at best.

Diffident/Indifferent *DIFFIDENT* is much like "reticent." It means to be reluctant to speak because of shyness or fear of being wrong. It can also apply to action--which *reticent* cannot. *INDIFFERENT* means to be neutral--neither one side nor the other. It can also mean uncaring, uninvolved. We say a person received an *indifferent* education, meaning the teachers really didn't care much what sort of schooling they were handing out.

Dilemma Here's another of those words with a built-in sense of number. A *DILEMMA* (note spelling) is a problem with two possible courses of action--both of them undesirable. That's what a *dilemma* is and nothing else. The cliché "on the horns of a *dilemma*" is quite accurate. You may choose one horn or the other--but you're still on a horn.

Diminish/Minimize *DIMINISH* means to reduce in size or quantity, but not to any particular degree. To *MINIMIZE* means to reduce as far as possible--to the minimum.

Diphtheria/Diphthong/Naphtha Note the spellings. These words all contain the *phth* combination of consonants, and, yes, they are pronounced: DIFF-theria, DIFF-thong, NAFF-tha. No matter how many years you have been saying and hearing others say DIP-theria and NAP-tha, it's wrong. Hardly anyone ever says *diphthong*, right or wrong. Recent dictionaries accept DIP as a secondary pronunciation. *See also* **Ophthalmologist.**

Dirigible *See* **Balloon.**

Disburse/Disperse These two almost sound-alikes need careful pronunciation. To *DISBURSE* is to make payments, to distribute the proceeds of, for example, a will. To *DISPERSE* is to scatter or spread about. It can also mean to evaporate.

Discomfit/Discomfort *DISCOMFIT* is another bad broadcast word because is sounds so much like *DISCOMFORT*. *Discomfit* means to disconcert or embarrass. *DISCOMFORT* can mean being uncomfortable in any way, not only through embarrassment.

Discover/Invent *DISCOVER* is sometimes mistakenly used when the writer wants *INVENT*. It is correct to say Madame Curie *discovered* radium. She uncovered something that was already there, but unknown. To *invent* means to create something that had not previously existed. Alexander Graham Bell, it is said, *invented* the telephone.

Discreet/Discrete These words are so frequently confused in the spelling that it appears not many writers know the difference. *DISCREET* has to do with behavior that is circumspect, not showy; prudent, cautious. *DISCRETE* refers to something or someone that is separate and identifiable as an entity. Something can be made up of *discrete* parts.

Disinterested/Uninterested *DISINTERESTED* means neutral, as a judge is expected to be, taking no sides. *UNINTERESTED* means having no interest in something, paying no attention.

Disorganized/Unorganized Something or someone that is said to be *DISORGANIZED* probably was organized at one point, but has gone into disarray. Something or someone said to be *UNORGANIZED* never had it together in the first place. A riot is *unorganized*, a disbanded fraternity is *disorganized*.

Dissect *See* **Bisect.**

Dissemble/Assemble We all know that *ASSEMBLE* means to bring together things or people. *DISSEMBLE* means to deceive in a subtle way, to overlook or ignore facts contrary to the impression desired. It's a bad broadcast word.

Divan *See* **Couch.**

Diverge/Diverse/Divert *DIVERGE* means to move away, to spread out, to turn from a course. *DIVERSE* means to differ, to be unlike one another. *DIVERT* means to turn aside, to distract as in *diverting* one's attention.

Dock/Pier/Wharf These words have been so thoroughly mixed up over so many years, there's probably no point in trying to unscramble them. But *DOCK* is a place in which a ship is moored--the watery space between piers, for example. The expression "come to *dock*" probably has led to the use of *dock* to mean the *pier*. *Dock* takes up a lot of dictionary space with its many and varied meanings. A *PIER* (note spelling) and a *WHARF* (the *h* is silent) are about the same thing--a structure extending out from shore against which a ship may lie while moored. I think most people would think of passengers when one says *pier* and of cargo at the word *wharf.* Maybe not.

Dog Days Those hot, steamy days of midsummer, usually from mid-July to the first of September in the Northern Hemisphere. The reference is to the rising of Sirius, the "Dog Star." The term has nothing to do with dogs, but many people, probably wisely, avoid annoying dogs in hot weather. Sirius is called the Dog Star because it is the brightest star in the constellation Canis Major, the Greater Dog. *DOG DAYS* is used metaphorically to refer to any period of inactivity or stagnation.

Dog-Eared We are usually referring to the condition of a book when we say something is *DOG-eared.* It refers to the practice of turning down a corner of a page to mark a place, folding the paper to resemble the ear of certain dogs. However, the phrase has come to mean shabby, worn, beat up.

Dominate/Domineer *DOMINATE* has to do with ruling or overseeing; command-ing presence. To *DOMINEER* is to tyrannize, to exercise overbearing control. *Dominate* is more-or-less neutral, *domineer* carries a negative connotation.

Down East Applies only to Maine; and in Maine, only to the coastal area.

Down Under Refers only to Australia and New Zealand. The reference is to their location south of the equator.

Draft/Draught/Drought *DRAFT* and *DRAUGHT* are both pronounced DRAFT and, in reference to drinking, share identical meanings. *Draught* is principally a British usage. *Draft* has numerous other meanings, mostly having to do with drawing, either on paper or on a rope. *Draft* also, of course, means the drawing of lots as in military conscription. *DROUGHT* refers to a prolonged period of shortage--usually of water. It is pronounced DROWT--rhymes with TROUT. Sometimes, but rarely, you will see it spelled *DROUTH,* but the pronunciation remains the same.

Drape/Drapery *DRAPE* is the verb--the lounging cat *drapes* over the sofa. The heavy (usually) fabric window covering is *DRAPERY.* The fire started in the wastebasket and spread to the *draperies.*

Dreamed/Dreamt Both are the past tense of *dream.* I prefer *DREAMT,* pronounced DREMPT, for broadcast use; *DREAMED* sounds precious, almost poetic.

Dredge/Dreg There is an occasional confusion between these two, usually the use of *DREDGE* when *DREG* is wanted. To *dredge* is to dig in a variety of ways: to *dredge* up obscure facts, or to *dredge* a new ship channel. The *dregs* (almost always expressed as a plural) are unwanted leavings, such as the residue on the bottom of a wine bottle, or metaphorically, the *dregs* of society.

Drier/Dryer *DRIER* is the adjective meaning less moist. *DRYER* is the noun, an appliance that removes moisture.

Drowned Do not precede with the verb *was*. That implies action by an outside force. "He was *drowned* by his wife" is OK grammatically, if not legally. But if he fell off the boat and didn't come up, he *drowned*.

Drugs/Medicine/Medication Be careful, in this day and time, of the use of the word *DRUGS*. There was a time when to say a person was taking *drugs* simply meant he was taking medicine. No more. *MEDICATION* is just a fancy word for *MEDICINE*. Use *medicine*.

Drunk/Drunken A person may be *DRUNK* but he is arrested for *DRUNKEN* driving. *Drunk* is a state of being; *drunken* is the adjective for actions while *drunk*.

Dual/Duel Careful pronunciation will distinguish these words for your listeners. *DUAL* has to do with twos--the *dual* wheels on a truck, for example. A *DUEL* is a fight, usually with arms, between two contestants. Note the notion of there being only two participants is built in. When dueling was accepted, it was usually a formal combat before witnesses. Today we use the term more metaphorically in speaking of contests between opposing persons, ideas, theories or banjos.

Due To *See* **Because.**

Dumb We usually hear DUMB used to mean stupid. But that's only a lesser meaning. *Dumb* means lacking the power to speak. *See* **Deaf-Mute.** And that's what the phrase "*dumb* animal" means. It does not mean animals are stupid; it means they cannot utter words.

Dwarf/Midget *DWARF* is pronounced as one syllable, not duh-WHARF. The plural is pronounced DWARFS, not DWARVES. A *dwarf* is a person exhibiting congenital deformities usually including a disproportionately large head, shortened and bowed extremities and, often, deformed hands and feet. Mental retardation is not part of the condition. Things other than people can be referred to as *dwarf*, such as certain plants which have been deliberately stunted in their development. A *MIDGET* is a person of abnormally small stature, but well-proportioned. *Midgets* often have high-pitched voices, which is not common among *dwarfs*.

Dwell/Live/Reside *DWELL* is quaint. *RESIDE* is stilted. Use *LIVE*.

Each/Either Any time you're tempted to use *EITHER* (pronounced, please, EE-thur), stop and think. It is perfectly correct to say "take *either* route." However, it is wrong to say "the flowers are on *either* end of the coffin." What you want in that phrase is *EACH*. *Either* carries the notion of choice.

Eager *See* **Anxious**.

Earmark An *EARMARK* is a notch or tag in the ear of an animal, usually a bull, cow or sheep, for identification purposes. As a verb, *earmark* is frequently used metaphorically to indicate something has been set apart for a specific purpose. "The profits from the state lottery are *earmarked* for education."

Earthquake/Richter Scale/Temblor We all know what an *EARTHQUAKE* is, but many of us aren't too sure about the *RICHTER* (pronounced RIK-tur) *SCALE*, or so it would seem from stories I have read telling me that the scale is a 10-point system for measuring the severity of an *earthquake*. In fact, there is no top limit on the *Richter scale*. Geologists tell me that nine is the theoretical maximum, because beyond that everything would be destroyed. The scale is set up so that four is not just double two, it is 20 times. So by the time you get to nine, it's all over. Note the spelling and pronunciation of *TEMBLOR*. That is the term for the actual shaking of an *earthquake*. It is pronounced just as it is spelled: TEM-blur. It is, however, a weird word and *trembler* or even *tremor* are acceptable and certainly more understandable.

Ecology/Environment Don't get these words mixed up. Actually, nearly everyone has had them confused for 30 years, but that's no reason to perpetuate the confusion. The *ENVIRONMENT* is just a part of *ECOLOGY*. *Ecology* is the study of the interrelationship of organisms and their *environment*. The *environment* is the surrounding conditions that influence the *ecology*. It's eh-KAH-luh-gee, by the way.

Ecstasy Although we usually think of *ECSTASY* as being related to joy, it applies to any strong emotion. It is possible to be *ecstatic* with rage. It is a state of overwhelming emotion, being beyond self-control, out of stasis.

Effect *See* **Affect**.

Effete/Elite Here we have a real misunderstanding. *EFFETE* means burned out, decadent, having lost stamina as a result of overrefinement or lax standards. *ELITE* refers to the choice part, the cream of the crop. *Effete* was given new life by Spiro Agnew's speechwriter in 1969. Let's forget it.

Effluent *See* **Affluent.**

Egoist/Egotist An *EGOIST* is one who acts in his or her own self-interest; self-directed action. An *EGOTIST* directs attention to oneself.

Eject/Evict People who are, through legal process, *EVICTED* from their homes, in fact are *EJECTED*. But the relationship of the two words in common use does not go the other direction. A person *ejected* from a restaurant, for example, should not be said to have been *evicted*. The idea of legal process is built into *evict*, but not *eject*.

Elder/Older Dictionaries tell us *ELDER* and *OLDER* are alternative words with the same meaning. However, in common usage *elder* or *eldest* refer only to people, while *older* and *oldest* can refer to anything, people included. Generally, too, one would say "the *elder* of two children" but "the *eldest* of three."

Elderly Here we run into a problem similar to that we encounter with *YOUTH*. Be careful who you designate as *ELDERLY*. Most newswriters are fairly young people and tend to look upon anyone over 50 as *elderly*. Most people around 50 don't think of themselves as *elderly*, and are offended when someone else does. I think *elderly* may be safe in referring to someone more than 75 or 80. *Elderly* often, in the context of news stories, carries a connotation of incompetence, dottering senility. "The *elderly* driver . . ."

Elicit/Illicit *ELICIT* means to draw out, to find from someone--as the judicial process attempts to *elicit* the truth. *ILLICIT* in most common use means illegal, unlawful or anti-social behavior.

Elude *See* **Allude.**

Embargo *See* **Wire Services.**

Embattled Most often used and well understood to mean under siege, receiving criticism. *EMBATTLED* actually means to be ready for battle, to be armed for conflict. I find only one source that accepts the sense of being under attack.

Emigrate/Immigrate One *EMIGRATES* from a country. One *IMMIGRATES* to another country. One leaving is an *emigrant*, while one entering is an *immigrant*.

Eminent/Imminent *EMINENT* means outstanding, prominent. *IMMINENT* means impending, soon to come, often with the connotation of threat.

Empty/Vacant The distinction here is fine, and possibly non-existent. I believe usage has it that an *EMPTY* house is one with no people in it and a *VACANT* house is one with nothing in it. But usage experts say no. An *empty* bottle or house has nothing in it, while *vacant* carries the idea of a temporary condition--the folks away from home will soon return. Take your pick.

Endive How do you pronounce the leafy green veggie? There seem to be at least three ways. I think most Americans call it EHN-dyv. Classier restaurants give it the French twist ahn-DEEV. At least one famous Midwesterner tries to have it both ways with ahn-DYV. Only in the remotest sense is it a French term. It may even come from the Egyptian, way back. Most dictionaries cite it as EHN-dyv. AHN-deev is recognized reluctantly.

Energize/Enervate I doubt this confusion occurs very often, but I have heard it. It is a dangerous confusion because the two words are exact opposites. *ENERGIZE* we all know. It means to give energy, to turn on the power. *ENERVATE* means to sap strength, to weaken, either physically or morally. *Enervate* is not a good broadcast word.

Enigma/Puzzle/Riddle An *ENIGMA* is a certain kind of *PUZZLE*. It is one that is stated in such a way as to be intentionally obscure--like a *RIDDLE*. It can also be a mysterious event. *Enigma* is not a good broadcast word--*puzzle* will usually do just fine.

Engine/Motor The two words are frequently used interchangeably, but there are distinctions. A *MOTOR* uses an outside source of power--such as an electric motor--while an *ENGINE* generates its own power by consuming fuel. Another distinction is that a *motor* is generally stationary, while an *engine* is used to move something about. That's not hard and fast, of course--we immediately encounter the stationary steam *engine*, and, after all, the *motor* vehicle. Let common usage determine which you choose.

Enormity *ENORMITY* is not the same as *enormousness*. *Enormity* refers to a monstrous offense against decency or order. An *enormous* lie.

En Route Pronounced ON ROOT. Why not write it "on route"?

Ensure/Insure   Some dictionaries say these two words, along with *assure* and *secure*, are synonymous, but I like the distinction between them. *ENSURE* means to make certain, to make safe. *INSURE* refers to obtaining insurance, and in current usage, unless you are talking about the insurance business, use *ensure*.

Envelop/Envelope   There is a pronunciation problem with these two closely related and common words. The verb *ENVELOP* is pronounced ehn-VEL-up. The noun *ENVELOPE* is frequently pronounced AHN-vuh-lohp, but dictionaries disagree. Let's stick with the English version: EHN-vuh-lohp.

Enthuse/Enthusiastic   *ENTHUSED* does not mean *ENTHUSIASTIC*. You cannot become *enthused*. It is a verb. You can certainly *enthuse* over something, but that usage is awkward and seldom used by serious writers, and certainly not by broadcast writers.

Enthusiasm   Take care with the pronunciation. It is ehn-THOOZ-ee-AZ-um. It is often mispronounced ehn-THOOZ-ee-IHZ-um.

Entomology/Etymology   Close sound-alikes that have nothing in common. *ENTOMOLOGY* is the study of insects. *ETYMOLOGY* is the study of word origins and histories along with changes in usage.

Epidemic   An *EPIDEMIC* is a rapidly spreading disease and must be declared by competent medical authority--such as a local health director. Just because a lot of people have it doesn't make it an *epidemic*. It is considered a "scare" word in some circumstances and should be used with great care.

Epitome   *See* **Acme.**

Epizootic   There are times when for the sake of precision we have to use technical terms--and this is a perfect example. *EPIZOOTIC* refers to a disease or condition that is widespread among a certain group of animals, and *epidemic* may be a more familiar substitute, but we generally think of epidemics occurring among humans. The word came in handy a few seasons ago when several million turkeys and chickens became affected by avian flu in the Shenandoah Valley--a major poultry producing area. When we used the word, we briefly explained what it meant. It is pronounced EH-pih-zoh-AH-tik.

Erstwhile   *ERSTWHILE* means former, once upon a time. The *erstwhile* mayor is the one who did not win re-election. It's a pompous word--not recommended for broadcast news.

Escapee/Fugitive Here's one that no amount of prattling on my part will ever change, but did you ever stop to think that the person who escapes from prison is the escapor, while the jailor is the *ESCAPEE*? In any case, avoid it--use *FUGITIVE*.

Espresso Note spelling. The strong steam-brewed coffee of Italian origin is *ESPRESSO*. It is NOT *expresso*.

Esquire In the United States, *ESQUIRE* is a title of respect following a person's name, usually in abbreviated form: *Esq.* It is used almost exclusively by lawyers. In Britain an *esquire* is a member of the gentry.

Ethics/Morals Books have been written on this one. For our purposes we'll simplify. *ETHICS* is the study of the ways we reach *MORAL* decisions. They are not synonymous. *Ethics* is always expressed as a plural, but treated as a singular--*ethics* is.

Everybody/Everyone Prefer *EVERYONE*.

Exacerbate/Exasperate The excited TV weatherperson during a recent rash of forest fires said the "gusty winds will *EXASPERATE* the fires." After the laughter subsided, it was realized what the poor man was trying to say was *EXACERBATE*, to make worse in degree. *Exasperate* means to frustrate, make angry. The winds undoubtedly *exasperated* the firefighters. *Exacerbate* is a very bad word for broadcast, just because this sort of confusion is possible, even likely in the case of excited weatherpersons.

Excessive/Extensive I recently heard it reported that the damage from a flood was *EXCESSIVE*. That may be true, but what the reporter meant to say was *EXTENSIVE*. *Excessive* means more than necessary. We speak of police sometimes using *excessive* force when they seem to overdo the violence needed in an arrest. *EXTENSIVE* means over a wide area and, in common usage, to a severe degree.

Excrement *EXCREMENT* is the waste of any animal, both solid and liquid. However, the term generally is used to refer to fecal waste.

Excuse *See* **Alibi**.

Exotic *EXOTIC* means coming from another country--foreign. It also has a secondary meaning of mysterious. The euphemism for "stripper" is "*exotic* dancer" which, like so many euphemisms, misses the mark completely.

Explicit *See* **Adult**.

Facade A false front--of a building or a person. Pronounced fuh-SAHD.

Facility A terribly overused word. *FACILITY* has to do with making things easier or more comfortable. Public toilets are correctly, although somewhat euphemistically, called *facilities*. A secondary meaning is something that is built for a specific purpose. A stadium is a "sports facility," I'm sorry to say; that's what sportswriters incessantly call them.

Factor Overused by lazy writers who want to say *ingredient, reason* or *component*. *FACTOR* is a perfectly good word in those senses, but I hear it too often. *Factor* also means agent--one acting in behalf of another. *Factor* is a favorite word with writers who feel a need to puff up their copy. Any time you are tempted to use *factor*, look at your sentence carefully to see whether you can do without it or use a more specific word.

Faint/Feint Both pronounced FAYNT, but with vastly different meanings. *FAINT* can mean to lose consciousness, but we most often use the word to mean indistinct, difficult to see or hear. *FEINT* is a defensive move--used by boxers, among others--to cause an opponent to make a wrong move. It can also mean any maneuver, physical or otherwise, to distract an opponent's attention.

Famous/Infamous/Notorious *FAMOUS* means well-known or much talked about. *INFAMOUS* (pronounced IN-fuh-muss) means having a detestable reputation, known to be a truly awful person or thing. *NOTORIOUS* applies to people or things and means well-known for a particular trait or characteristic. It has a generally unsavory connotation.

Farther/Further Many experts on usage are about to give up on the distinction, saying *FURTHER* is winning out. I think the distinction is worth preserving. *Farther* has to do with space or distance, while *FURTHER* can mean "moreover" or going beyond--as *"further* education." Please do not use the phrase "all the *farther* (or *further*)." That is unrecognizable as English.

Fathom A measure of the depth of water, usually of the ocean. A *FATHOM* is six feet. It also means to get to the bottom of something--to understand completely. Most often used in the negative: "I just can't *fathom* that."

Faze/Phase Two exact sound-alikes that have nothing in common. *FAZE* means to worry, disconcert, bother. It is often seen in the negative sense: "The weather did not *faze* him." *PHASE* refers to a stage of development, a subdivision of time, place or completion, such as a *phase* of the moon.

February/Library Note spellings and the fact that both have two *r's* that are pronounced. It's FEB-roo-airy and LY-brair-ee. Elster is strong on this point, taking great umbrage at authorities who would condone dropping the first *r* to come up with feb-yoo-AIR-ee and LY-berry. Correct pronunciation of even these difficult words is the mark of a cultured, educated speaker and professional broadcaster.

Feel *See* **Believe.**

Felony/Misdemeanor A *FELONY* is a serious crime for which a lengthy jail term can be handed down. A *MISDEMEANOR* is a less serious offense and usually carries only a short jail term, if any. There are, of course, specific definitions of both which vary from state to state and are also to be found at the federal level.

Fettle An odd word that probably is rarely used in serious writing, but is sometimes useful. It means to be in good health and almost always is accompanied by *fine*. He was in "fine *FETTLE*." *Fettle* also has to do with the lining of a furnace, but that's specialty jargon, even though it's in the dictionary.

Fever/Temperature Everyone has a *TEMPERATURE* and if all is well it will be about 98.6 F. If it is elevated we are said to have a *FEVER*. It is colloquial at best to say "I have a *temperature*." Of course you do.

Fewer/Less OK--one more time. *FEWER* refers to number while *LESS* refers to quantity. The illiterate commercial that tells you a certain beer is *less* filling (correct) because is has *less* calories (wrong) is an abomination. I suppose the language in those commercials is a cynical attempt to reach to the "common man"--the beer drinkers. I have seen another commercial--this for light wine, in which the same phrase is used only slightly altered: "*Less* filling because it has *fewer* calories." Correct all the way. It gives you an idea of what sorts of stereotypes are current on Madison Avenue. The problem is these illiteracies creep into serious newswriting.

Fiancé/Fiancée Both are pronounced fee-awn-SAY, and their meanings are identical--except for gender. The male of the couple engaged to be married is the *FIANCÉ*, while the female is the *FIANCÉE*.

Figurative/Literal If you use *LITERALLY* you'd better mean it. To write "The woman was so embarrassed, she *literally* died" means the lady is really dead. *FIGURATIVELY* has a metaphoric sense--where one thing is made to stand for another. In the example above, "The woman was so embarrassed she *figuratively* died" is correct, but silly.

Filipino/Philippines Note spellings. A *FILIPINO* is a male native or citizen of the Republic of the *PHILIPPINES*. The feminine equivalent is *FILIPINA*.

Filling/Gas/Service Station At one time virtually all places where one bought gasoline also had service bays and did mechanical or other work on motor vehicles. Today, as we all know, there are places that do nothing but pump gas (often do-it-yourself). The preferred term once was *SERVICE* station. Today, that's no longer precise. If we must have a single word for such places, let's call them all *GAS* stations.

Fin/Finn A *FIN* can be an appendage on a fish, part of a rocket or old slang for a five-dollar bill. A *FINN* is a native of Finland.

Firm Not all businesses are *FIRMS*, but you wouldn't know it listening to broadcast news (or reading newspapers, for that matter), where everything becomes a *firm*. A *firm* is a business involving a partnership of two or more members. Therefore, a trucking business owned by one man is not a *firm*. Neither is the city-owned bus company. However, modern dictionaries recognize *firm* as a generic term for business enterprise.

Firmament A quaint old word often misused. *FIRMAMENT* has nothing to do with firmness. In fact, it's about as far from that as you can get. It means the sky, the "Heavenly Arch."

First Annual An impossibility. If it's the *FIRST* it cannot be *ANNUAL*--not yet, anyway. The phrase is full of hope, but not good sense.

Firstly/Secondly/Thusly, Etc. Don't. Please don't!

First Such . . . Of Its Kind If it's the *FIRST SUCH* then *OF ITS KIND* is illogical--if it's the *first* there is no *kind*. There are other similar constructions. Watch for them.

Fission/Fusion Easy to confuse and with exactly opposite meanings. Usually we use these words in connection with nuclear energy, but they both have other meanings. *FISSION* means to split apart, to divide, from which we get *fissure*--a crack. *Fusion* means to come together; two dissimilar things merging to form a new thing. We speak of the *fusion* of political groups.

Flagrant *See* **Blatant.**

Flair/Flare *FLAIR* has to do with style or talent--a *flair* for doing something. *FLARE* is a signal, a bright light to call attention. It is also used figuratively as: "his cold symptoms *flared* up." Fires *flare* when they ignite an especially flammable substance.

Flammable/Inflammable Isn't our language wonderful? These both mean the same thing, and there are many other similar seeming contradictions--words that begin with what we normally think of as a negative, but turn out not to be at all. *FLAMMABLE* and *INFLAMMABLE* both mean capable of burning, with the usual sense of being highly volatile. For broadcast use *flammable*.

Flash *See* **Wire Services.**

Flash In The Pan I recently saw this phrased as *splash in the pan*. That doesn't make any sense. The reference is to what would occasionally happen with flintlock weapons, when the flint spark would ignite the priming powder in the pan, but would fail to fire the gun--creating a *FLASH IN THE PAN* but without result, a misfire. The current sense of the phrase is in reference to someone or something that comes briefly to public notice but amounts to nothing.

Flaunt/Flout Often confused. *FLAUNT* means to make a showy display, usually in a vulgar manner. *FLOUT* means to defy authority in a contemptuous manner, to mock.

Flautist/Flutist For some reason we have two words for one who plays the flute. *FLAUTIST* is considered the "correct" one by serious musicians and others. *FLUTIST* is probably better understood by other folks. Webster's lists both, but prefers *flutist*.

Flay/Fray *FLAY* means to remove the skin or surface from someone or something. The usual sense is a violent skinning process. One can also *flay* someone with harsh language. A *FRAY* is usually a fight of some kind, but also means a wearing away, such as a *frayed* shirt collar.

Flew/Flied Only in baseball is *FLIED* the accepted past tense of fly. "He *flied* out," for some reason, is OK on a ball diamond, except for the batter who did it.

Flotsam/Jetsam These terms were once limited to applying to shipwrecks. The *FLOTSAM* was the floating wreckage and the *JETSAM*, certain cargo or other things tossed overboard (jettisoned) in an attempt to save the ship, and which eventually washes ashore. Today, they are used to describe almost anything floating or drifting about as if on water. We speak of "street people" as being the *flotsam and jetsam* of society.

Flounder/Founder *FLOUNDER*, in addition to being a tasty flat fish, means to thrash around, to be out of control. *FOUNDER* is usually used in reference to ship sinkings. Its primary meaning is to fill with water and sink. Note that the idea of sinking is built in. It is redundant to say "The ship *foundered* and sank." Today we speak of businesses *foundering*. That's certainly apt.

Flu *FLU* is an informal way of saying *influenza*, and that's not the sniffles. Influenza is a serious disease. Do not report that someone missed a meeting, for example, because of a "touch of the *flu*." There is no such thing as a "touch" of influenza. It is not a common cold.

Fluorescent Mostly, look at the spelling.

Forbade The past of *forbid*. It is preferably pronounced for-BAD.

Forceful/Forcible *FORCEFUL* means to be full of force, as one might expect. Effective, as in *forceful* language. *FORCIBLE* means to use force, as in *forcible* entry; breaking in.

Forecast The past form is also *FORECAST*, although some dictionaries permit *forecasted* as a secondary pronunciation. Prefer *forecast* in all tenses.

Foreign Words Many very useful and colorful *foreign words* and phrases have found their way into our daily speech. You should not avoid using them, as long as they are generally familiar. Be careful with the pronunciations, though--many such words have retained at least some of the foreign accenting, such as *pizza* (PEET-zuh) and *espresso*. *See also* **Zucchini**.

Forego/Forgo Both spellings are considered correct. *FOREGO* (the spelling I prefer) means to pass up, to let go by, to abstain. It also means to go before. I prefer that spelling, because it just looks right, and to my eye at least, *FORGO* doesn't. It looks too much like the city in North Dakota.

Foreword/Forward *FOREWORD* has to do with words that go before, the *foreword* of a book, for example. *FORWARD* means to move ahead in space or time. It is also a team position in a number of sports, and what one does when a document or message is sent on to a secondary recipient. While we're on the subject, a *foreword* to a book is often written by someone other than the principal author. An introduction is written by the author of the main text, as is a preface.

Forging/Uttering This will come up in forged check stories as well as others. *FORGING* is the actual writing of a check or other document with intent to defraud. *UTTERING* is the attempt to cash the check or exercise a forged document. The charge is usually expressed with both terms: *forging and uttering*.

Former/Latter   Neither term should be used in broadcast copy to refer to something already stated. It's all right to identify someone as a *"former senator,"* but not to name two persons in paragraph one, then refer to them as the *FORMER* or *LATTER* in paragraph two. The listener doesn't have time to figure it out. *Former* and *latter*, by the way, are used only when you are dealing with two persons or things. When more than two are involved, use *first* and *last*.

Formidable   Pronounced FORM-id-ih-bul.

Fortuitous   A *FORTUITOUS* event is not necessarily a good thing. *Fortuitous* does not imply good fortune, only accident or fate--occurring by chance. A secondary meaning is "lucky."

Forward   *See* **Afterward**.

Fracas   Pronounced FRAY-kus. It means a minor but physical encounter and can involve two or more individuals. Be careful not to write yourself an unintended double entendre--"The woman was shot in the *fracas*." It's a good old word, but has something of a slangy sound. It's fine for describing a brawl.

Frankenstein   *FRANKENSTEIN* was the fictional doctor, not the monster he constructed. If you ever have cause to use this to describe something that got out of hand, call it *"a Frankenstein's* monster."

Fractious   A terrible word for broadcast. It means to cause trouble by disobedience or unpredictable behavior.

Frantic/Frenetic   One who is *FRANTIC* may act in a *FRENETIC* way. *Frenetic* means wild, intense activity. Originally it meant insane. *Frantic* usually carries with it the notion of fear or anger--*frantically* searching. Both words come from the same Middle English root.

Fugitive   *See* **Escapee**.

-Fuls   Most authorities now tell us the plural of spoonful is spoonfuls. Other *-FULS* are treated similarly. My recollection of early education is that the correct plural was "spoonsful," which makes more literal and logical sense. Oh well. *Spoonfuls* seems to me to be very much like saying mother-in-laws or attorney generals, neither of which is acceptable.

Fulsome Recent dictionaries claim *FULSOME* has as its first meaning "in great abundance." This is a very new primary meaning. The word historically has meant offensive to the senses, disgusting. Be very careful how it is used.

Fundamental *See* **Basic.**

Funeral Home *See* **Mortuary.**

Funeral Service A redundancy. A *FUNERAL* is a *SERVICE.*

Funny/Peculiar Don't use *FUNNY* when you mean *PECULIAR* or strange. *Funny* has to do with humor.

Furlong One-eighth of a mile. Used mainly in horse racing. Literally, the length of a furrow.

Fusillade/Fuselage A *FUSILLADE* (pronounced FYOOS-ih-lahd) is a hail of something, often bullets. A firing squad creates a *fusillade*. A *FUSELAGE* is the body of an airplane.

Gaff/Gaffe *GAFF* has numerous meanings, most having to do with a spear or pole used for some specific purposes--such as *gaffing* fish or raising a sail. A *GAFFE* (still pronounced GAFF) is a social blunder.

Gage/Gauge We sometimes see *GAGE* used where *GAUGE* is needed. A *gage* is the cap or glove that's thrown on the ground to invite an opponent to fight. A *gauge* is usually a measuring device. The verb form "to *gauge*" refers to measuring or judging. *Gauge* also refers to the diameter of shotgun barrels, hypodermic needles and the width of railroad tracks, among other things, all having to do with measurement or size.

Gala There are three pronunciations. Most preferred is GAY-luh. Also recognized are GAL-uh and GAH-luh. Take your pick. *GALA* is both a noun and an adjective; an event may be called a *gala*, or may be referred to as a *gala* event.

Game/Sport Is there a difference? Certainly many *SPORTS* include playing a *GAME*, but there are *games* that do not include physical activity. I do not think checkers or chess are *sports*, even though there may be formal competition involved. Likewise, it seems unlikely that a professional boxing match can rightly be called a *game*, although many activities are informally referred to as *games*: the dating *game*, for example.

Gamut/Gantlet/Gauntlet The correct phrase, although a cliché, is "to run the *GANTLET*." It is frequently and, I believe, incorrectly phrased as "run the *GAUNTLET*." Webster's accepts the usage. A *gauntlet* is a long glove such as a welder or horseman might wear. A *gantlet* is formed by two rows of people between which someone runs while being beaten with sticks. Another thing we seem to run a lot is a *GAMUT*. That means to run the whole range of something. It originated as a musical term--to run the *gamut* meant to run the whole musical scale from one extreme to the other.

Garnish/Garnishee *GARNISH* and *GARNISHEE* are related words, as one might expect. In modern usage, however, they are far apart. *GARNISH* is a verb meaning to embellish, usually having to do with placing a bit of pretty on food. It is also a noun, of course; the bit of something is called a *garnish*. *GARNISHEE* is usually a verb meaning to attach a debtor's salary or property. As a noun, a *GARNISHEE* is one who garnishes. A *garnishee* is also one whose property is garnisheed. Certainly it's confusing. The point here is it is wrong to say a court has *garnished* a debtor's salary. A sprig of parsley in the pay envelope, maybe?

Gas Station *See* **Filling Station**.

Gauge *See* **Caliber, Gage**.

Gender/Sex Both words refer to the difference between males and females, and *GENDER* also refers to certain linguistic formations. In broadcast copy, *SEX* is preferred, as it is almost anywhere.

General Public A redundancy. Nothing can be more *general* than the *public*.

Generic/Genetic These words are related, both stemming from *genus*. Something that is *GENERIC* is characteristic of the whole genus. Thus, it has been extended to include such things as *generic* drugs, bread and cigarettes--sold without brand names. *GENETIC* refers to genes and to origins and can be applied to all living things.

Genteel/Gentile A *GENTEEL* person is one who is polite, stylish. It also means living in an elegant manner. A *GENTILE* is a non-Jewish person, usually a Christian.

Genuine Pronounce it JEN-yoo-in.

Gila (monster) HEE-luh. It is a venomous lizard with beady scales found in the desert southwest and in Mexico. The *Gila* is also a river in Arizona. The name is Spanish in origin, meaning "salty water." The *g* gets an *h* sound.

Girlfriend *See* **Boyfriend.**

Girl/Woman *See* **Boy.**

Glamour This is among the few words in American English to retain the British *-our* ending. It is, however, pronounced GLAM-ur. The adjective form is *glamorous.*

Glance/Glimpse The error here is to use *GLANCE* for *GLIMPSE.* A *glance* is the physical act of *glimpsing.* You get a *glimpse* of something when you *glance* at it. The *glance* is the quick sidelong look, the quick sight you get is the *glimpse.* Got it? Don't work too hard at it; in common use the words are almost interchangeable.

Golf/Gulf Pronunciation problems with these words. The game is pronounced GAHLF; the abyss or body of water is pronounced GUHLF.

Gondola It is pronounced GAHN-duh-luh. It is the famous romantic boat of the canals of Venice and also several other things. It was recently reported that some passengers were spilled from the *GONDOLA* of a hot air balloon. What the reporter was after there was basket. A *gondola* of a balloon must be enclosed. *See* **Blimp.** Some railroad cars, such as coal hoppers, are also called *gondolas.*

Gorilla/Guerrilla Another pronunciation problem. The great ape is pronounced guh-RILL-uh. The irregular soldier is pronounced gehr-ILL-uh, in American English. It's a Spanish word meaning, literally, "small war."

Got/Gotten These are ugly-sounding words when spoken--avoid them in broadcast copy. Often *got* is used unnecessarily. Some folks in Pennsylvania are stuck with auto license tags that read "You've *got* a friend in Pennsylvania." Leave out the got and you still have: "You've a friend in Pennsylvania," which says exactly the same thing in a much nicer way. I have seen Pennsylvania tags with the *got* taped over. That's gratifying.

Gourd Dictionaries give GORD as the first pronunciation, but also accept GOORD. I've always thought of the latter as a mispronunciation based on spelling. Use GORD. The botanical family includes squash and pumpkins, but in general use the term refers to smaller, inedible fruits often dried for decorative items or used as water dippers.

Gourmand/Gourmet A *GOURMAND* is a person who likes to eat--usually a lot. A *GOURMET* (pronounced goor-MAY) is a person who knows a lot about and appreciates good food, but is not necessarily a heavy eater. *Gourmet,* although widely used as an adjective, is usually recognized only as a noun. It is technically incorrect to speak of "*gourmet* food." "*Gourmet* cooking" sounds like cannibalism to me. Webster's says it may be used as an adjective. Try to avoid that usage.

Graduate   You are "*GRADUATED* from" a high school or institution of higher learning. It is an action taken by the school. Think about the word--it has to do with making the grade. It is non-standard to say "He *graduated* from . . . ." It is correct to say "He was *graduated* from . . . ." Never say "He *graduated* college."

Granada/Grenada   *GRANADA* is a city in Spain and is pronounced gruh-NAH-duh. *GRENADA* is an island in the West Indies and is pronounced greh-NAY-duh. Note the different spellings.

Graffiti/Graffito   Note spellings--two *f*'s, one *t*. *GRAFFITI* is the plural. The singular form *graffito*, is rarely used because it's rare to find just one mark on a wall.

Gratuitous   *GRATUITOUS* means unearned or unnecessary. It has nothing to do with graciousness and is only distantly related to gratitude when used in the sense of something that is given without cost to the recipient. The word is related to *grace* in the theological sense; something that simply comes without our bidding or deserving. We speak of *gratuitous* violence (unnecessary) in TV action programs. A waiter's tip is called a *gratuity*.

Greasy   The pronunciation varies regionally. GREE-see is most acceptable. GREE-zee is heard in some places. Prefer GREE-see.

Greenwich   Always pronounced GREN-itch. It is a city in England, near London, which is the commonly agreed-upon 0 degrees longitude--the prime meridian from which standard time is derived. *Greenwich* Mean Time. Also a city in Connecticut, and a section of New York City called *Greenwich* Village. Often simply called "the Village."

Grill/Grille   This is a distinction without much of a difference. A *GRILL* usually has to do with cooking food or the place that serves grilled food. A *GRILLE* is a barred structure forming a gate or screen. It's also the front of an automobile above the bumper. *Grill* can be used for either. Don't worry about it too much.

Grip/Grippe   *GRIP* means to hold firmly, and in television you will find a person who assists a photographer known as the "key *grip*." His job is to set up or hold lights, string microphone cables and generally be around to lug equipment. *GRIPPE* is a viral disease resembling influenza, still pronounced GRIP.

Grisly/Gristly/Grizzly   A bloody scene, such as a bad highway crash, can be described as *GRISLY*. A tough piece of cartilage in meat is said to be *GRISTLY* and is pronounced GRIZ-uh-lee. The bear is the *GRIZZLY*.

Groundhog Day   It is not *Groundhog's Day*. We are so accustomed to naming several holidays for saints (Valentine's, Swithin's, etc.) that the possessive seems to come naturally. But the hibernating critter who is supposed to appear on February 2 and predict the remaining winter doesn't own the day. It's expressed as *Groundhog Day*.

Guadaloupe/Guadalupe   *GUADALOUPE* is an island in the West Indies. *GUADALUPE* is an island owned by Mexico off the coast of southern California, among other things and places. Both are pronounced gwah-duh-LOOP.

Guardrail/Guiderail   There may be such things as *GUIDERAILS*, but they are not found beside highways--those are *GUARDRAILS*.

Guest Host   This apparently contradictory phrase is well understood whenever a talk show host goes on vacation. Watch for oxymorons; they will creep in. An oxymoron is a figure of speech that is internally contradictory. It comes from the Greek meaning "sharply foolish." Webster's gives *cruel kindness* as another example.

Guide/Guy Wires   A frequent error. The cables that support towers, bridges and so on, are *GUY WIRES*, not *GUIDE WIRES*.

Gun/Weapon   *See* **Automatic.**

Gutted   It's slangy and crude, but accepted, to say fire *GUTTED* a building--burning out the entire interior. However, we cannot extend that usage to say fire *gutted* 35 acres of woods.

Gynecology   A branch of medicine relating to the health of women, usually associated with the reproductive organs. It is pronounced GYN-eh-CAHL-eh-jee, with a hard *g*. Virtually all other words beginning with *gy* are pronounced with a soft *g*, such as *gyroscope, gyration, gypsom*. Another linguistic mystery.

Habit/Practice   Don't say *HABIT* when you mean *PRACTICE*. *Habit* implies fixation or compulsion, not simply doing something in a predictable way. For instance, it is misleading to say "He's in the *habit* of driving to work along Main Street." A habitual act occurs without thinking or planning.

Habitable/Inhabitable/Uninhabitable Here we hit another of those weird words. *HABITABLE* and *INHABITABLE*--both mean the same thing: capable of being lived in. *UNINHABITABLE* means you wouldn't want to live there. I think in a broadcast script I would use *inhabit* as the verb and *habitable* as the adjective.

Hail/Hale *HAIL* is the frozen precipitation, the greeting and the salutation as in "all *hail* the chief." *HALE* means healthy and also means to haul someone into court. Now, may we talk about the size of *hail*? I think it is common for untrained volunteer weather observers in rural areas, who are often consulted by TV weatherpersons, to exaggerate a variety of conditions: how deep is the snow, how much did it rain, how strong was the wind. And, too, how big was the *hail*. It has become common to compare *hail* to the size of a variety of round objects. We begin with BBs or peas, move to cranberries, come up to Ping-Pong balls, then to golf balls. That's about the limit of my credulity for the average *hail*storm. Hailstones of more than seven inches in diameter have been reliably reported, but such things are very rare and make the record books. Baseball-sized hailstones would probably be fatal to any creature struck by one, certainly heavily damaging to automobiles and structures. Any dense object falling from a substantial height will strike the earth at terminal velocity, about 125 miles an hour. When one considers the formation of *hail*, an object the size and weight of a baseball would seem to be a rare occurrence. *Hail* is formed by falling, then being lofted into the high atmosphere to pick up more moisture and ice, then falling again. It would take quite an updraft to toss a baseball several thousand feet in the air. I'm not saying it would not be possible for such hail to develop--indeed it has-- only that broadcasters should be cautious in reporting such an event on the basis of a telephoned report from a viewer.

Half-Mast/Half-Staff Flags on land are flown at *HALF-STAFF*. It is, after all, a flag*staff*. At sea, flags are most often flown from a mast, so there they are said to fly at *HALF-MAST*. *Half-staff* or *half-mast*, flags are so flown to indicate mourning.

Halley's Comet After a disappointing appearance in 1986, *HALLEY'S COMET* has returned to deep space not to reappear to spectators on earth until 2062. What you need to know in the intervening years is this: it rhymes with *valley*.

Hallowe'en Note the spelling. It is a contraction of All Hallows' Eve, the night before All Saints' Day. The pronunciation is often HAHL-oh-ween. It is correctly HAL-uh-ween. Webster's accepts the spelling *Halloween*, without the apostrophe. Why not?

Halve To divide in half. It's a fine word, but not for broadcast, because it sounds just like have. "The Mayor says he will *halve* the staff next week." What did the mayor say? It will probably take more words to work around *halve*, but do it anyhow.

Handkerchief Pronounced HAND-ker-chif. Be careful not to drop the "d" so it comes out "hanker-chif." Elster says it's a HANG-ker-chif. So do the dictionaries. Am I alone in fully pronouncing the HAND?

Hangar/Hanger Aircraft are stored and repaired in a *HANGAR*. The most common use of *HANGER* is to refer to clothes *hangers*--but it has a number of other uses as well.

Hanged/Hung A condemned person is said to have been *HANGED*, while a picture is *HUNG* on the wall.

Hang Glider/Ultralight It was reported on several occasions that someone had flown a *HANG GLIDER* over the Berlin Wall when it was still in place, or over some other such barrier either out of or into forbidden territory. My bet is it was not a *hang glider* at all, but an airplane known as an *ULTRALIGHT*. A *hang glider* is not powered and cannot "fly" anywhere unless launched from a high point such as a cliff or towed aloft. An *ultralight* looks much like a *hang glider* to the uninitiated eye, but has a small gasoline engine to propel it and is capable of taking off from a level and short runway.

Happen/Occur/Transpire Accidents don't *HAPPEN*, they *OCCUR*. *Occur* is the preferred verb when the action is spontaneous or accidental. The words are very similar in meaning, but *occur* is preferred when referring to the unexpected. *TRANSPIRE* is a pompous word for "to take place," and is usually used incorrectly. It means, literally, "to exhale across." It is used to mean to come to light, to expose, to become known. It does not mean to *happen* or *occur*.

Hara-Kiri A Japanese form of ritual suicide. The term is often seen as *hari-kari*. Harry Caray is a baseball announcer. I believe there was an actor named Harry Carey. Pronounce it carefully, please. It is HAH-ruh KEE-ree.

Harass Often misspelled and perhaps mispronounced. It is spelled as you see it here, and its pronunciation is huh-RASS, especially in military boot camp. I prefer HAR-uss. Dictionaries disagree on the preferred pronunciation. Elster says either is acceptable, but HAR-uss is the older, more traditional pronunciation.

Harbor/Port A *HARBOR* is any safe haven on a coastline where a ship can enter to be protected from the open sea. A *PORT* is usually located in a *harbor* and is the complex of *docks* (which see), *wharfs* and *piers* against which ships may moor. The idea of *port* extends to the city itself.

Harebrained Note the expression is not "hair" brained. It means flighty, easily excited, like a hare or rabbit. A *HAREBRAINED* idea is one that has not been thought through, that is likely to be wrong or lead to failure.

Hare/Rabbit Except in informal usage, a *HARE* is not a *RABBIT*. They look very much alike, but are different in detail. The *hare* is generally larger than a *rabbit* and its young are born with eyes open and fully furred. A *rabbit's* young are born blind and naked. Both have a double row of incisors, which differentiates them from rodents which have only a single row. So, regardless of Elmer Fudd's long-standing feud with that "waskally wodent," Bugs Bunny, the rabbit is not a rodent. *Hare* has a sort of Old World sound to it. It's not a familiar reference, so probably you'll do OK calling any such animal a *rabbit*.

Headline Words There are numerous words that headline writers, especially those of more sensational publications, adore because they are short and have come to mean things that are more accurately expressed with longer words. Many of them are words rarely, if ever, heard in conversational speech. Broadcasters will do well to avoid them, or at least select them with great caution. There are many such words. A few examples are *FOE*, *WOE*, *PANEL* (for committee), *HIKE* (as in price hike), *CUT* (as in tax cut), *PREXY* (old slang for college president), *DEB* (for debutante), *SLAY, SLAIN, TALKS* (for negotiations), *FLEE, COP, VOW, NAB* (Cops Nab Cut Foe; Vows to Flee), *EYE* (Prexy Eyes Fee Hike), *TEST* (for election, contest, fight, etc.), *FACE* (for confront, as in Panel Faces Hike Test), *SET* (for schedule), *SHAM, SPUR, CLAIM* (Wreck Claims Deb), *PACT, BID, MUM, MARK, NIP, LINK* (Cops Link Prexy, Deb), *HEIST, RAZE, PARLAY, NIX, BLAST* (for criticize), *RIP, FLAY, INK* (for sign), *SLATED, SOLON* (for senator), *LEVY* (tax), *SCAM, COED* (Prexy Ripped in Coed Scam). And, of course, there's the local all-purpose superhero: AREA MAN who, with his family, gets involved in all sorts of wonderful and horrible things: Area Man Arrested In Drug Sweep, Area Couple Dies In Crash, Area Boy Wins Swim Meet, Area Girl Is Twirling Champ. We can go on and on. It's fun, but there's a serious side, too. Many of these words are ambiguous and can lead to confusion. Be as precise as you can be.

Headlong/Head-On It was reported in connection with a horrible bus wreck that a pickup truck hit the bus *HEADLONG*. I think what the reporter wanted was *HEAD-on*. *Headlong* means rushing in a reckless manner, out of control, going head first. *Head-on* refers to two objects or ideas colliding head to head or front to front.

Healthful/Healthy A distinction is normally drawn between *HEALTHFUL* and *HEALTHY*. *Healthful* is taken to mean promoting or contributing to health. We speak of *healthful* foods. *Healthy* is a state of being free of disease and functioning properly. New lines of low-fat, -salt and -sodium foods, along with their advertising, may soon destroy this distinction with their illiterate insistence on "*healthy* foods."

Heart Attack *See* **Coronary.**

Height Note spelling. It is not *heighth* as many people seem to believe, influenced, no doubt, by *width* and *depth*. Webster's says *HEIGHT* may be pronounced HEIGHTH, but I don't like it. And it's not spelled that way.

Heinous Pronounced HAY-nuss. It means shocking, grossly evil.

Heir Someone has to die before there can be an *HEIR*. It is technically wrong, but commonly done, to refer to the *heir* to the throne before the reigning monarch has died. What is wanted in that instance is "*heir* apparent" or *scion* (which see).

Helicopter Pronounced HELL-ih-copter. People who persist in saying HEEL-ih-copter are probably just shy of saying HELL. The term is derived from the helical pattern formed by the rotation of the blades--and that's pronounced HEEL-ih-kul.

Hemorrhage To bleed profusely, possibly to death. It's pronounced HEM-uh-ridj. Often heard as HEM-ridj, but for broadcasters, that's just lazy pronunciation.

Heroin/Heroine These words are identically pronounced HAIR-oh-win. Be careful not to refer to the brave lady as a *heroin*.

Historic/Historical If something is said to be *HISTORIC* it is a famous or important thing, such as a crucial meeting between heads of state. Something that is *HISTORICAL* has a place in history. A building, such as Independence Hall for example, can be both old and important. The adjective you choose in that case would depend on the context of your story. To be *historic* does not necessarily imply age. What is termed *historic* will likely find a place in history books.

HIV Human immunodeficiency virus. It is written "*H-I-V*"--it is hyphenated because it isn't a pronounceable acronym. It refers to a group of viruses that cause *AIDS* (which see). Be careful not to write "*H-I-V* virus," thus saying "virus" twice.

Hoar/Whore *HOAR* is frost. An old person with white hair is said to be "hoary-haired." We all know what a *WHORE* is. I would urge you to use either word with great caution.

Hoard/Horde To *HOARD* is to gather up large quantities of food or other materials against possible future shortages. During World War II when rationing was imposed, *hoarding* was a serious offense. The word carries with it the implication of greed. *Hoard* is also used as a noun as in "a *hoard* of gold." A *HORDE* is a large number of people; the sense of being unorganized is built in.

Hoi Polloi Many people seem to think the *HOI POLLOI* are the fancy folks, the elite. Not so. The *hoi polloi* are the common folks--the masses. Pronounced HOY puh-LOY. Often used as a term of contempt.

Holocaust Originally *HOLOCAUST* referred to sacrifice by fire, then destruction by any big fire. It has come to mean the destruction of European Jews by the Nazis, and perhaps has been pre-empted from other uses. That's what happens to a dynamic language. It's too bad, perhaps, but such words as *gay* and *queer* have also been nearly lost in their original senses.

Home/House A *HOUSE* is not always a *HOME*. A *house* is a structure intended to be lived in but which may or may not be occupied. A *home* is any place a person or group of persons lives; a house, apartment or tent.

Home . . ./Hone In On A fairly common careless usage. *HOME IN ON* . . . refers to focusing or aiming, as in radar homing in on a target, or a homing pigeon finding its way. *Hone in on* . . . means nothing. To hone is to sharpen or whet.

Homicide/Manslaughter/Murder To cause the death of any human being by whatever means is a *HOMICIDE* (note spelling). It is preferably pronounced HAHM-ih-syd. *MANSLAUGHTER* is the unlawful killing of another person without malice or premeditation. A *MURDER* is the unlawful, willful, malicious or premeditated killing of another human being. There are, in most states, several "degrees" of *murder*. A *murder* involves only a human life. A newspaper headline referred to a man who *murdered* seven pigeons. Not so. He killed them.

Hoof The plural is pronounced and spelled HOOVES, not HOOFS.

Hopefully Do not use *HOPEFULLY* as an adverb in the sense of "it is to be hoped" at the beginning of a sentence: "*Hopefully*, the car will arrive on time." That means the car is full of hope. There's a deep urge in all of us, I think, to use *hopefully* and *thankfully* that way. Don't.

To A Hospital Use *TO A HOSPITAL* rather than "to the hospital," or name the specific hospital to which someone is taken. A word of caution: In most localities in which there is more than one hospital, one will develop into the "emergency" hospital. Logically, that is the place where most accident victims and other emergency cases will die. If you name the hospital each time, it will soon become known to the public as a pesthouse--the place you go to die. Just a thought.

Host *See* **Author**.

Hot Cup Of . . . Some authorities are saying it is sheer sophistry to insist that it's not a *HOT CUP OF* something, but a "cup of hot" something. But I still like the precision. It is not the cup that is hot (at least initially), but rather what is in it.

Hot Water Heater Same thing here. It is not a *HOT WATER HEATER*, but a *water heater*.

Hudson Bay The huge body of water north of Canada is *HUDSON BAY*, not "Hudson's Bay." The British trading organization that developed the region for fur trading and later for virtually all commercial purposes is The Hudson's Bay Company.

Humongous The word is a combination of *huge* and *tremendous*, I'm told. It is slang. There it is, right in the dictionary. Don't use it.

Hungary Pronounce the European country with three syllables: HUHN-gur-ee.

Hurdle/Hurtle These words have similar sound and meaning and are often confused. *HURDLE* means to leap over an obstacle. *HURTLE* means to plunge rapidly as in "the rocket *hurtled* through space." Careful pronunciation is needed.

Hurricane *See* **Cyclone**.

Hyper/Hypo *HYPER* as a prefix means above, in excess; as an adjective it means overexcitable. *HYPO* is the opposite; it means below, less than normal. We speak of *hypo*thermia when the body temperature is severely below normal, and *hyper*tension when the blood pressure is seriously elevated.

If/Whether *WHETHER* has a built-in sense of "or not," implying an alternative. If that is the sense of your idea, then use *whether*. Otherwise, use *IF*. Most often, "or not" is not needed with *whether*. Test your sentence to see whether you can leave out the "or not."

Ilk It's not what you think, if you think it means something like "people he associates with." Your *ILK* are those of your family--with the same name. It's an old Scottish word, heard infrequently and mostly pejoratively these days. "MacDonald and his *ilk*."

Ill/Sick Prefer *ILL* most of the time when referring to physical indisposition. But "the scene *sickened* even the hardened police" is much stronger than "the scene made even the hardened police *ill*." Commonly, and especially in England, *sick* means specifically a stomach upset--*nauseated* (which see).

Illicit *See* **Elicit.**

Illusion *See* **Allusion.**

Immature/Premature *IMMATURE* means unfinished, not fully grown or developed. *PREMATURE* means before it's time, unexpectedly early. In referring to *premature* babies, there are two measures: born before the full gestation period is complete, or with lower than normal birth weight, regardless of the gestation period.

Immigrate *See* **Emigrate.**

Imminent *See* **Eminent.**

Immolate We became familiar with this word during the Vietnam War when Buddhist monks were said to have committed self-*IMMOLATION* when they burned themselves to death publicly. That is a correct use of the word, but many people now think *immolation* necessarily involves burning. An *immolation* is a sacrifice, sometimes involving killing oneself or someone else, but the word can also be used symbolically, and *immolation* does not necessarily involve fire.

Immoral *See* **Amoral.**

Impeach When a public official is charged with official misconduct he is said to have been *IMPEACHED*. Note that an *impeachment* involves ONLY the bringing of charges. It is similar to an *indictment* (see **Indict**). Under the U.S. Constitution, the House of Representatives, after hearings, may *impeach* a sitting president. But the actual trial on the *impeachment* (charges) is conducted by the Senate. The president may be found either guilty or innocent of the *impeachment*.

Imply/Infer The easiest way to handle this confusion is to remember that the speaker *IMPLIES* and the listener *INFERS*. It's not always oral communication, of course.

Impotent/Imprudent/Impudent The pronunciation of *IMPOTENT* is IM-puh-tunt. Therefore, it is often confused with *IMPUDENT* which is often confused with *IMPRUDENT*. *Impotent* means powerless, helpless, weak. *Impudent* means cocky, bold, without regard for others, disrespectful. *IMPRUDENT* means lacking caution, without regard for consequences.

Incipient/Insipid Here are a pair of almost look and sound-alikes that have very different meanings. *INCIPIENT* means something that is about to come into being. A person about to be graduated from a teachers' college, for example, is an *incipient* teacher. *INSIPID*, way on the other hand, means dull, lacking in taste. The word can be applied to people or things, such as soup.

Incorporated *See* **Corporation.**

Indecision *See* **Ambivalence.**

Indict An *INDICTMENT* (pronounced in-DYT-munt) is carried out by a grand jury. An *indictment* is a statement that a crime has been committed and there is sufficient evidence to bring the accused to trial. It is not a finding of guilt or innocence. The finding of a grand jury to bring the accused to trial is called a *true bill*. If there is not an *indictment* the finding is called *no bill*. The proceedings of grand juries are usually secret, including the identities of the members. Incidentally, a grand jury is said to "hand up" an *indictment*, while a judge "hands down" a sentence. The image is the judge sitting above the courtroom. The grand jury hands the *indictment* up to the judge, who later hands down a sentence.

Indifferent *See* **Diffident.**

Infamous *See* **Famous.**

Infant *See* **Baby.**

Infectious *See* **Contagious.**

Inflammable *See* **Flammable.**

Informant/Informer Both have the meaning of "one who informs." However, *INFORMER* is the word of choice when speaking of someone who "squeals." "The police *informer*."

In Front Of *See* **Before.**

Inhabitable *See* **Habitable.**

Inhuman/Inhumane These mean about the same thing, but it seems to me that *INHUMAN* refers to actions affecting people, while *INHUMANE* relates to animals. They both mean "to be cruel and insensitive to the feelings, comfort or safety of others." *Inhuman* also means not human--lacking the qualities that mark a human being.

Inimical/Inimitable Sound-alikes that are entirely unrelated. *INIMICAL* means unfriendly, dangerous. *INIMITABLE* refers to something that cannot be imitated, frequently used to describe a singer's style. Neither is a good word for broadcast news.

Injured *See* **Damaged.**

Inmate *See* **Convict.**

Innocent/Not Guilty There is a difference between *INNOCENT* and *NOT GUILTY*. The verdict of a court will be *not guilty*, it will not be *innocent*, because innocence is a state of being, not an official finding. In broadcasting we do better to say a person was "acquitted" rather than found *not guilty*, because of the possibility of being misunderstood.

Inoculate Note the spelling--just one *n*.

Inquire *See* **Ascertain.**

Inquiry/Question *INQUIRY* has the sense of being more than just asking a *QUESTION*. An *inquiry* is the seeking of truth or facts and the examination of that information. One would ask *questions* while conducting an *inquiry*.

Inside/Outside Do not use with *of* unless *INSIDE* or *OUTSIDE* is used as a noun. "The *inside of* the boiler was damaged" is correct. But "He tossed the body *inside* of the boiler" is not. "I am painting *outside* the barn," tells a different story from "I am painting the *outside* of the barn."

Insidious/Invidious Both are unpleasant. *INSIDIOUS* means cunning, deceitful, creeping slowly with, most likely, a hidden effect. *INVIDIOUS* means defamatory, likely to cause discontent, jealous.

Insoluble/Insolvable Both can be used to mean "incapable of being solved." However, *INSOLUBLE* also means "incapable of being dissolved." When you are referring to a problem that seems to have no solution, use *insoluble,* to avoid a possible ambiguity in some contexts. *Unsolvable* is also accepted.

In Spite Of *See* **Despite.**

Instantaneously/Instantly *INSTANTANEOUSLY* is what we usually want when we say *INSTANTLY. Instantaneously* means with no perceptible lapse of time. *Instantly* means without delay, at once, with urgency. It is probably incorrect to say a person died *instantly* in a wreck. But it is almost always used that way.

Insure *See* **Ensure.**

Intended/Intentional What is *INTENDED* is what is meant by or expected from some speech or action. *INTENTIONAL* means deliberately--on purpose.

Inter/Intra *INTER* as a prefix means among or between, as in *inter*national or *inter*relation. *INTRA* means within, inside, as in *intra*venous injection or *intra*mural.

Interpretative/Interpretive These are synonyms, each equally acceptable. I'd suggest for broadcast using the shorter: *INTERPRETIVE. INTERPRETATIVE* seems a bit pretentious. *See also* **Preventative.**

Introduction *See* **Foreword.**

Inundated *INUNDATED* means flooded. To write "*inundated* by floodwaters" is a redundancy.

Invent *See* **Discover.**

Irregardless *IRREGARDLESS* of how many times you've seen this word--it is not a word. The word wanted is *REGARDLESS.*

Irrevocable Pronounced eer-REV-uh-kubl. Study the *ir-* words in a good dictionary. Pronunciation of many is tricky.

Isle Of Wight In the United States probably the only people who need to worry about this are those in Virginia where there is an *Isle of Wight* County and a town of the same name. The original is an island in the English Channel. The thing to note here is the spelling and pronunciation--it is WIGHT--not WHITE.

Israeli/Israelite A modern native of the Republic of Israel is an *ISRAELI*. A member of one of the ten Hebrew tribes of ancient times is called an *ISRAELITE*.

Its/It's *ITS* is the possessive and is formed without an apostrophe. *IT'S* is the contraction of "it is." This is confusing, because most possessives are formed with an apostrophe, as in "Murphy's Law." I seem to recall in early education to have been taught that the possessive was formed as *its'* but not so any longer.

Jail/Prison/Penitentiary Some dictionaries claim *JAIL* and *PRISON* are synonymous, but usage dictates a distinction. A *jail* is a local lockup where newly arrested persons are held pending trial, or where short-term prisoners are housed (*see* **Convict**). A *PRISON* is a state or federal penal institution where convicted prisoners are incarcerated. A *PENITENTIARY* is the same as a *prison* and refers to a major Big House. One would not refer to the city *prison* or the state *jail*. *Penitentiary*, of course, comes from *penitent*--a place one goes to feel sorry for committing a crime. Most often I would suggest avoiding the word, unless it is part of the official name of the prison.

Jerry/Jury Something done for temporary or emergency purposes is said to be *JURY RIGGED*, such as a spar erected on a ship in place of a broken mast. Something that is hastily or sloppily done is said to be *JERRY-BUILT*. It is a term of contempt. Some authorities believe it stems from World War II, when German troops were referred to as *Jerries*, but the usage dates to the 19th century.

Jetsam *See* **Flotsam**.

Jibe/Jive I was going to leave this one out, figuring everyone knows the difference, then the error showed up in an AP newsletter. To *JIBE* is to agree with in the sense that your opinion *jibes* with mine. A *jibe* can be a sharp, slyly critical remark. A *jibe* is also a maneuver performed with a sailboat in which the stern is brought across the wind and the sail swings from one side to the other, usually with some force. Sometimes it is spelled *gybe*. *JIVE* on the other hand is a slang term for certain kinds of talk; glib, deliberately deceptive. It also refers to certain kinds of music and dancing popular during and just after World War II. *Jive* can also mean to tease or mislead. "Don't *jive* me, man!"

Join Together A redundancy.

Judge/Jurist/Juror We all know what a *JUDGE* is, but we get confused over *JURIST*. A *jurist* is not a member of a jury. A *jurist* is a person skilled in the law. He might be a *judge* or an *attorney* (which see), or not. A person serving on a jury is a *JUROR*. Pronounce it JOOR-ur, not JOOR-or.

Judgment Note spelling--not *judgement*. That's OK in Britain, however. A former U.S. president, I'm sure, spelled it the British way because he pronounced it as three syllables: judge-uh-ment.

Judicial/Judicious *JUDICIAL* has to do with the process of judging, the administration of justice. Court proceedings are said to be *judicial* actions. *JUDICIOUS* refers to the exercise of sound judgment, not necessarily in connection with court actions. Characterized by reasoning and sound logic. *Judicious* carries the notion of caution.

Juggler/Jugular A *JUGGLER* is a person who can keep several objects in the air seemingly at the same time. It is used literally to describe someone putting on a show, and figuratively to describe a busy person with many projects under way at once. The *JUGULAR* is any of several large blood vessels in the neck that, when severed, allow a person (or animal) to rapidly bleed to death. To say a person is "going for the *jugular*" means that person is out to literally or figuratively kill an opponent. Note it is a three-syllable word: JUHG-yoo-luhr.

Junction/Juncture A *JUNCTION* is a place of meeting, in its most common use. A railroad *junction* is a point where two or more rail lines come together. A *JUNCTURE* is most often used to indicate a point in time, but it also can mean a coming together, a seam.

Junta A *JUNTA* is a group of people, usually military, who are placed in control of a government following a *COUP* (which see). It is a Spanish word, therefore pronounced HOON-tah or HUN-tah. Prefer HUN-tah.

Karat *See* **Carat.**

Ketchup *See* **Catsup.**

Kill *See* **Wire Services.**

Killed After This is one we see and hear with frightening regularity. The man was *KILLED AFTER* his car struck the tree. Did they run over him with the ambulance? He may have *died after* the wreck, but he was not *killed after* the crash. *Killed when* is what is usually wanted in a case of instantaneous death.

Kilo Pronounced KEE-loh. It is an abbreviation of *kilogram*, usually. A *KILO* is one-thousand grams or approximately two and a half pounds.

Kilometer Pronounced kuh-LAHM-uh-tur or KIL-oh-mee-tur. It is the metric system's equivalent of the mile and is 1,000 meters or approximately six-tenths of a U.S. mile. The pronunciation is up for grabs. Elster has a lengthy discussion in which he cites usage expertise on both sides. He prefers KIL-oh-mee-tur. I still prefer kuh-LAHM-uh-tur.

Kinetic The kind of energy derived from motion. There is a frequent misconception that *KINETIC* energy is that which creates motion. It's the other way around. Overactive children are sometimes called by anxious parents hyper*kinetic*, which is not an accurate use of the term. It really means abnormally increased muscle movement--twitching.

Knot One nautical mile. It is a measure of speed, not of distance. The sense of time is built in. A ship is said to be making 10 *knots*, not 10 knots an hour. A nautical mile is approximately one and one tenth statute miles.

Koala Probably one of the "cuddliest" of the animal kingdom. Often called a *KOALA BEAR*. It's not a bear, although it does have considerable resemblance to a stuffed toy bear. It really looks very little like a true bear. It's a marsupial, native to Australia.

Kudos Always written as if plural. It refers to praise offered following an achievement. Mostly limited to public performances. The audience heaped *KUDOS* on the actor.

Lady/Woman Don't use *LADY* when you are simply referring to a female person. *Lady* is a term of respect or honor. It is the companion of *gentleman*, not *man*. Say *WOMAN*.

Laid/Lain/Lay/Lie So, here we go. *LAID* is the past participle of *LAY*, *LAIN* is the past participle of *LIE*. See how easy it is? *LAY* has many meanings, but the most common usage would be the act of laying something down. In that use, *lay* is a transitive verb that requires an object: "*Lay* down the gun." *LIE* is a verb that does not take an object (an intransitive verb): "I will *lie* down." People have problems mostly with the past tense and past participle of these words. The past tense of *lie* is *lay*, and the past participle is *lain*. The past tense and participle of *lay* are both *laid*. Look to your dictionary for further discussion. The whole mess is admittedly confusing.

Laissez-Faire Pronounced LESS-ay FAYR. It means to let things find their own way, without government direction. It is a doctrine of certain economists.

Lama/Llama A *LAMA* (pronounced LAH-muh) is a lamaist monk, chief among whom is the Dalai Lama. The belief system is found chiefly in Tibet and Mongolia. A *LLAMA* is a South American beast of burden. *Llama* is pronounced LAM-uh or LAH-muh in American English, but elsewhere it is pronounced YAH-muh.

Languish *LANGUISH* means to be depressed, to become feeble. I believe a lot of people think it means to lie passively, in comfort. The image may come from some novels that refer to Southern belles *languishing* in the shade.

Larynx The voice box. Note the spelling and pronunciation. It is LAHR-inks, not LAHR-nix. The *LARYNX* is a structure in the throat that contains the vocal cords. It is sometimes the site of a cancerous lesion and must be removed. The procedure is called a *laryngectomy*. *Laryngitis* is a more common problem with the *larynx*.

Last But Not Least A horrible and predictable cliché used often by those introducing members of a group of people. Someone has to be last which, in itself, does not constitute a ranking. Avoid the phrase.

Last/Latest Both have the meaning of "most recent," but *LAST* also means "final." One's *latest* breath and one's *last* breath are very different things, indeed.

Lath/Lathe A *LATH* is a thin strip of wood used primarily for the underlayment of wall and ceiling plaster. A *LATHE* (pronounced LAYTH) is a machine for turning and shaping wood or metal.

Latitude/Longitude *LATITUDE* is a measure of distance north or south of the equator. *LONGITUDE* is the distance east or west from Greenwich, England. Both are expressed in "degrees," "minutes" and "seconds." *Longitude* is also expressed as time. One degree of *latitude* varies from approximately 69 miles at the equator to approximately 70 miles at the poles. One degree of *longitude* varies from approximately 69 and a half miles at the equator to zero at the poles.

Latinates These are the many words in our language that derive from Latin roots. Their plurals often cause problems because in common usage the Latin rules have broken down. For example, we once had one *agendum*, but two *agenda*. Today, *agenda* is the accepted singular, and we rarely hear *agendum*. The common plural is *agendas*. Still clinging to life, but by an ever-thinning thread, is *datum* as the singular and *data* as the plural. Only the most pure of the purists still insist on *stadia*. And for broadcast use we would refer to *referendums* and *curriculums* even though academicians shudder. *Media* is plural. The only time you would refer to *mediums* is when there is more than one person conducting a séance. We are often called upon to use *criteria*. Always remember, it is plural. The singular is *criterion*. If the occasion ever arises that you feel compelled to use the plural of *syllabus*, you have a real problem. Both *syllabi* and *syllabuses* sound "sylly." If you have doubts, consult Webster's.

Latter *See* **Former**.

Laudable/Laudatory A *LAUDABLE* act or event is one that is praiseworthy. What is said about the praiseworthy act or event is said in *LAUDATORY* language--expressing praise.

Lawyer *See* **Attorney**.

Lease/Rent A *LEASE* is a contract arranging to *RENT* something. You do not *lease* an apartment; you sign a *lease* to *rent* the apartment.

Leave/Let *LEAVE* me alone and *LET* me alone do not mean the same thing. *Leave* means just that--go away and leave me here by myself. *Let* means stop bothering me.

Lectern *See* **Dais**.

Legalese The language of the law is filled with jargon, much of it based on Latin. Your job as a broadcast newswriter is to interpret, not to parrot. Do not inform Aunt Tillie that "a fiduciary has been named," nor that "a writ of certiorari is on file." She, and most other people (including you and me), have no idea what you're talking about. Get a copy of a good legal dictionary for your newsroom. And use it.

Legible/Readable In common use *LEGIBLE* and *READABLE* mean the same thing--capable of being read. Use *readable*. We most often use the negative form--*illegible*. That's a tongue twister for a lot of people. *Unreadable* is much easier.

Legislator/Legislature A frequent source of pronunciation confusion. A *LEGISLATOR* is a representative of the people elected to sit in the

LEGISLATURE, which is the governing body of a state or nation. It is an inclusive term, encompassing members of both houses--the state *legislature*.

Lend/Loan Some authorities are saying that *LOAN* is becoming accepted as a verb. There is a nice distinction between *loan* and *LEND* that I think should be preserved: *lend* is the verb and *loan* is the noun. *"Lend* me your book." *"I took out a *loan*."* Kilpatrick suggests that *lend* applies to animate things as in *"lend* me a hand," while *loan* applies to inanimate objects. I don't know where that came from. Many dictionaries and usage guides are accepting *loan* as a verb.

Less *See* **Fewer.**

Liable/Libel Easily and often confused. To be *LIABLE* is to be obligated or responsible for something, or less formally, to be likely to be exposed to something--a teacher is *liable* to catch students' colds. *LIBEL* is a form of defamation. If a journalist defames the subject of a news story, he is *liable* to be sued for *libel*.

Libel/Slander Both are forms of defamation. The difference lies in how widespread the defamation becomes. Defamation when published, either in print or by broadcast, is *LIBEL*. Defamation that is unpublished, as in a conversation or in private correspondence, is usually, but not always, considered *SLANDER*. Both generally require that what is said is maliciously false and damaging to the subject's character and reputation. *Libel* law is complex and frequently changes. As a broadcaster, you will do well to keep up with it. (*See* Part Three, "The Law.")

Library *See* **February.**

Lighted/Lit Either is considered an acceptable past tense of the verb to light. For broadcast, prefer *LIGHTED*.

Lightening/Lightning *LIGHTENING* has three syllables--LY-ten-ing. *LIGHTNING* has only two--LYT-ning. *Lightening* has to do with making something less heavy or less dark. *Lightning* is the electrical accompaniment to a thunderstorm.

Like *See* **As If.**

Like/Such As Dictionaries accept the use of *LIKE* in the sense of *SUCH AS*. However, confusion can result, so let's use *such as*, even though it may sound a little more formal. Kilpatrick makes a strong case for the distinction. He says "places *like* New York's Bellevue Hospital Center" refers to other similar places, but excludes Bellevue, while "places *such as* New York's Bellevue Hospital Center" includes Bellevue and other similar hospitals. He offers several other examples and a good discussion.

Limbo *LIMBO* is a place, especially in Roman Catholic theology, where the souls of those who had not been baptized repose. The word, of course, is used frequently to refer to people who are wandering or awaiting a decision as to their fate. It was recently reported that some out-of-favor politicians were "in a limbo." *Limbo* is a place, not a thing. *Limbo* is also the name of a somewhat bizarre West Indian dance.

Lingerie It's pronounced lahn-zhur-AY. Feminine undergarments. Elster reluctantly accepts this pronunciation, preferring LAN-zhu-ree or lan-zhu-REE, as being closer to the original French, but he concedes they are incomprehensible to most Americans.

List To *LIST* is to lean to one side, in the meaning we're talking about here. Dictionaries approve of a general sense of leaning over, but suggest it may be specifically intended to refer to ships. I would prefer to keep that narrow meaning. It's a bit out of the ordinary to refer to railcars *listing* after a wreck. They are *tilting*.

Litany/Liturgy Frequently confused. A *LITANY* can be part of a *LITURGY*. A *litany* is the ritual repetition of incantations or prayers. It has come to mean the detailing of any list, as in: "He reeled off a *litany* of wants and needs." *Liturgy* is a rite prescribed for public worship services, specifically in Christian churches, done in observance of traditional form.

Literally *See* **Figuratively.**

Live *See* **Dwell.**

Livid Some authorities (such as Kilpatrick) are giving up on this one. Most people, for some reason, believe that *LIVID* means reddish. It does not. *Livid* means ashen, pale gray. When a person is said to be "*livid* with anger" he is so angry he has gone white, not red. Fine writers such as Capote and Whitman have used *livid* to mean red or blue. What's a writer to do?

Loath/Loathe *LOATH* means a reluctance to do something; *LOATHE* refers to an intense dislike, hatred. The *th* sounds differ. *Loath* gets a short sound, as in "Smith." *Loathe* gets a longer sound, as in "with."

Love A score of nothing in tennis. It was recently reported in connection with baseball that "the score is three-*love*" in the sense that the score was tied at three each. That's plain wrong. What the sportswriter wanted was "three-*all*."

Luxuriant/Luxuriate/Luxurious *LUXURIANT* refers to abundance, usually of plant growth. We speak of *luxuriant* fields of wheat. *LUXURIATE* in the common use means to live in luxury, in which case you would be living in *LUXURIOUS* surroundings.

Macduff, Lay On The phrase from Shakespeare's *Macbeth* is frequently misquoted as "lead on, *Macduff*." It's not. It's *LAY ON, MACDUFF*, meaning to begin the battle or fight. The phrase is a challenge: "Come on, do your worst."

Mad *See* **Angry**.

Maddening/Madding Thomas Gray's phrase is "far from the *MADDING* crowd." We often, perhaps most often, hear it as "far from the *MADDENING* crowd." *Madding* means going mad, the crowd is becoming riotous. *Maddening* means driving someone nuts. The crowd may, indeed, be *maddening*--that is, driving you mad--but that's not what Gray had in mind. If you're going to use quotations, make sure they're widely understood, and make sure you get them right.

Magic/Miracle Take care in serious writing that *MAGIC* and *MIRACLE* are used in the proper context. There are very, very few *miracles* these days, and *magic* is sleight of hand. A *miracle* would be something that happened beyond human comprehension, supernatural. The rescue of the victim of a near-drowning, for example, might have been difficult or spectacularly carried out, but it would not be called a *miracle*. Almost a miracle, perhaps. *Magic* is trickery, an illusion. They don't REALLY saw the woman in half, you know.

Majority/Plurality A *MAJORITY* is a number greater than half the total. A *PLURALITY* occurs when, for example, there are more than two candidates running for the same office. The one winning among the three holds a *plurality*, not a *majority*, unless one alone polls more than half the total of all three. *Majority* applies only to things you can count. It is nonstandard to refer to a *majority* of your writing. It is not a synonym for "the major part" or "the largest portion."

Mantel/Mantle Sound-alikes that have quite different meanings. A *MANTEL* is the trimming around and shelf above a fireplace. A *MANTLE* is, among other things, a robe or shawl, a cloak. We also speak of the earth's *mantle* that portion of the interior between the crust and the core. A *mantle* is something that surrounds or covers. It is also used symbolically: "He assumed the *mantle* of office." That's pompous and not a good metaphor for broadcast. We often see the fireplace decoration referred to as a *mantle*, and that spelling may be emerging as acceptable.

Manual Labor/Physical Labor *MANUAL LABOR* has to do with working with one's hands. It is not necessarily strenuous work. *PHYSICAL LABOR* is generally considered to be hard work involving the whole body. Grinding lenses is *manual labor*, digging ditches is *physical labor*.

Manslaughter *See* **Homicide**.

Margin/Score A *SCORE* of 9 to 5 is not a *MARGIN*. In that example, the *margin* would be four. The *margin* is the difference between the two.

Marginal Do not confuse *MARGINAL* with *small*. *Marginal* means, in one sense, near the lower limits of acceptability, just barely qualifying. That may be where the idea that *marginal* means "small" comes from. But it doesn't mean "small." It means near the margin, on the edge.

Marine/Nautical The word *NAUTICAL* pertains specifically to ships or navigation. It is not standard to refer to "nautical life." What is meant is *MARINE* life. *Marine* refers to both ships and other aspects of the sea. It has been extended to refer to fresh water as well.

Marital/Martial/Marshal/Marshall *MARITAL* (having to do with the state of being married and pronounced MAIR-ih-tul) and *MARTIAL* (having to do with the military and pronounced MAR-shul) need to be clearly marked in broadcast copy because they are so very easy to confuse. Sound-alikes *MARSHAL* and *MARSHALL* are also easily confused. *Marshal* is a military rank or someone who leads a public event, such as a parade. It also has to do with preparing, getting things in order, as *marshal* your forces. *Marshall* is someone's name.

Marriage/Wedding *MARRIAGE* is a state of being in which a man and woman are legally bound together. The ceremony is a *WEDDING*. Of course, we commonly refer to the ceremony as a *marriage*, but that's not precise. Let's call the ceremony a *wedding*.

Mass/Service A *MASS* is a *SERVICE* in certain churches. The *services* in those churches (usually Catholic) are always referred to as a *mass*. A *mass*, depending on the church and the type of *mass* it is, is said to be read, sung or celebrated, but never preached.

Masterful/Masterly *MASTERFUL* implies dominance--a strong personality, imposing one's will on others. *MASTERLY* implies competence, doing something with the skill of a master. Neither implies **maleness**--and can be applied to either men or women.

Material/Materiel *MATERIAL* has a number of meanings, most having to do with physical objects, such as cloth, paving *materials* and so on. *MATERIEL* is a much narrower term referring to supplies for a military operation. It is pronounced muh-TEER-ee-ELL.

Matinee A *MATINEE* is a performance, so to say *"matinee* performance" is redundant. A *matinee* is, by definition, a daytime performance, usually in the afternoon, although its root is *matin*, which means "morning."

May *See* **Can.**

Mayonnaise There are three syllables here--MAY-uh-NAYZ. It is not MAN-ayz or any such variant.

Meaningful So overused as to be *nauseating* (which see).

Meanwhile Be careful of using *MEANWHILE* as a transition to mean "at the same time." *Meanwhile* suggests an interval, during an intervening period of time. It also implies some connection between events. It is careless writing to use *meanwhile* as a general transition simply to show two things happening at about the same time.

Media If you learn nothing else here, learn this: *MEDIA* is plural! *Mediums* is not the proper plural of *medium*. *See* **Latinates.** It is "the TV *medium*" but "the mass *media*."

Median/Medium The grassy divider between two highways is called the *MEDIAN*, not the *MEDIUM*. "*Median* strip" is a redundancy. A concrete barrier between two roadways is, however, correctly called a "*median* divider."

Medical Examiner *See* **Coroner.**

Medication *See* **Drugs.**

Medicine *See* **Drugs.**

Melee This is often mispronounced. It is correctly MAY-lay. It means a fight among several people. It's probably better to call a fight a *fight*.

Melt/Thaw To *MELT* is to go from a solid state to a liquid. Ice *melts*. To *THAW* is to go from the frozen state to a solid or liquid state. We *thaw* frozen foods.

Thaw is also a noun. In northern climes there is a period known as "the spring *thaw*."

Memento This error occurs too often to be a mere typo, although that's what it looks like. The word is *MEMENTO*, meaning something to remember me by, an object that stirs memory. There is no such word as *momento*. Incredibly, some dictionaries recognize *momento* as a variant spelling. Others call it what it is: a misspelling of *memento*. Probably influenced by *momentum*.

Memo An acceptable abbreviation of *memorandum*.

Memoranda/Memorandums Take your pick for the plural of *MEMORANDUM*. Purists will stick with the Latinate, but those striving for conversational speech will use the English version. There are many words from the Latin that pose similar problems. Usage will eventually level them out. *See* **Latinates.**

Meretricious/Meritorious Two look-alikes that have very different meanings. *MERETRICIOUS* means to exhibit attractions based on deceit or pretense, originally relating to a prostitute. *MERITORIOUS* means deserving of merit, worthy of reward.

Metal/Mettle *METTLE* is most often used to suggest strength or stamina: "he proved his *mettle*." It also refers to temperament, strength of character. *METAL*, of course, refers to any metallic substance, such as iron or aluminum.

Meteor/Meteorite/Meteoroid *METEOR* has to do first with the atmosphere, hence *meteorology*, the study of weather. Most often, however, when we say *meteor* we're talking about a small particle of orbiting matter that enters the earth's atmosphere and burns, producing what is commonly known as a "shooting star." A *METEORITE* is the remains of a meteor that survives the entry and is found on earth. A *METEOROID* is a particle in orbit around the sun that may someday become a *meteor*.

Meticulous Not a compliment. A *METICULOUS* person is one who is fussily painstaking for fear of error or criticism.

Midair There is no such place. Undoubtedly a headline word. Certainly planes may collide in flight, or in the air, but not in *MIDAIR*. Webster's accepts it and claims it dates from 1667.

Midget *See* **Dwarf.**

Milestone Be careful what you do with a *MILESTONE*. It's a useful metaphor, but be sure you use it right. One does not "mark a *milestone*." One "reaches a *milestone*." A *milestone* is a marker.

Milieu Pronounced meel-YEU (second syllable rhymes with the *eu* in *Europe*) or meel-YOO. It's a narrow environment--the social setting, for example. A bad broadcast word. "Social *milieu*" is a redundancy.

Minimize *See* **Diminish.**

Minion We frequently hear police referred to as *MINIONS* of the law--with the sense that *minion* means upholder or enforcer. Not so. *Minion* means either one who is admired or a subordinate--a follower, dependent. Yes, it is confusing, not to mention contradictory.

Minuscule Note spelling. Pronounced MIHN-ih-skyool. It comes from the same root as *minor*, not from the root of *miniature*. *MINUSCULE* does mean a very small amount, however, as does *minute* (pronounced myn-YOOT). Use *miniature* if it fits. You certainly would not refer to "a miniature amount," however.

Minutiae The little details. Probably unimportant stuff. The sort of things we leave out of broadcast news stories. It is usually pronounced mih-NOO-shuh, but properly mih-NOO-shee-ee. Not a good broadcast word--too obscure.

Misanthrope/Misanthropy A *MISANTHROPE* is a person who believes humankind is evil or untrustworthy. It is pronounced MIS-an-THROAP. The error here is pronouncing *misanthrope* as *MISANTHROPY* which is what a misanthrope does. Neither word is good for broadcast. *Misanthrope* is an odd word that does not seem to follow normal English "rules." Why not "philanthrope" instead of *philanthropist*?

Misdemeanor *See* **Felony.**

Mishap *See* **Accident.**

Monday, Etc. When pronouncing the days of the week--fully pronounce *-day*. It is MUN-day, not MUN-dee.

Mongoloid Idiot Avoid this phrase. In the past it was accepted as a common adjective for a sufferer of mongolism or Down's syndrome. It is now considered insensitive and derogatory. Not all Down's victims are *idiots*, although mental retardation is common.

Monk The person who lives in a monastery is a *MONK*, which I prefer to pronounce MAHNK, whereas the diminutive word for monkey, usually spelled *munk*, is pronounced MUHNK. This distinction is not supported by Webster's, but I think it's needed.

Monstrous Yes, *MONSTROUS* means huge, but it also means grossly abnormal, horrifying. The sense is an act or thing that is deliberately or inherently evil--a *"monstrous* lie."

Morals *See* **Ethics.**

Morbid/Sordid *MORBID* in common use can mean susceptible to gloom or depression. It also means gruesome, diseased. *SORDID* means either filthy or gross, vile.

More Than/Over Picky editors will land on this one every time. *MORE THAN* refers to quantity, *OVER* refers to a spatial relationship. Therefore, to say *"over* one-million-dollars" will earn you a nasty look from Ed.

Mortgage Pronounced MOHR-gidj.

Mortuary A funeral home. Also called a funeral parlor or chapel. Literally, *MORTUARY* means "place of the dead." I suppose it's understandable that morticians resort to euphemisms to describe much of what they do.

Most *See* **Almost.**

Motor *See* **Engine.**

Murder *See* **Homicide.**

Naked/Nude Both mean "without clothing," but for broadcast prefer *NUDE*. *NAKED* has other usages, such as "the *naked* truth." Trees in winter are said to be *naked*. *Nude* has to do almost exclusively with unclothed or uncovered human beings or representations of them.

Namesake Technically, anyone with the same name as yours is your *NAMESAKE*. Usually, however, a *namesake* is one specifically named for someone else: Junior is the *namesake* of senior.

Naphtha *See* **Diphtheria.**

Nation *See* **Country.**

National Institutes Of Health In Washington, D.C. Note it is expressed as a plural. Within the Department of Health and Human Services, it is made up of about a dozen biomedical research units. (*See also* **Centers For Disease Control**.)

Nauseated/Nauseous You become *NAUSEATED* when you see or smell something *NAUSEOUS*. You cannot feel *nauseous*. Please pay attention to this--it's a frighteningly common misuse. Webster's disagrees with the distinction and seems to base its acceptance on the fact that a lot of people use the term. That doesn't seem to me to be a good reason to accept the usage--just because a lot of people make the same error. Other dictionaries list the usage as "colloquial." Feeling *nauseous* was considered an obsolete usage a few years ago. Have we witnessed a resurrection? Please use *nauseated*.

Nautical *See* **Marine**.

Naval/Navel *NAVAL* is a term referring to the navy only, not generally to ships. A *NAVEL* is a belly button, or a certain kind of orange that has a scarlike depression that looks like an "outsie" where the blossom once was.

Near Miss OOPS. We hear this phrase in air traffic stories often--it is a nonsense phrase. Think about it. If it was nearly a miss, it was a hit! What happened was a near collision, not a *near miss*. Sure, it's use is ubiquitous and universally understood. It just offends logic.

Negotiate Pronounced nuh-GOH-shee-ayt. It is not nuh-GOH-see-ayt. Elster blames broadcasters for perpetuating the mispronunciation. When all else fails, blame the media!

New Innovation A redundancy--an *INNOVATION* is new by definition.

New York *See* **State Of . . .**

News/Press Conference We broadcasters run very few presses. Let's refer to the occasions as *NEWS* conferences, rather than the more restrictive *PRESS* conferences. "The *press*" is used generically to refer to all journalists, of course. I wish there were another word.

Nice A waffling adjective. Find a better one.

Nobody/None/No One They all mean *NO ONE*, or "*not one*." Use *no one* or *not one*. Note they are all treated as a singular: "*None* is going."

Noisome A common and quite understandable confusion surrounds *NOISOME*. It refers not to noise, but to smell. Something that smells offensive is said to be *noisome*. It is not necessarily poisonous, so don't confuse *noisome* with *noxious*, which is something that is harmful, but does not necessarily smell bad. *Noisome* is not a good broadcast word.

Nominal *NOMINAL* has to do with naming, forming nouns. In a remote meaning it has to do with things going according to plan, satisfactorily. That's the way we hear it used most frequently. During the age of experimental manned space flight, things were referred to as being *nominal* when they were within acceptable limits.

Normalcy/Normality Both mean the state of being normal. For broadcast purposes, prefer *NORMALITY*, because it is the more commonly used. Many usage experts claim *normalcy* is unacceptably substandard.

Not Guilty *See* **Innocent.**

North America In most usages, *NORTH AMERICA* refers to the United States and Canada. Technically, it also includes what we usually call Central America--everything north of the border between Colombia and Panama. Hawaii is not considered part of *North America*, even though it is one of the United States. *North America* does include Greenland.

Notorious *See* **Famous.** Note spelling--it is not *nortorious*.

Noxious *See* **Noisome.**

Nuclear Pronounce it with three syllables: NOO-klee-uhr.

Nutritional/Nutritious Related but not synonymous. *NUTRITIONAL* has to do with the mechanism by which living things take in nourishment--it refers to the process. *NUTRITIOUS* refers to the nourishment value of that which is taken in. A *nutritional* diet includes *nutritious* foods.

Observance/Observation An *OBSERVANCE* usually has to do with a ceremony, the carrying out of a ritual. An *OBSERVATION* is the act of taking notice. However, in certain contexts, *observation* can be used as a synonym for *observance*.

Occult Most people believe things that are *OCCULT* have to do with witchcraft or sorcery. Maybe so, but it's a much broader term than that. It means hidden, obscure. In medicine there is *occult* bleeding--coming from an unknown source.

Occupation/Vocation Not every *OCCUPATION* is a *VOCATION*, although, as with many other words, they are frequently treated as synonyms. An *occupation* is generally seen as the principal work of one's life, so studying can be the *occupation* of a student. A *vocation* is, as the word implies, a calling--a strong summons to do certain work. Members of the clergy are often said to follow a calling, a *vocation*. Journalists, too, very often see themselves as "called" to do what they do. Heaven knows, very few of them are in it for the money!

Occur *See* **Happen**.

Oculist/Ophthalmologist/Optician/Optometrist All these folks work with the eyes or eyeglasses. An *OCULIST*, *OPTICIAN* and *OPTOMETRIST* have varying levels of training and specialize in examination of the eyes and the fitting of eyeglasses. An *OPHTHALMOLOGIST* is a medical doctor who specializes in diseases of the eye, but may also fit eyeglasses. Note the *Phth* combination in the spelling. It is fully pronounced.

Official Not everyone who talks to the media is an *OFFICIAL*. Police, although properly called *officer*, are not all police *officials*. An *official* is one who holds an office, especially a public office. Please don't refer to rescue squad personnel or all hospital spokespersons as *officials* unless they really are.

Off Of/On To Most often *of* and *to* are unnecessary baggage.

Often The *t* is silent. Pronounce it OFF-un.

Older *See* **Elder**.

On/Onto Test the usage. "The band marched *ON* the field" and "the band marched *ONTO* the field," tell entirely different stories.

One Of The Only . . . An assault on logic. If something is *ONE* it must be the *ONLY*. What's wanted here is "One of the few . . . ." I see otherwise excellent writers (and editors!) using this phrase.

Only, Etc. *ONLY* and many similar modifiers, such as *just* and *even* are frequently, possibly more often than not, misplaced. "I will *only* go to the store tomorrow" means that I will go to the store tomorrow and not come back. What you probably want in this example is "I will go to the store *only* tomorrow," meaning that's the *only* day I'll be going to the store. The problem with misplacing modifiers is the danger of ambiguity--not knowing what the sentence really intends to say. One of the guiding rules of editors is: "*Only* is always in the wrong place."

Only Time Will Tell . . . A waffling phrase. So is "We'll just have to wait and see." Avoid them. They have no place in straight news, anyway. "Remains to be seen," it has been pointed out, can be found at a funeral home. (*See* **Mortuary.**)

Oneself This is the spelling preferred by publishers, but it looks very odd to me. I think in scripts to be read aloud the spelling *ONE'S SELF* is helpful to the reader. It is acceptable as English.

Onset/Outset An *ONSET* is an assault, such as the *onset* of a disease, the first symptoms. *OUTSET* refers to a beginning, a starting out. One would not refer to the first day of classes as the *onset* of the semester, yet I hear learned professors use the word every term.

On The Day/Season Sports people, tell me what this means? It is a vogue phrase and should be avoided by serious writers.

Opossum Pronounced, y'all, POSS-um. Nawthuners often pronounce the *o*. It's silent, or nearly so. Whatever sound there is comes closer to "uh" than "oh." The common *opossum* is a marsupial found in the Eastern United States. It is considered a nuisance. There are similar animals in other parts of the world. Note the odd spelling--one *p*, two *s's*. The word is Algonquin in origin.

Oral/Verbal *ORAL* has to do with the mouth, so something spoken can be said to be *oral*. *VERBAL* has to do with words, written or spoken, but most often written. Just to add to the confusion, we can toss in *AURAL*, which sounds almost like *oral* but has to do with hearing, of all things. A frequent misuse is in the description of an agreement as a "*verbal* contract" when there is no written document. What is meant is "*oral* contract."

Ordinance/Ordnance Watch the spelling closely. An *ORDINANCE* is a law governing a locality. Only cities, towns and counties enact *ordinances*. *ORDNANCE* is military hardware, usually weapons and explosives.

Oregon Favor OAR-eh-gun as the pronunciation.

Oscillate *See* **Alternate.** *See also* **Osculate.**

Osculate To kiss. An overeager auto salesman recently told the author that a desirable new car had an *OSCULATING* fan built into the dashboard. Tough love!

Ought *See* **Aught.**

Outside *See* **Inside.**

Over *See* **More Than.**

Pago Pago   The capital city of American Samoa is pronounced "PAWN-go PAWN-go," no matter how it's spelled. "PAW-go PAW-go" is a secondary pronunciation. Let's stick with "PAWN-go PAWN-go." It was once spelled Pango Pango, which explains the pronunciation.

Paid/Payed/Played   A loan is *PAID* out, a rope is *PAYED* out and a drama is *PLAYED* out. The common error here is to say a rope is *played* out. If, however, you have used all the rope, it is common in some parts of the country to say "the rope has *played* out." "A rope is *payed*" out when it is released and allowed to run. *Out* always accompanies *payed* in that sense. Newswriters will often write *payed* when they mean *paid.* "I got *payed* on Friday."

Palate/Palette/Pallet   The *PALATE* is the roof of the mouth, an artist keeps his paints on a *PALETTE* and heavy materials are stacked on a *PALLET* so a forklift can get under them. All are pronounced PAL-ut.

Palm/Pawn   A confusion arises here when the sense is to pass the buck. What is done is to *PALM* off, not *PAWN* off. The idea is to slyly shift, as in *palming* a card. A *pawn* is a chess piece, or an act of securing a loan with property. *Pawn* may also be used metaphorically to indicate a person or thing used to the benefit of someone else, often without their knowing it.

Palpate/Palpitate   When the doctor thumps on your back, he's *PALPATING.* When your heart goes "pitty-pat" it's *PALPITATING.* To *palpate* is to touch, to feel. To *palpitate* is to quake, tremble, beat faster than normal or irregularly. It usually refers to the heartbeat.

Papier-Mâché *See* **Chaise Longue.**

Parity/Parody   *PARITY* has to do with equality. Or evenhanded treatment. Broadcasters worry about having First Amendment *parity* with the print media. A *PARODY* is writing, music or drama in an imitative manner for humorous effect.

Partially/Partly   Both have the meaning of "not entirely." Prefer *PARTLY. Partial* also has to do with a bias or preference.

Passed/Past The problem here is in the spelling. *PAST* has numerous meanings and uses, including to go by. *PASSED* is a verb and means only to go by. "The car *passed* the truck." "The truck roared *past*." We say students *passed* the course, and make other uses of the word, all meaning to progress by or through.

Past Experience A redundancy. All *EXPERIENCE* is *PAST*.

Pathologist *See* **Coroner.**

Patient Conditions This is a personal bugaboo with me. There are only four *PATIENT CONDITIONS* in a hospital environment. They are *good, fair, serious* (or *poor*) and *critical*. There are no such conditions as *grave, satisfactory* or *stable*. *Stable* has come into use only in the past few years and seems to mean nothing. The only possible meaning could be that the patient is not getting any worse. To say a patient is in "*critical* but *stable* condition" is a contradiction in terms. "*Critical* condition" means, by definition, the vital signs are unstable. *See* Appendix IV.

Patron *See* **Client.**

Peculiar *See* **Funny.**

Pedal/Peddle/Petal You *PEDAL* a bicycle, you might *PEDDLE* vegetables on the street--it means to sell informally--and, of course, flowers are made up of *PETALS*.

Pendulum Pronounced as if spelled with a *j*--PEN-juh-lum.

Peninsula Don't say "surrounded on three sides." *Surround* means completely around. A *PENINSULA* is bounded on three sides, usually by water. It is preferably pronounced pen-IN-suh-luh--not pen-INCH-uh-lah.

Penitentiary *See* **Jail.**

People/Persons *PEOPLE* is not always the plural of *person* and neither is *PERSONS*. Use *persons* as the plural when you are speaking of a specific number of individuals--no matter how large a number--but use *PEOPLE* when the number is indefinite. "Three *persons* were injured in the crash." "The *people* of New York continue to flock to Yankees games." Using *persons* in this way recognizes the humanness--the dignity--of the individuals involved. There have recently been downright vehement, almost bitter, objections to using *persons*. AP never uses *persons* as a plural for *person*.

Per/Via   Avoid the Latinates. "Miles an hour," "came by truck" are just fine. Sure, we use M-P-H for miles an hour. What I'm suggesting is avoiding the word *per*.

Percent   Write it as one word.

Perfect   In its most common use, *PERFECT* means flawless. If so, can it be qualified? I guess it can. One of our national treasures speaks of forming "a more *perfect* union." In most uses, however, keep it unqualifiable.

Perfunctory   Note the spelling. It is not *pre*; it is *per*. It means something done only as a duty or superficially. It's a terrible word for broadcast.

Perish   *See* **Die/Perish.**

Perquisite/Prerequisite   Don't get confused. A *PERQUISITE*--the beloved "perks" of certain occupations--is a privilege, such as a company car, extra fees or a key to the executive washroom. A *PREREQUISITE* is a requirement in advance. You must have taken Introduction to Reporting as a *prerequisite* to Advanced Reporting.

Persecute/Prosecute   *PERSECUTE* means to follow or hunt down, to harass. *PROSECUTE* means to bring to trial, in modern usage. Another use of *prosecute* is in the sense of to follow to completion.

Perspective/Prospective   There's more than just a pronunciation problem with these two similar words. Several times an interoffice memo has arrived telling me to expect a meeting with a *PERSPECTIVE* student. That would be wonderful. One meaning of the word is to view things in their true relations or importance. *Perspective* has to do with seeing--especially seeing within a realistic framework. *PROSPECTIVE*, what the memo really wanted to say, means expected, likely to come about, relating to the future.

Perspiration   Note that it is not PRESS-pur-ay-shun. It is PURS-pur-ay-shun. It is a euphemism. Use *sweat*.

Petite Fours   *See* **Chaise Longue.**

Phase   *See* **Faze.**

Philippines   *See* **Filipino.**

Physical Labor   *See* **Manual Labor.**

Picaresque/Picturesque Not even remotely related. I would suggest *PICARESQUE* is a word never to be heard in a broadcast news story. *Picaresque* refers to an attractive rogue such as Tom Jones (the title character in a novel by Henry Fielding), frequently the lovable but facile hero of a story. *PICTURESQUE* has to do with pictures or scenes. A *picturesque* coastline is one that would make an attractive picture.

Pidgin English *PIDGIN* is an artificial language mostly found in the South Pacific. It has nothing to do with the bird. It's thought *pidgin* is a pidgin word for *business*, because that's why the language was developed--so people could deal with each other even though they didn't speak the same language. It is not always associated with English, although it borrows heavily from it. *Pidgin* (or in pidgin *tok-pisin*) is the official government and business language of Papua New Guinea. It is not just an argot; it has developed into a formal language, with rules of grammar, tenses and so on.

Pier *See* **Dock.**

Pimento The red stuff in green olives. Regardless of how it's spelled, it's preferably pronounced puh-MEN-toh. It is a very mild red pepper.

Pincers A military maneuver in which one army is surrounded by another. It is always expressed as a plural. It is pronounced PIN-serz, not PINCH-erz.

Pistol *See* **Automatic.**

Pitiable/Pitiful There is barely a distinction between these two. Both mean capable of arousing pity, and both carry a sense of mixed pity and contempt: "a *PITIFUL* performance." I would suggest using *pitiful* in broadcast scripts, but use either with great care as the connotation often can be pejorative.

Pit Viper Several venomous snakes, such as the rattlers, moccasins, copperheads and others, are referred to as *PIT VIPERS*. The name refers not to their living quarters, but to sensory *pits* on each side of the head. It is best not to get close enough to inspect for *pits*.

Pizza Pie A redundancy. A *PIZZA* is a *PIE*.

Plaintiff/Plaintive You need to be careful with the pronunciation here. A *PLAINTIFF* is one who has a complaint against someone else--it is usually associated with civil court cases. *PLAINTIVE* is an adjective expressing sadness, melancholy. The two words are related through *plaint*, which has a use in law as well as mean an utterance of lamentation.

Plantar Wart The often painful growth on the sole of the foot is called a *PLANTAR WART*, not a planter's wart. *Plantar* has to do with the sole of the foot. It is often pronounced just like *planter*.

Pleaded/Pled *PLED* until recently was considered non-standard English. For broadcast use *PLEADED*.

Plurality *See* **Majority**.

Plus Avoid using *PLUS* as a conjunction, with the sense of furthermore as in "He is a careful driver *plus* a good mechanic." A phrase often heard in commercials is "*plus* there's more!" *Plus* is the French for "more." So that phrase says "More there's more!" In school we are all taught "two plus two equal four." Technically, that's illiterate.

Podium *See* **Dais**.

Police Among other things, be careful with the pronunciation. It is puh-LEES, not PLEES or POH-lees.

Poinsettia The latest dictionaries (at least some of them) now say the preferred pronunciation of this showy Christmastime plant is poyn-SET-uh. That pleases me, because that's the way I've always said it. Other dictionaries, however, insist that not only is poyn-SET-ee-uh preferred, it is the only pronunciation. It certainly is spelled for the four-syllable treatment. Elster says that's the only way to say it.

Pore/Pour You *PORE* over a book, but *POUR* a cup of coffee. You have *pores* in your skin.

Port *See* **Harbor**.

Portrait Pronounced POHR-triht, for broadcast purposes.

Posthumous It means after life ends and is pronounced PAWS-choo-muhs.

Post Mortem *See* **Autopsy**.

Potpourri A mixture, specifically of herbs and flowers, but used to describe any conglomeration of dissimilar things. It comes from the French and is pronounced POH-purr-ee, in English.

Practically/Almost *PRACTICALLY* means for all practical purposes--as in "the bucket is *practically* empty." It also has the sense of *ALMOST*. For broadcast, use *almost*.

Practice *See* **Habit.**

Pray/Prey Today, *PRAY* almost always has the sense of imploring a deity. *PREY* is something that is hunted. The insect is a *praying* mantis because of the attitude of its forelegs, even though it is a voracious predator.

Precipitate/Precipitous *PRECIPITATE* means to fall out of or to cause. *PRECIPITOUS* means with a lack of caution, to act in haste. A steep slope is referred to as *precipitous*, but that derives from *precipice*.

Predominant/Predominate Something that is *PREDOMINANT* is a thing that is most frequent or common, "the *predominant* culture." A thing or person that *PREDOMINATES* is a force that controls. *Predominant* is the adjective form and *predominate* is the verb.

Preface *See* **Foreword.**

Preferable Preferably pronounced PREF-er-uh-buhl.

Prefixes Hyphenate freely in scripts, especially to separate vowel strings as in "co-operate," "anti-aircraft," "re-election," "co-education," "bi-ennial."

Prelude How do we pronounce this familiar word? Well, it seems there are several ways. Dictionaries give at least five versions: PREL-ood, PREL-yood, PRAY-lood, PRAY-lyood, PRE-lood and so on, depending on the sense in which it is used. Elster says PREL-yood is the traditional and preferred version. Primarily, *PRELUDE* means something that comes before the main action, preparing for what is to come, usually in music. The use has become extended to include nearly anything that precedes something else.

Premature *See* **Immature.**

Pre-recorded A seeming nonsense word; after all, something cannot be post-recorded. But it may be a useful word in the phrase "Parts of the preceding were *pre-recorded*." To say "Parts of the preceding were recorded" could have an entirely different meaning. Even so, for the sake of precision, I prefer the latter.

Prescribe/Proscribe   Look-alikes that have directly opposite meanings. To *PRESCRIBE* is to direct that something be done. To *PROSCRIBE* is to forbid the doing of something.

Present   Be careful of creating redundancies such as "the *PRESENT* incumbent." Test the use of *present* and *current* to see if they are really needed. Many times they are not.

Presently   *See* **Currently**.

Presume   *See* **Assume**.

Pretense/Pretext   A *PRETENSE* is, as the word implies, the act of pretending--an action intended to deceive. A *PRETEXT* is an excuse. The words are closely similar. Some dictionaries say they are synonymous.

Preventative/Preventive   Some say these are equally acceptable synonyms, but most dictionaries prefer *PREVENTIVE*. It is certainly the more familiar and easier on the tongue. It's also the shorter of the two words and therefore preferred for broadcast. *See also* **Interpretative**.

Price Hike   Please avoid using *HIKE* or similar words when you mean "increase." It's a headline word that has no place in working English in that sense. *See* **Headline Words**.

Principal/Principle   These are distantly related words that are often confused. *PRINCIPAL* means foremost, the chief, the one who holds a leading position--the high school *principal*. *PRINCIPLE* refers to a basic law or truth, a rule. Both words have other more narrow meanings. It's best to consult a dictionary when in doubt. While we're on the subject, even very sophisticated speakers often mispronounce these identically sounding words as PRINCABLE. Take care.

Prison   *See* **Jail**.

Prisoner   *See* **Convict**.

Problematic   If a thing is said to be *PROBLEMATIC*, it means it is in doubt or difficult to solve--not necessarily that there is a problem with it.

Proboscis   Used humorously for a big nose. The late comedian Jimmy Durante made much of his *PROBOSCIS*. It is really a long snout, such as an elephant's trunk or the sucking tube of butterflies and other insects. Pronounced pro-BAH-sis.

Produce *PRODUCE* has two distinctly different meanings and three different pronunciations. *Produce* (pronounced PRAW-doos or PROH-doos), the noun, refers to a product, usually a farm product, most often fruit and vegetables. *Produce* (pronounced pruh-DOOS), the verb, means to manufacture, to create or bring to light.

Prognosis *See* **Diagnosis.**

Prone/Supine *PRONE* means inclined, bent toward some attitude or action. When one inclines all the way, he is *prone*--lying facedown. Rifles are fired from the *prone* position. The point is, to be *prone* one must be facedown. Lying faceup is *SUPINE*, a word we rarely hear.

Proportion, Out Of All A *PROPORTION* is an expression of relationship, comparison. The media are frequently accused of taking an issue *all out of proportion*. What the complainer is trying to say is *out of all proportion*. In other words, treating the issue as being more important than it really is. A *proportion* is also a share, a portion of something. In this latter sense, use *portion*.

Prostate/Prostrate The *PROSTATE* is the very useful, but often troublesome, gland in males. To be *PROSTRATE* is to be lying horizontally in submission or, metaphorically, to be helpless or in a humble position.

Protein Note spelling. It is pronounced PROH-teen.

Prototype Model A redundancy. A *PROTOTYPE* is a *MODEL*. It is, in fact, a first model, often experimental.

Proved/Proven Both are acceptable past forms of *prove*. For broadcast, *PROVEN* is to be preferred in most instances, except in such uses as "he *proved* his point." *Proved* is the verb, *proven* the adjective. "It is a *proven* fact."

Psychiatrist/Psychologist A *PSYCHIATRIST* is a medical doctor who practices psychiatry. A *PSYCHOLOGIST* is a student of the mind, often one who practices counseling or clinical psychology. A *psychologist* may be a medical doctor, but most often is not.

Pulitzer Prize Prestigious awards given to journalists annually for outstanding work in a variety of ways. It is often pronounced PYOO-lit-zer, but it is preferably pronounced PUHL-it-zer. Think of the young chicken having just laid her first egg: pullet surprise. (I'm sorry, it was too good to let go by. It's not original with me. I don't know where it came from.)

Pull Out All The Stops To go after a goal with everything at one's command. The reference is to a pipe organ which will put out its maximum voice when all the stops are pulled out. I wonder what image was in the mind of the writer who recently said *"pulled out all the stoppers."*

Pupil/Student Although dictionaries say *PUPIL* and *STUDENT* are synonyms, usage dictates a distinction. Use *pupil* when referring to a young student--usually in elementary school. High school and college inmates are called *students.*

Put To Sleep This is a common euphemism for *kill.* In the case of animals that are killed to put them out of misery, I would prefer the word *destroy. PUT TO SLEEP* might be proper when an animal or human is put under anesthesia but is expected to awaken.

Puzzle *See* **Enigma.**

Quadruple Be careful with the pronunciation. It is kwahd-ROOP-uhl, not kwahd-RIHP-uhl. It means to increase fourfold.

Quantum It has become fashionable to characterize anything that increases or moves forward as having taken a *QUANTUM* leap or some other such verb. *Quantum* has distinct meanings in physics, but in the language of the rest of us it refers to bulk or gross quantity. It is possible to have a tiny *quantum* of something. Avoid the word.

Quart/Quarter Watch your pronunciation of these. Why is it people who can pronounce *quartz* just fine, will pronounce *QUART* as KORT? It's KWORT and KWORT-ur.

Quash/Squash Both words have the sense of putting down--to *QUASH* or *SQUASH* a rebellion, for example. However, I think *squash* denotes some sort of crushing action, while *quash* can be less violent. Of course, *squash* has a number of additional meanings, such as the well-known vegetable and the racquet game. When speaking of a rumor being put down, I would use *quash.*

Quebec The province in eastern Canada is pronounced kweh-BEK, in English. French speakers in Canada pronounce it kuh-BEK.

Quebecois KEH-beh-KWAH. As the Quebec separatist movement developed in recent years, the French-speaking residents of that province became known as the *QUEBECOIS.* It means simply "a person living in Quebec," but pertains primarily to the French-speaking element. A non-French resident of Quebec resents the name.

Question *See* **Inquiry.**

Rabbit *See* **Hare.**

Rabid The state of having rabies. Do not speak of a *RABID* sports fan. What you mean is *avid*. In one sense, *rabid* means with intense feeling or violence, but let's not use it that way. The association with the disease is too strong to get subtle with the word.

Radio The wireless transmission and reception of electromagnetic energy modulated so as to contain information. With that definition, any electromagnetic energy emitted into the atmosphere is a *RADIO* transmission, even TV pictures. The frequency range on which radio transmissions are practical in the electromagnetic spectrum is called the *RF band*, meaning radio frequency. It extends from below three kilohertz to 300 gigahertz, and lies between the audio frequencies and the infrared frequencies. It's possible you can earn your living as a broadcaster without knowing this, but I think you should have some idea of the basics.

Raffle Off The *OFF* is unnecessary.

Raise/Rear Some authorities are surrendering on this one, but the purists hang on. You *REAR* children, but *RAISE* other things. But there's the common colloquial cliché: "born and raised."

Ramshackle *RAMSHACKLE* means to be in a state of disrepair, ready to fall down. It was mistaken for *random* in a report that said a section of a city had grown in a *ramshackle* way, without benefit of zoning laws.

Ration The preferred pronunciation is RASH-uhn. RAY-shun is acceptable.

Ravage/Ravish *RAVAGE* means to ruin, destroy; violent devastation. *RAVISH* means to carry away, kidnap, usually a woman with rape in mind. Some feminists object to the built-in notion of rape, but there it is. Oddly, *ravishing* means having great beauty or attractiveness, when used as an adjective.

Reaction/Response A *REACTION* is an unthinking, spontaneous response to a stimulus. A *RESPONSE* is any action brought on by a stimulus, but for our purposes, limit it to a thought-out answer, or other action. Therefore, an answer to criticism by a politician is not a *reaction*, but rather a *response*.

Readable *See* **Legible.**

Realtor A member of the National Association of Realtors--not just someone who happens to sell real estate.

Rebellion/Revolution/Revolt There's a difference. Why do we call it the American (or French) *REVOLUTION*, but the Boxer *REBELLION*? Because a *revolution* (a turning around) is a *rebellion* that was successful. A *rebellion* usually does not succeed. A *rebellion* is open defiance of authority, but not necessarily with the intent of overthrowing that authority. *REVOLT* also comes from the idea of turning over and means a turning away from established authority or rule.

Rebut/Refute *REBUT* in common use means to oppose by legal argument, to counter another's claim. *REFUTE* means to bring forth evidence or logic to overthrow another's claim and prove it wrong. A *rebuttal* may not be convincing or successful; a *refutation* is.

Record When one sets a *RECORD*, that's it; it is not a *"new record."* Nor do we break *"old records."*

Red-Haired/Redheaded Prefer *Red-Haired* when referring to people. It is a *Redheaded* woodpecker, however.

Referee/Umpire Generally used synonymously with the sense of judging. Commonly, usage depends on the sport involved. Baseball has *UMPIRES*, football and boxing have *REFEREES*, for example. Both terms are used outside sports, as well. There are, for example, *referees* in bankruptcy and *umpired* art shows.

Regina The capital city of Saskatchewan is pronounced ruh-JYN-uh.

Reign/Rein A monarch has a *REIGN*, a horse is controlled by a *REIN*. To give one *"free rein"* is to release controls and give a person free will. It is not *"free reign,"* although that would seem to carry the same idea.

Relatively *See* **Comparatively.**

Relic A *RELIC* is, by definition, old. *"Old relic"* is a redundancy. So is *"old tradition."* A *relic* is something left after the life or usefulness of an object is past. A skeleton, for example. Attics are places where *relics* are found.

Reluctant/Reticent *RELUCTANT* means unwilling or hesitant to act. *RETICENT* means unwilling or hesitant to speak. *Reticence* has to do only with restraint in expression or communication.

Remiss *See* **Amiss.**

Remorse/Sorrow One feels *REMORSE* as a sense of guilt over one's own actions. *Remorse* is not a general sense of *SORROW* which one might feel over the loss of a friend.

Rend/Render To *REND* is to tear or split violently. To *RENDER* is to reduce, melt down, such as animal fat that is *rendered* into lard. *Render* also has many other meanings, the most common being to reduce to helplessness, to *render* unconscious. A touching scene is "heartrending" not "heartrendering."

Rent *See* **Lease.**

Reparable Capable of being fixed. It is pronounced REP-ur-uhbl.

Repeat Again A redundancy. *REPEAT* means to do it *AGAIN*. If your sense is to *repeat* for a second or third time, then *repeat again* would be appropriate.

Replenish Yes, the word meaning to resupply or to fill is related through its Latin root to *plenty*, but there's no *t* in it. Pronounce it ree-PLEHN-ish.

Replete This is a word more often misused than not. *REPLETE* means to have something in great abundance--it does not have the sense of being complete, even though it sounds as though it does. A recent advertisement informed us that an apartment was "*replete* with a microwave oven and stove." A correct usage would be "Iowa farms are *replete* with corn." *With* always accompanies *replete*.

Replica *See* **Copy.**

Reported/Reputed Take away the *-ed* endings and you will readily see the difference. *REPORTED* means the transmission of information, the telling of the story. *Reportedly* has come into use as a substitute for *REPUTED*. *Repute* has to do with reputation, esteem, which can be either high or low. The use of *reputed* for *reported* may result from a confusion with *putative*, which is a related word and means assumed to be true, or accepted as fact.

Reprise Pronounced ruh-PREEZ. Play it again, Sam. A repeat performance in the most common use.

Repugnant/Repulsive *REPUGNANT* means to be opposed to, incompatible. *REPULSIVE* means disgusting, repelling.

Reputable Pronounced REP-ewe-tuh-buhl.

Reside *See* **Dwell**.

Resin/Rosin For practical purposes the same thing. Athletes use *ROSIN* on their shoes or hands, violinists rub it on their bowstrings. *RESIN* is mixed in paints, varnishes and plastics.

Retaliation The noun form of the verb *retaliate*, to get even, to strike back in anger. *RETALIATION* requires that it be preceded by *in*, in most constructions. You should not write "His action was *retaliation of . . . .*"

Restaurateur One who owns or operates a restaurant. Note the spelling and the pronunciation. In its preferred spelling there is no *n* as there is in *restaurant*. It is REHS-tuhr-uh-TOOR.

Restive/Restless *RESTIVE* means stubborn, unwilling to submit to authority, inflexible. In other words, wishing to stay at rest. *RESTLESS* has to do with discontent, or constant motion, nervousness. The terribly common misuse is saying *restive* when *restless* is clearly needed. Please watch for it.

Retch/Wretch To *RETCH* is to gag or throw up--to vomit; actually the heaving action just before vomiting. A *WRETCH* is a pitiable person, one who lives in degradation.

Revolve *See* **Center On**.

Revolver *See* **Automatic**.

Richter Scale *See* **Earthquake**.

Riddle *See* **Enigma**.

Riffraff/Riprap This confusion probably doesn't happen often because *RIFFRAFF* is a pejorative term meaning those of low esteem, and *RIPRAP* would not likely come up in the news frequently. *Riprap* is the layer of heavy stones dumped on a riverbank or lake or ocean shore to prevent erosion.

Rile/Roil There is a close relationship between *RILE* and *ROIL*. Some authorities consider them synonymous. For precision, however, there is a distinction to be drawn. *Rile* means to stir up emotionally, to make angry. *Roil* means to stir up physically, to turn a liquid cloudy; by roiling the muddy bottom of a pond, for example.

Ring Off The Hook This is a terribly overused metaphor used when one has received a large number of phone calls. It's a cliché that no longer makes sense. Telephones haven't had *hooks* for a generation. Avoid the phrase. Also avoid referring to switchboards that "light up like a Christmas tree." It's just too familiar a simile. Find something else.

Rio *RIO* means "river." Don't write "the *Rio* Grande River." *Rio Grande* means "big river."

Risk *See* **Weather Words.**

Robbery *See* **Burglary.**

Roof The plural is pronounced ROOFS, not ROOVES.

Route Pronounce it ROOT.

Ruffed Grouse The game bird is a *RUFFED* grouse--not "ruffled."

Rug *See* **Carpet.**

Sahara *SAHARA* means "desert." Refer to "The *Sahara*" not "the *Sahara* Desert."

Salmon *See* **Almond/Salmon.**

Sam An acronym of surface-to-air missile. Take care not to say "*SAM* missile," thereby saying "missile" twice.

Sanitarium/Sanitorium These are probably the same thing--a hospital for long-term care--but usage has brought a distinction. A *SANITARIUM* is a facility for housing the mentally ill. A *SANITORIUM* is a facility for housing those with other chronic illnesses, such as tuberculosis. It is a fine distinction and probably not important. What is important is knowing how the institution in your story refers to itself.

Sanction One of those odd words that seems to mean two exactly opposite things. As a noun, a *SANCTION* is a coercive action designed to enforce a law or social norm. To disapprove. As a verb, to *sanction* means to approve of, to ratify, to make valid.

Sandwich Come on, folks! How can you mispronounce *SANDWICH*? Some do manage, however. SAND-widge is most common, heard not only in general speech, but in TV commercials by people who get paid a lot of money to talk right. Could they be golfers influenced by "sand wedge"? Some bloody fools even say SANG-wich (or -widge). Elster is especially hard on those who say SAN-wich. It is pronounced as written: SAND-wich.

Sapling A small tree. But, I believe, a tree with leaves, not an evergreen. It would be at least uncommon to refer to a Christmas tree as a *SAPLING*. Technically, a *sapling* may be no more than four inches in diameter at chest height. Bigger than that, it's a tree. Anybody care? Probably not.

Sao The Portuguese equivalent of the Spanish *San* or the French/English *Saint*. In English we can get close to the pronunciation with SOWN (rhymes with sound). Yes, there's an *n* sound, regardless of how it's spelled. It is most likely to be encountered in stories involving Sao Paulo, Brazil's largest city.

Saving/Savings You put your money in a *SAVINGS* account, but it is Daylight *SAVING* Time. No final *s*. Some authorities say the account is a *saving* account; what is in it is *savings*. Take your pick on that distinction, but remember *DST* is singular.

Scare Words It's difficult in this day and time to think of *SCARE WORDS*--words that in themselves can cause panic. There are a few, however. Be very careful with *epidemic* (which see), *tornado* (which see), *riot*, things to do with escaped dangerous criminals, lunatics and so on. Report the events, of course, but do not unnecessarily stir up the populace--unless of course, there is imminent danger--such as the local dam about to burst. In that case, panic is the order of the day.

Scared/Scarred A frequent spelling error that can really mess up a news program. Be careful.

Scat Yes, *SCAT* is an irritated command to a cat. But the word also means the fecal excrement of animals. Hence *scatological*, the use of sexual or excremental references in humor. Caution: Locally, there is an activist organization known by the acronym *SCAT*. I think that's pretty funny.

Schism Preferably pronounced SIZZ-uhm, but SHIZ-uhm and even SKIZ-uhm are accepted as secondary versions. It means a division or discord, especially when involving factions within a church.

Scholar Today, a *SCHOLAR* is usually found at a university and is someone who has obtained a great depth of knowledge in a specific, even narrow, field.

Scion Pronounced SIGH-uhn. It means, literally, a child or descendant. However, its use is usually in the sense of heir, and not just an inheritor of family wealth, but also its social position and power.

Score *See* **Margin.**

Scotch/Scots/Scottish Anyone with a name such as mine gets sensitive about the misuse of these words. First, please don't use *SCOTCH* to mean "cheap" or "stingy." That's plain offensive. *SCOTCH* refers to the *whisky* (which see) and other products of Scotland. The people are properly referred to as the *SCOTS*, or *SCOTTISH*. *Scottish* also refers to all things having to do with Scotland. *Scotch* also has the informal meaning of to quell, such as a rumor.

Scrip/Script *SCRIP* is the paper currency issued following an emergency--a war, for example--when the basic economy has been wrecked. A *SCRIPT* is, among other things, what broadcast newswriters create several times a day.

Sculpt/Sculptor/Sculpture To *SCULPT* is to create a *SCULPTURE*. The one who does it is a *SCULPTOR*.

Seasonable/Seasonal Something that is *SEASONABLE* is typical of the season. Temperatures are said to be *seasonable*. Something that is *SEASONAL* varies with the season. Skiing is a *seasonal* sport.

Secondly *See* **Firstly.**

Sectarian/Secular *SECTARIAN* usually has to do with a sect, most often a religious sect, or a person devoted to a sect. *SECULAR* has to do with worldly things, things not related to religion. Pointedly not church related.

Semiweekly *See* **Biweekly** .

Senile *See* **Anile.**

Sensual/Sensuous *SENSUAL* carries a sense of gratification of the senses and usually is used to relate to sexual attractiveness. *SENSUOUS* has a more aesthetic sense, to be inwardly appreciative of such things as art and music.

Septic *See* **Antiseptic.**

Service *See* **Mass.**

Service Station *See* **Filling Station.**

Sew/Sow It's hard to see how this confusion can occur, but it does with some frequency. *SEW* has to do with stitching--needle-and-thread work. *SOW* has to do with seeding, especially by spreading seed. Both are pronounced SOH. The female swine, and females of some other animals, are called *SOWS*, pronounced SOWS (rhymes with COWS).

Sewage/Sewerage The network of pipes and pumps that takes care of a city's waste is called a *SEWERAGE* system. The stuff that flows through the system is called *SEWAGE*. Thus the *sewage* treatment plant is the last stop in the *sewerage* system.

Sex *See* **Gender**.

Sherbet/Sherbert/Sorbet These are frozen confections. *SHERBET* is the preferred spelling and pronunciation; however, *SHERBERT* is sometimes accepted. Elster says flatly SHUR-burt is wrong. *SORBET* certainly looks French and is most frequently pronounced sohr-BAY. Sorry, that's wrong. Both of these come from the Persian. It is correctly pronounced SOHR-but. But, everyone will think you are an uncultured clod if you pronounce it that way. Such is life.

Ship *See* **Boat**.

Shore *See* **Bank**.

Sick *See* **Ill**.

Sierra *SIERRA* means "sawtooth mountains," and it is plural. It is the "*Sierra* Nevada" not the *Sierra* Nevadas or *Sierra* Nevada Mountains. On second reference, however, "The *Sierras*" is considered proper.

Sight *See* **Cite**.

Similar Means having characteristics in common. *SIMILAR* should not be used as a synonym for "identical." It is more closely related in meaning to analogous, comparable. Note also the spelling and pronunciation--it is not SIM-yoo-lur, it is SIM-ih-lur.

Simultaneous *See* **Coincident**.

Since *See* **Because**.

Site *See* **Cite**.

Skeptic *See* **Cynic.**

Skid Road/Skid Row *SKID ROAD* was originally a rough road along which logs were skidded. Later, that part of town frequented by loggers became known as *Skid Road*. *SKID ROW* is a part of town frequented by vagrants and addicts, said to be "on the *skids*." The terms are used interchangeably, but prefer *skid row*, when referring to the place where the bums hang out. Be very cautious with this one--people don't like to be considered residents of *skid row*.

Slew/Slough In most senses, these are pronounced SLOO. *SLEW* always is. It means, among other things, to swerve or skid around--as an automobile does on ice. *SLOUGH* is pronounced SLOO or SLOW (rhymes with COW) when it refers to a swamp or mire, which is the usual meaning. However, peeling skin--such as following a bad sunburn--is said to *slough* off, and in that case, it is pronounced SLUFF. Got that?

Sloth Pronounced SLOHTH, SLUHTH or SLAHTH. Dictionaries prefer SLOHTH. I think it sounds odd. I have always said SLAHTH for the animal, but SLOHTH-ful for the human behavior. Time to change my mind--I'll go with SLOHTH in all cases. It is a South and Central American animal that lives in trees and moves very slowly. Applied to humans, the term means inactive, indolent. A favorite tongue twister to try on neophyte (and experienced!) broadcasters is saying quickly "Three-toed tree *sloth*." Try it.

Small-Businessperson Always hyphenate so as to make clear that *SMALL* refers to the size of the *BUSINESS* and not the size of the *PERSON*.

Smithsonian Institution In Washington, D.C., the *SMITHSONIAN* includes a number of the national museums and galleries. Note, it is NOT "Institute."

Sniper A *SNIPER* is a gunman who shoots from concealment at an exposed enemy. I do not think it is correct to refer to a "police *sniper*" in a hostage situation where an officer shoots the hostage-taker. Call him a "police sharpshooter" or "marksman." *Sniper* has a negative connotation; suggests cowardice.

Socialization/Socializing It was recently reported in a campus newspaper that there was "too much *SOCIALIZATION* at fraternities." What the writer was after, of course, was *SOCIALIZING*. He was euphemistically referring to partying. *Socialization* is what anthropologists are interested in: bringing young members of a group into full participation. *Socializing* is simply being social--OK, taking part in fraternity parties.

Socks/Stockings *SOCKS* are generally considered to be short foot coverings, reaching midcalf. *STOCKINGS* in common use refers to long foot and leg coverings worn primarily by women. However, anyone--man or woman--who is without shoes is said to be in *"stocking* feet."

Sofa *See* **Couch.**

Solder A method of bonding two pieces of metal by melting a metallic alloy in the joint. Pronounced **SAW**-dur. One may *SOLDER* a relationship in a metaphorical sense.

Sordid *See* **Morbid.**

Spar In nautical circles a *SPAR* is a wood or metal pole above decks, such as a mast, boom, gaff or yard used to support sails or other rigging. In boxing, a *sparring* match is one for practice or exhibition. One can also *spar* with an opponent verbally, as in a debate.

Specie/Species *SPECIE*, usually pronounced SPEE-shee, refers to coins--money. *SPECIES*, pronounced either SPEE-sheez or SPEE-seez (Elster says NOT SPEE-seez), refers to a biological type, a variety of life.

Spectators *See* **Audience.**

Spitting Image This somewhat crude, but colorful phrase is also seen as "the *spit* and *image.*" It means an exact likeness and is often used to compare a child to a parent.

Spinster Originally *SPINSTER* referred to a woman who worked as a spinner. Today, it refers to an unmarried woman past the age where she is likely to marry--an old maid. I would urge you not to use the term to describe a living person you're writing about.

Sport *See* **Game.**

Spree Usually avoid *SPREE* in reference to a series of crimes. The word means overindulgence or an outburst of any activity, but to me it carries the idea of having fun: a shopping *spree*. I don't think a person engaged in serial killings is having much fun. No doubt a headline word.

Stalking Horse We would rarely use the first meaning of this term--the horse behind which a hunter hides while stalking game. We hear it often, however, in its metaphorical sense: a political candidate who comes forward to divide the opposition or to cover up who is actually running.

Stanch/Staunch *STANCH* means to stop the flow. We speak of *stanching* blood. Note that the idea of stopping a flow is built into the word, so to say "*stanching* the flow of blood" is redundant, although commonly heard. To be *STAUNCH* is to be steadfast, loyal, strongly supportive.

Stars And Stripes The flag of the United States of America. The phrase is capitalized as "The *Stars and Stripes*." Sometimes confused with "Stars and Bars," which is the term for the Confederate flag of Civil War times, still to be seen in some southern states. *Stars and Stripes* is also the name of a military newspaper.

Start Treaty A redundancy. *START* is the acronym for Strategic Arms Reduction Talks. To say "*START Talks*," you are saying "talks" twice. You need to watch acronyms closely for this trap.

State Of . . . Needed only when referring to Washington or New York to differentiate from the cities of the same name. In other cases, just name the state.

Stationary/Stationery There is a slight variation in pronunciation between *STATIONARY*--at a standstill, unmoving--and *STATIONERY*--writing materials and office supplies. The final vowel sound in *stationary* is -airy, while in *stationery* it is -erry. As I say, the difference is slight.

Stifle To *STIFLE* (STY-ful) is to strangle, to cut off the air supply or to prevent speech in other ways. It is not correct to say traffic was *stifled* by a wreck that blocked the highway.

Sting *See* **Bite.**

Straight/Strait We all know the many meanings of *STRAIGHT*. Note the different spelling of *STRAIT*--a narrow body of water between two land masses--the "*Strait* of Gibraltar," "Torres *Strait*." *Strait* means confined, in a narrow place, tight.

Straitjacket The word *STRAITJACKET* refers to a restraining device. Note the spelling of *strait*.

Strangle/Strangulate These both have the same basic meaning--to cut off the oxygen supply until death results. *STRANGULATE* has a broader meaning in medical circles, where a "*strangulated* hernia" is so swollen that the blood supply to the tissue is cut off and the tissue dies.

Strangled To Death A redundancy. *See* previous entry.

STRATEGY/TACTICS A *STRATEGY* is a master plan, either military or not. *TACTICS* are part of that plan--how one goes about achieving the goals of the plan.

Student *See* **Pupil.**

Subsequent *See* **Consequent.**

Successive *See* **Consecutive.**

Such As *See* **Like.**

Suicide Be careful in *SUICIDE* stories not to write what is probably a non sequitur--"He died of self-inflicted wounds." It's very unlikely there would be more than one wound, although such has been known to happen.

Suit/Suite Both mean set or group. *SUIT* usually refers to clothing, except in court or on a card table, and is pronounced SOOT (rhymes with BOOT). *SUITE* is often used to refer to a set of musical compositions or groups of rooms or furniture and is pronounced SWEET. *Suit* has numerous additional uses. See your dictionary.

Supine *See* **Prone.**

Suppress/Surpress *SUPPRESS* means to conceal or hold back. There is no such word as *SURPRESS*, which we often hear when the speaker wants *suppress*. It probably derives from the word being so similar to *surprise*.

Surprise *See* **Astonish.**

Suspected *See* **Accused.**

Sustain A favorite word of the writers of accident or crime stories. *SUSTAIN* means to survive, to withstand. Therefore, "He died of injuries *sustained* in the crash" is nonsense. If he *sustained* the injuries, he survived. Sustain does not have the same meaning as "suffered" or "received," except in the sense that the army *sustained* heavy losses. That still means the army survived despite the losses.

Swimsuit *See* **Bathing Suit.**

Syrup The sticky sweet stuff is pronounced SUHR-up, not SEER-up.

Tack/Tact The cliché has it: "Take a different *TACK*," that is to say, go in a different direction. It's a nautical term, specifically relating to sailing craft when changing course. The phrase is now used to mean any change in direction. For some reason, people use *TACT*, which has to do with behavior, usually relating to circumspection, good manners, diplomacy. *Tact* may get confused with *tack* from its seemingly close relation to *tactic*. The words are not related. *Tack* is also the generic term for saddles, bridles and other items associated with riding horses.

Take *See* **Bring**.

Tantamount This is a word Virginia newspeople once used frequently. *TANTAMOUNT* means just as good as, equal to. During the state Democratic primary process it was considered deeply wise to point out that receiving the Democratic nomination for certain state offices was *tantamount* to election. Which it was. The political climate has now changed and being nominated by either party is no longer a guarantee of election. *Tantamount* is a nice old word, though. It makes you sound a lot smarter than you probably are.

Tarmac The paved area in front of an airport terminal or hangar is called the *TARMAC*. It's really short for Tarmacadam, a trade name for a certain kind of paving developed by Scottish engineer John MacAdam early in the 19th century. The term does not apply generally to airport pavement--only the "apron" near the terminal or hangar. Webster's says it includes the runway, but I don't think it does.

Tarpaulin A large sheet of plastic or canvas to protect something from the weather. It has only three syllables: tar-PAHL-ihn. Frequently mispronounced tar-PAHL-ee-uhn.

Teen-Age Dictionaries recognize *TEEN-AGED* as a secondary spelling, but please don't use it. The term is always hyphenated in broadcast copy. *See* the discussion under **Boy/Man**.

Telephone Poll A poll taken by telephone is probably properly called a *TELEPHONE POLL*, but that's really confusing. Try to find a better way to describe it. Call it a "survey."

Temblor *See* **Earthquake**.

Temerity/Timidity Good grief! Don't get these mixed up as did a learned university economist on a recent TV program. *TEMERITY* means reckless courage, defiance of odds, foolhardiness, rashness. "He had the *temerity* to challenge the police." *TIMIDITY* means just the opposite--lacking in courage, shy.

Temperature *See* **Fever.**

Tennessee *See* **Detroit.**

Tenterhooks When one is anxiously awaiting something, uneasy, one is said to be on *TENTERHOOKS*. The word is often jocularly pronounced *tenderhooks*, but that's a joke. A *tenter* is a wooden frame on which fabric is stretched. It has many small sharp nails around the perimeter to hold the fabric. They are called *tenterhooks*. So the image is of one so strained as to be stretched on a frame.

Test Out The *OUT* is unnecessary.

That *THAT* causes problems. Broadcasters should avoid the excessive use of *that*. Too many *thats* create a "machine-gun" effect: That-a-that-that. Test each sentence in which *that* appears to see whether it might read just as well and mean the same thing without the *that*. Most of the time *that* can be left out without damaging the sense of what you are trying to say. "The prime minister said that the navy is in full alert." "The prime minister said the navy is in full alert." There are times, however, when *that* is needed for clarity, in which cases, of course, leave it in.

That/Which This one puzzles even the best of writers. My way of handling which word to use is to decide whether the phrase being introduced is to be set off by commas or parentheses. If the setting off is needed, then use *WHICH*. If it will not be set off (that is, the phrase is necessary for the understanding of the sentence), then use *THAT*. There are formal rules of grammar that give you the technicalities, but I think my way works fine. By the way, *which* normally refers to things, while *that* refers to people or things and *who* only to people. I find referring to a person as *that* to be grating.

Thaw *See* **Melt.**

Theater It is pronounced THEE-uh-tur, not thee-ATE-ur. And let's spell it *theater*, not *theatre*. *Theatre* is British and is being taken up pretentiously by those in the American theater.

Think *See* **Believe.**

Thoroughbred Only horses are *THOROUGHBREDS*. It is a specific breed of race and show horse. The word is used informally to describe other domestic animals and sometimes people. Dogs and other animals are properly called *purebred*. Webster's says *thoroughbred* is a synonym for *purebred*. Horse people would not agree.

Threat *See* **Weather Words.**

Throe/Throw *THROE* has to do with violent struggle; death *throes*, the *throes* of revolt. *THROW* is the act of flinging, primarily, but *throw* has numerous other meanings, such as *throw* a fit, or be *thrown* from a horse.

To All Intensive Purposes One of many gaffes to show up on student term papers and quizzes. Another of my favorites is "It's a doggy dog world." Ranking close behind are "Fair to midland" and "hare's breath." What the writers were after, respectively, was "*TO ALL INTENTS AND PURPOSES*," "it's a dog-eat-dog world," "fair to middling" and "hairbreadth." College professors collect these things.

Toddler *See* **Baby.**

Tomato Where you come from plays a large part in what you call this fruit (it is a fruit, by the way, not a vegetable). I believe the only correct pronunciation is tuh-MAY-toh; that's the way I say it. A close associate of mine calls it a tuh-MAH-toh. That's chiefly British, and some people would say it's affected. It is heard most frequently in New England. My mother persisted in calling it a tuh-MAT-oh, which may be limited to a now-abandoned lumbering town at Lincoln Gap, Vermont, where she spent a number of her formative years. Elster says tuh-MAT-oh is Canadian. I'll go along with him.

Tornado *See* **Cyclone.**

Tortoise/Turtle A *TORTOISE* is, in fact, a *TURTLE*, but it is one that lives entirely on land. A *turtle* is an amphibian, which spends most of its time in the water, including its overwinter hibernation. Both are reptiles. The race of fable, by the way, involved a *tortoise* and a *hare* (which see), not a *turtle* and a rabbit. Oddly, a *terrapin*, regardless of what its name might suggest, is a water-dwelling turtle. The name is of North American Indian origin.

Tortuous/Torturous A *TORTUOUS* road is one that has many twists and bends. The word also refers to anything that is devious. There is usually a connotation of danger inherent in the word. *TORTUROUS* has to do with torture--physical abuse. Another sound-alike is *tortious*. It is a legal term meaning unlawful; having to do with torts. You wouldn't want to use *tortious* in a news program; maybe not ever.

Totaled The Car This is an informal phrase at best. It means damage was so great the cost of repair would be more than the value of the vehicle, so damage was declared *total*.

Toward *See* **Afterward.**

Tract *See* **Acre.**

Trademarks And Names We frequently find the need to refer to things in the news that are familiarly called by their *trade names*. We must keep in mind that these names are valuable property and should not be used as generic names for those sorts of things. I refer to calling all photocopiers "Xerox" machines, all plastic tape "Scotch" tape, all tissues "Kleenex," and so on. If these *trade names* become generic, they are lost to the owner. There are many cases in which that has happened. The media play a large role in either retaining the owner's interest or helping him lose it. Other examples that come immediately to mind are: TV Guide, Coke and Coca-Cola, Popsicle, Tabasco, Day-Glo, Caterpillar, Drygas, Cook's Tour, Rolodex, Weight Watchers, Velcro, Vise-Grip, Frigidaire, Breathalyzer, TelePromTer and Heat-o-lator. There are many others.

Transpire *See* **Happen.**

Treachery/Treason *TREACHERY* is a violation of trust or confidence; to cheat. We usually think of *treachery* as being serious business. *TREASON* is usually used to indicate *treachery* against one's country. It is, under certain circumstances, punishable by death.

Triple Crown In horse racing and baseball only. The *TRIPLE CROWN* in racing is made up of the Kentucky Derby, the Preakness and the Belmont Stakes. In baseball, the *triple crown* is worn by the player who leads a league in batting average, home runs and runs batted in for a season.

Triumphal/Triumphant A celebration following a victory of some sort can be referred to as *TRIUMPHAL*. The person basking in the glow of victory is said to be *TRIUMPHANT*.

Troop/Troops/Troupe When referring to military personnel, the reference is always to *TROOPS*, it is not used as a singular. *TROOP* used to refer to a unit of mounted cavalry equivalent to a company of foot soldiers. *Troop* has a number of other meanings as well. Actors come in *TROUPES*.

Truck We all know what a *TRUCK* is--the vehicle. But *truck* has other meanings as well, many of them having to do with moving things. Some uses seem slangy, and are probably not good for broadcast. *Truck* has to do with bartering small goods, but most often we use it to mean rubbish, trash. "Get out of here with that *truck*." It can also apply to nonsense speech, and is usually used in a negative way: "I don't believe that *truck*."

Trustee/Trusty Take care with this, *trusty* reader. They are frequently confused and therefore misused. A *TRUSTEE* (pronounced truss-TEE) is a person who has been given a great deal of responsibility over the funds or affairs of others. A *trustee* of a bank, for example, or a member of a university's board of *trustees*. A *TRUSTY* is a prisoner who, because his behavior has been good, is given a certain degree of freedom in exchange for performing some jailhouse tasks. It is pronounced TRUSS-tee. *Trusty* also means faithful, trustworthy, as in "my *trusty* rifle."

Try And/Try To *TRY AND* implies two actions. I will *try and* I will do. Most of the time you will want *TRY TO*. But, if you indeed do have two things in mind, then of course use *TRY AND*.

Turbid/Turgid *TURBID* means cloudy, impure, polluted. Water that has been *roiled* (which see) is *turbid*, and so is air filled with smoke. *TURGID* (pronounced TER-jid) means swollen or distended or, when referring to writing style, overly embellished, pompous.

Two In A Row This can't be. It takes three, at least, to make a row. To say "Temperatures will top 90 degrees for the second day *in a row*" is illogical.

Typhoon *See* **Cyclone.**

Umpire *See* **Referee.**

Under Way/ -Weigh The term is nautical in origin--it means to have *weighed* (hoisted) the anchor and to be moving. Today's usage, however, has it spelled *UNDER WAY* which makes more sense when speaking of anything but boats.

Uninhabitable *See* **Habitable.**

Uninterested *See* **Disinterested.**

Unique *UNIQUE* is one of those words, such as *pregnant*, that cannot be qualified. Something is one of a kind or it's not. "Very *unique*" or "nearly *unique*" are just plain wrong. Once again, Webster's and I depart company. There is a lengthy discussion of certain circumstances under which the dictionary believes *unique* may be modified. I prefer to leave it unqualifiable.

University *See* **College.**

Unloosen/Unravel These look wrong, but they are OK. For some reason we often seem to need two words that mean the same thing. *UNLOOSEN* means to *loosen. UNRAVEL* means to *ravel. Unloosen* and *unravel* seem to carry the sense of deliberate acts, while *loosen* and *ravel* are accidental or occur spontaneously, I think. *Unloose* means to set free, to relax constraints. *Unravel* means only to come apart and can be applied to knitted sweaters, mental stability or complicated plans.

Unorganized *See* **Disorganized**.

Untimely It means premature or inopportune. It is often used as in *"UNTIMELY* death." Keep in mind that from the point of view of the deceased, many deaths are *untimely.*

-Up Almost never needed, as in "fix up," "warmed up," "catch up" and so on. Test each *-up* to see if you can live without it.

Upcoming A redundancy to be avoided.

Uppermost/Upmost/Utmost Although *UPMOST* is a perfectly good word, meaning of the highest rank or order, use *UPPERMOST* which means the same thing and avoids confusing the sense with that of *UTMOST*, which means most extreme--at the farthest point, of the highest degree of intensity. "Of the *utmost* importance." *Uppermost* is also used to indicate the physically highest thing--the *uppermost* branch of a tree, for example.

Urgent *See* **Wire Services**.

Use/Utilize Generally, *UTILIZE* is to be considered pretentious and avoided in broadcast copy. There are times, though, when *USE* just doesn't make the grade. In such cases, use *utilize.*

Utility Pole Instead of guessing what it was the car ran into--use *UTILITY POLE* rather than "power pole" or "telephone pole." Actually, it's a rare pole these days that does not carry several different kinds of cable and wires.

Uttering *See* **Forging**.

Vacant *See* **Empty**.

Vacuum Note the spelling--one *c*, two *u's*. It is pronounced with three syllables--VAK-yoo-um.

Variety This is a plural noun meaning a collection of similar but different things. It is frequently used to refer to one of several differing things, as in "the russet is a *VARIETY* of apple." One of a group of things thought of together.

Vascillate *See* **Alternate.**

Vase A vessel, usually associated with flowers. How is it pronounced? VAYS or VAHZ? Elster is very firm. VAHZ is British and not acceptable American English. VAYS or VAYZ are fine.

VDT Terminal The same sort of redundancy we encountered with *START Talks*. The abbreviation VDT means video display terminal. You don't want to say "terminal" twice, do you?

Vehicle The *h* is silent. Pronounce it VEE-uh-kul.

Velocity An expression of speed AND direction. *VELOCITY* is commonly used to denote speed only. Technically, however, *velocity* considers both qualities: the *velocity* of a baseball is an expression of its speed through the air and the direction toward home plate. Don't worry overmuch about this one.

Venire Mispronounced almost always. It is vuh-NEER-ee. A *VENIRE* is the whole group of people called for possible jury duty from which a jury is drawn. Totally unrelated to *veneer*, a thin layer, usually of wood, to present a fine surface. *Veneer* is sometimes used metaphorically when describing people who are not what they seem to be on the outside.

Venom *See* **Antivenin.**

Venue A location, but a specific kind of location. Usually associated with the site of a trial. *VENUE* has become a vogue word to describe the location of nearly any activity or event. It was especially noticeable during a recent Olympic games, where it was used correctly, but too often. It describes a place where large crowds gather.

Verbal *See* **Oral.**

Veritable/Virtual *VERITABLE* has to do with verity, truth. It means actual, not false, the thing actually named. It is often confused with *VIRTUAL*, which means to be functionally or effectively something--"*virtually* the same as sugar."

Vermont *See* **Detroit.**

Via *See* **Per**.

Viable *VIABLE* means capable of living without outside support. The word is badly overused in current American idiom as in *"viable* alternative" and other constructions. Please use it with care, if at all.

Vice/Vise A *VICE* is an evil habit or practice. Be careful not to condemn some habits as *vices* when they may be addictions, which are considered medical problems and not moral issues. A *VISE* is a device for clamping or holding material being worked on. Both are pronounced VICE.

Viper *See* **Pit Viper**.

Vis-à-Vis Literally, "face to face." A useful French phrase for comparing opposites or likenesses. Pronounced VEEZ-aw-VEE.

Vital Signs In terms of patient conditions, the *VITAL SIGNS* are the rates of the pulse and respirations, temperature and often blood pressure. In hospital jargon, PTR (pulse, temperature and respiration).

Vital Statistics Governments, especially on the local level, keep detailed *VITAL STATISTICS*, which include births, deaths, marriages, divorces and figures having to do with health and disease. Many other records, such as real estate transfers, property tax assessments and business licenses, are also maintained but are not referred to as *vital statistics*. *Vital* has to do with life.

Vocation *See* **Occupation**.

W Pronounce it DUB-ul-you. In broadcasting we are frequently called upon to pronounce the name of our station. Don't say DUB-yuh. Of course, there are many stations whose call signs begin with *K*, but you still need to know how to pronounce *W*.

Wacky Related to *whacky* but not spelled or pronounced that way. It means pretty much the same thing--erratic, silly. *Whacky* comes from "whack-head"-- someone who's been stupefied by a blow to the head--punch-drunk.

Wait For/Wait On If your sense is to be awaiting something or someone, use *WAIT FOR*: *"Wait for* me on the corner." If your sense is of service to another, then use *WAIT ON*: "He *waits on* her hand and foot."

Wane/Wax These terms are frequently found in referring to the phases of the moon, but are figuratively used to express the idea of any gradual coming and going. *WANE* means to slowly fade away, while *WAX* means to gradually increase. Do not confuse *wane* with *wan* (pronounced WAHN), which means pale, sallow.

Wangle/Wrangle *WANGLE* usually has to do with obtaining something through trickery, deceit or pleading. The teen-ager *wangles* the keys to the family car. *WRANGLE* has a similar sense, but usually carries the connotation of a struggle or physical threat. A cowboy is called a *wrangler* because it's sometimes necessary to physically push a cow around.

Was A Former . . . As long as someone is alive, that person remains a former of whatever that person was. To say a living person *WAS A FORMER* senator, for example, is to imply that person is dead.

Washington *See* **State Of . . .**

Wasp White Anglo-Saxon Protestant. Often used derisively. *WASP* refers to an American of English or northern European descent who is a Protestant. Note that the term does not apply to the Highland Scots, Welsh or Northern Irish, who are Celtic, not Anglo-Saxon. *See* **Celt.**

Weather Words Some of these terms already have been discussed, but we'll look at them again. The forecast from the Weather Service in winter will often include the term *bitterly cold*. That's about as subjective as one can get. In fact, the terms *hot* and *cold* mean very different things in different parts of the country and at different times of year. *Bitter* has as one sense, harsh, causing discomfort or pain. That's probably what *bitter cold* means. Once again, *currently* and *presently* do not mean the same thing. Do not say "the temperature is *presently* 60 degrees." *Presently* means soon. *Cyclone, hurricane, tornado* and *typhoon* have already been discussed--*see* **Cyclone.** Even though the Weather Service people may refer to forecasting as *progging*, please resist the temptation. It is jargon and should be avoided. *See* **Seasonable.** I object to weatherpeople's referring to a *threat* or *risk* of some weather feature. It's a natural phenomenon and rarely is there any great danger. If the air is not moving, there is no *wind*. Avoid saying "the *wind* is calm." And, worse yet, "The *winds* are calm." That's a contradiction in terms. If the wind is blowing, there is a *wind chill index* involved. That is the effect of wind on the skin, making the effective temperature lower than that measured by a thermometer. Do not say "the wind chill index is minus three degrees." Say "with the wind chill index, the temperature is minus three degrees." Do you know what *POP* is? It is the probability of precipitation. Do you know what that means? Most people don't. It is expressed as a percentage and it means the likelihood of rain or snow. It is derived from computer analysis of weather data over a 100-year period. When this particular set of weather conditions has existed in the past, it has brought on precipitation this percentage of the time. It does not mean it will rain that percentage of the day, nor over that percentage of the area. The term has been phased out of official forecasts. They will now simply state a percentage of precipitation chance, but it still means the same thing. Please don't say, as the official forecast may, "a near-zero percent chance of precipitation." That sounds awful. Just leave it out. There are two levels of severe weather notices used by the Weather Service. They are *watch* and *warning*. *Watch* means that conditions are right for certain kinds of severe weather to develop; *warning* means that the severe weather has been sighted nearby or is almost certain to develop. In summer, these usually have to do with severe thunderstorms, wind and hail. These conditions can develop in a spotty fashion and sometimes cannot be seen to be approaching. In winter, the alerts usually have to do with approaching heavy snow, which can be seen and accurately predicted. You should be very careful to use the proper level in any story related to severe weather, perhaps even explaining what they mean. A *blizzard* in everyday language describes a long heavy snow, but it is generally used to describe a heavy snow accompanied with strong winds. The formal definition is heavy snow, with winds of at least 35 miles an hour and visibility of no more than a quarter of a mile. There is a phenomenon known as a *ground blizzard* in which high winds blow snow already on the ground, although it is not actually snowing at the time.

To give you an idea of how necessary it is to translate what comes out of the weather bureau, the following is an exact quotation from a severe weather watch notice as sent from the Weather Service to the Associated Press:
"THE SEVERE THUNDERSTORM WATCH AREA IS ALONG AND 70 STATUTE MILES EITHER SIDE OF A LINE FROM 45 MILES SOUTH OF FLORENCE SOUTH CAROLINA TO 35 MILES EAST OF RICHMOND VIRGINIA."
I defy anyone without a detailed map to refer to, to explain where the watch area is. The frightening thing about this is the AP sent it exactly as it was received. And, it was undoubtedly read exactly that way on the air by disc jockeys up and down the line.

Weapon *See* **Automatic.**

Wedding *See* **Marriage.**

Weep *See* **Cry.**

Welt/Whelk/Whelp The raised bruise on the skin that results from a stroke of a whip or some other sharp blow is called a *WELT*. A *welt* is also the seam on a leather shoe that attaches the sole to the upper. Many people refer to the bruise as a *WHELP*, but that's wrong. A *whelp* is a young animal, usually a puppy. A *WHELK* is a sea creature. In fact many sea creatures are called *whelks*. Their shells are much prized by collectors.

Wench/Winch This confusion occurs too often to be mere accident. A *WENCH* is an old word meaning peasant girl or serving girl. It is now used only humorously. A *WINCH* is a device containing a spool of cable or rope used to lift or pull heavy things.

Wharf *See* **Dock.**

Whereabouts Is treated as a singular. "His *WHEREABOUTS* is unknown."

Whether *See* **If.**

Which *See* **That/Which.**

Whiskey/Whisky If it is *Scotch* (which see) it is *WHISKY*; if it is any other kind it is *WHISKEY*. Both pronounced the same.

Whore *See* **Hoar.**

Wide *See* **Broad/Wide.**

Widow In stories involving the death of a man, say "he leaves his wife," not his *WIDOW*. She's the *widow*, all right, but when he left, she was his wife.

Wind *See* **Weather Words.**

Windchill Index *See* **Weather Words.**

Windfall A *WINDFALL* is a surprise good fortune. Originally, it referred to (and still does in some places) tree branches blown down by wind, which became free firewood for those willing to pick them up. Today, a *windfall* can be any unexpected benefit. "Unexpected *windfall*" is a redundancy.

Wire Services Special features of the *wire services* are discussed in Appendix II. It is important that a broadcast newswriter be familiar with the ins and outs of *wire service* operations and what comes into the newsroom from them.

Woman *See* **Lady.**

Wounded *See* **Damaged.**

Wrack/Wreak/Wreck   Although colorful, the phrase *"WRACK* and ruin" is a redundancy. *Wrack* means ruin, destruction, violent damage. *WREAK* (pronounced REEK) means to bring down punishment, to indulge in a violent manner, to bring about harm. We all know what a *WRECK* is.

Wrest/Wrestle   When your sense is to describe the taking of something through effort, use *WREST*, as in "He *wrested* the title from his opponent." To *WRESTLE* is to physically grapple, to throw an opponent by force. One can also *wrestle* with an idea, a dilemma or a stubborn bag of lawn food.

Xerox *See* **Trademarks**. You know it's pronounced ZEE-rocks, don't you? In fact, many words that begin with *x* are pronounced as though they are spelled with a *z*.

X-Ray   It is pronounced as written--not EX-uh-ray. Always hyphenate.

Yacht   A *YACHT* doesn't have to be a luxurious boat. For insurance purposes, any pleasure boat more than 16 feet long is considered a *yacht*. By definition, a *yacht* is a pleasure craft. It's pronounced YAHT.

Yankee   There is some confusion over just what constitutes a *YANKEE*. Being a native of the Deep North, I have more than a passing interest. Somewhere years ago, I read a definition that I believe to be accurate: "Elsewhere in the world, a *Yankee* is someone from the United States; in the United States, a *Yankee* is someone from north of the Mason-Dixon Line. North of the line, it is someone from New England. In New England, a *Yankee* is someone from Vermont and in Vermont a *Yankee* is a person who has pie for breakfast." A Vermonter would find that amusing. Probably no one else, however.

Yoke/Yolk   A *YOKE* is part of a harness used with oxen that functions much the same as a horse collar does. It is usually wooden. There are also *yokes* designed to make it easier for humans to carry heavy loads, although I haven't seen one in years outside antiques shops and museums. *YOLK* is the yellow part of a chicken egg. The color varies with other kinds of fowl.

Youth *See* **Boy**.

Yucatán   A peninsula on the east coast of southern Mexico, often mispronounced as YUK-uh-tan. It's correctly YOO-kuh-tan (or -tahn). Perhaps the error comes from the semitropical plant, the yucca, which is pronounced YUK-uh.

Zapping/Zipping Terms used to describe certain practices of TV viewers. *ZAPPING* refers to muting the sound during commercials, much to the distress of commercial advertisers. *ZIPPING* has two meanings: to switch rapidly from channel to channel (also called *grazing*) and also the practice of fast-forwarding a videotape through commercial breaks, also to the distress of advertisers. When a program has been videotaped for future viewing, it is said to have been *time-shifted*.

Zealot Pronounced ZELL-uht. Often pejorative. A person exhibiting excess zeal toward a point of view or belief, often fanatically or in an intensely partisan manner.

Zeppelin *See* **Balloon.**

Zoology Although the study of animals might cause one to think of a zoo, the word is pronounced zoh-AW-luh-gee. That's the whole point of the title of Elster's "There Is No Zoo in *Zoology.*"

Zoom *ZOOM* implies an upward motion--a jet plane *zooms* to its cruising altitude. It is technically incorrect, although frequently heard, to say the eagle *zoomed* down on its prey. In broadcasting, *zoom* has its own meaning: to refocus a camera lens either "in" or "out," changing the size of the image.

Zucchini The ubiquitous dark green summer squash, as everyone probably knows. The word, pronounced zoo-KEE-nee, does provide some important insights into the pronunciation of vowels and consonants in Italian. Most Italian (and many other) words that end with a vowel receive stress on the next-to-last syllable. Vowels normally receive their "natural" sound: U=OO, I=EE, E=EH, A=AW, O=OH. There is no *k* in the Italian alphabet. The sound is achieved by the spelling *cch* or *ch*, followed by a vowel. The *ch* sound is spelled simply *c*, again followed by a vowel. The family name *Cecchini* is pronounced cheh-KEE-nee. Ciao, baby!

APPENDIXES

Radio-Television News Directors Association Code of Broadcast Ethics

The responsibility of radio and television journalists is to gather and report information of importance to the public accurately, honestly, and impartially.

The members of the Radio-Television News Directors Association accept these standards and will:

1. Strive to present the source or nature of broadcast news material in a way that is balanced, accurate and fair.

   A. They will evaluate information solely on its merits as news, rejecting sensationalism or misleading emphasis in any form.

   B. They will guard against using audio or video material in a way that deceives the audience.

   C. They will not mislead the public by presenting as spontaneous news any material which is staged or will identify people by race, creed, nationality or prior status only when it is relevant.

   D. They will clearly label opinion and commentary.

   E. They will promptly acknowledge and correct errors.

2. Strive to conduct themselves in a manner that protects them from conflicts of interest, real or perceived. They will decline gifts or favors which would influence or appear to influence their judgments.

3. Respect the dignity, privacy and well-being of people with whom they deal.

4. Recognize the need to protect confidential sources. They will promise confidentiality only with the intention of keeping that promise.

5. Respect everyone's right to a fair trial.

6. Broadcast the private transmissions of other broadcasters only with permission.

7. Actively encourage observance of the code by all journalists, whether members of the Radio-Television News Directors Association or not.

The Wire Services

Virtually every newsroom will have at least one national broadcast wire circuit--either AP or UPI. There are certain things you need to know about them.

The Bureaus

First, most states have at least one "bureau," often more than one. The bureaus are the collection and dissemination points for news in their states.

Schedules

Each main bureau--usually in the state's capital city--has a schedule it follows for sending out news of statewide interest. You should have a copy of that schedule posted in your newsroom so you will know what to expect and when.

The state bureau feeds the wire circuit about 20 minutes of each hour. The rest of the time the circuit is carrying the output of the national wire service, and there is also a schedule of the routine news and features that come down the wire from national.

Advisories and Notes

There are certain things that "move" on the wires that are not intended for broadcast--notes to editors, news directors or station managers--various advisories, schedules of audio feeds and the like. These should be saved and passed on to the people who need to see them. Newsroom computer systems "collect" wire service copy and hold it for a specified time. In such cases there is normally no printer pumping out a paper copy.

Warnings on Content

Sometimes a story will be preceded by a note. Often the note will indicate that the story contains material some people might find objectionable. In that case you read the story carefully to decide in your rewriting whether the material is really all that bad. If you think it is, leave it out.

Embargoes

Other times the note might indicate that the story is "embargoed" for broadcast until after a stated time. Usually the embargoes are imposed by the source. The governor, for example, might not want the advance story on his speech to be broadcast before he delivers it. Embargoes should be strictly observed. No one is held in lower esteem by fellow journalists than the person who "breaks" an embargo. Once broken, however, the story is out and everyone is free to use it.

Kills

Always obey any "KILL" notice. That indicates the story in question either is wrong or is in serious doubt and must not be used. If it is used after a KILL advisory is sent on the wire, any subsequent action, such as a law suit, will be taken against the broadcaster who used the story.

Alerts

The wire services have established several levels of alerts which are signaled by a series of bells on the printer, if a printer is present. With computer wire collection systems, the alert is signaled by a series of "beeps," and usually an on-screen notice that such a message has been received.

Three bells indicates a story coming that is slugged "URGENT." It doesn't sound it, but it is the lowest level of alert and may be a story about a late-breaking development, but not necessarily something of overriding public importance.

The next level is "BULLETIN" which is preceded by five bells. A bulletin is usually the first news about a major story.

The highest level is "FLASH." It is reserved for only the most shattering stories. It is preceded by ten bells and is usually very tersely worded: PRESIDENT SHOT. A flash is a very rare thing, indeed.

Sharing News with Your Wire Service

Both the AP and the UPI depend on member stations to share their news--called "protecting" them. That means that when you develop a local story that might have wider interest or appeal, you send it on to the state bureau--after you have used it yourself, of course. That also goes for any audiotapes that might accompany the story. Some newsrooms subscribe to both wire services, so it's up to the local news director to decide which he will "protect" on a given story. Both wire services provide small monetary rewards for protecting them on stories, and really cooperative news departments may receive an award at the annual meeting.

Police "10-Code"

Law enforcement agencies at all levels across the nation make use of this "10-Code." The 100 entries encompass most of the things police get involved in as well as routine messages. The 10-Code is used to speed communications and to standardize messages.

10-0	Caution	10-16	Domestic problem
10-1	Unable to copy--move	10-17	Meet complainant
10-2	Signal good	10-18	Complete assignment
10-3	Stop transmitting	10-19	Return to . . .
10-4	OK (acknowledgment)	10-20	Location
10-5	Relay	10-21	Call . . . by telephone
10-6	Busy--stand by	10-22	Disregard
10-7	Out of service	10-23	Arrived at scene
10-8	In service	10-24	Assignment complete
10-9	Repeat	10-25	Report in person
10-10	Fight in progress	10-26	Detaining subject
10-11	Dog case	10-27	License information
10-12	Stand by (stop)	10-28	Vehicle registration
10-13	Weather/road report	10-29	Check for wanted
10-14	Prowler report	10-30	Illegal use of radio
10-15	Civil disturbance	10-31	Crime in progress

10-32 Man with gun

10-33 EMERGENCY

10-34 Riot

10-35 Major crime alert

10-36 Correct time

10-37 Suspicious vehicle

10-38 Stopping suspicious vehicle

10-39 Urgent, use light, siren

10-40 Silent run, no light, siren

10-41 Beginning duty tour

10-42 Ending duty tour

10-43 Information

10-44 Request permission to leave patrol for . . .

10-45 Animal carcass at . . .

10-46 Assist motorist

10-47 Need emergency road repair

10-48 Traffic standard needs repair

10-49 Traffic light out at . . .

10-50 Accident (F, PI, PD)*

10-51 Wreaker needed

10-52 Ambulance needed

10-53 Road blocked at . . .

10-54 Livestock on highway

10-55 Intoxicated driver

10-56 Intoxicated pedestrian

10-57 Hit-and-Run (F, PI, PD)*

10-58 Direct traffic

10-59 Convoy or escort

10-60 Squad in vicinity

10-61 Personnel in area

10-62 Reply to message

10-63 Make written copy

10-64 Message for local delivery

10-65 Net message assignment

10-66 Message cancellation

10-67 Clear for net message

10-68 Dispatch information

10-69 Message received

*F, PI and PD mean, respectively, fatality, personal injury and property damage.

10-70 Fire alarm	10-85 Delayed due to . . .
10-71 Advise nature of fire	10-86 Officer/operator on duty
10-72 Report progress of fire	10-87 Pick up/distribute checks
10-73 Smoke report	10-88 Advise present telephone number of . . .
10-74 Negative	10-89 Bomb threat
10-75 In contact with . . .	10-90 Bank alarm at . . .
10-76 En route	10-91 Pick up prisoner/suspect
10-77 ETA (estimated time of arrival)	10-92 Improperly parked vehicle
10-78 Need assistance	10-93 Blockade
10-79 Notify coroner	10-94 Drag racing
10-80 Chase in progress	10-95 Prisoner/suspect in custody
10-81 Breathalyzer report	10-96 Mental subject
10-82 Reserve lodging	10-97 Test signal
10-83 Work school Xing	10-98 Prison-jailbreak
10-84 If meeting . . . advise time	10-99 Records indicate wanted

Most larger localities will have their own list of special "code" signals, many duplicative of the 10-Code, but including, as well, locally significant sites or activities. There might be a special code for a civic center demonstration, for example. There are usually special codes for airport problems, as well. Many times local police units are reluctant to provide these special codes to the public. Most newsrooms, however, find ways to obtain them. You cannot know what the police radios are saying without a copy of the codes.

Most newsrooms will be equipped with so-called "public service" radio receivers. These are the police, fire and other emergency units' communications systems. You will hear a great deal of useful information on them. But what you hear may be used only as a tip. You may not, under federal law, use directly any information you may gather that way. It is considered a serious offense and carries a heavy fine.

Patient Conditions

Patient conditions are defined by the American Hospital Association, and are recognized and followed by most hospitals.

Good Vital signs are stable and within normal limits. Patient is conscious and comfortable; indicators are excellent.

Fair Vital signs are stable and within normal limits. Patient is conscious but may be uncomfortable; indicators are favorable.

Serious (sometimes **Poor**) Vital signs may be unstable and not within normal limits. Patient is acutely ill; indicators are questionable.

Critical Vital signs are unstable and not within normal limits. Patient may not be conscious; indicators are unfavorable.

A spokesman for the AHA told me, "The use of the phrase 'in critical but stable condition' is, in my view, contradictory."

I recommend attributing anything but the above condition reports directly to the source: "As a nursing supervisor put it, [patient] is in critical but stable condition."

The Military

Comparative Organization by Service

ARMY	NAVY	AIR FORCE
Division	Fleet	Division
Brigade	Task Force	Wing
Regiment	Task Group	Group
Battalion	Task Unit	Squadron
Company		Flight
Platoon		
Squad		

Comparative Rank by Service

ARMY	NAVY	AIR FORCE
General of the Army	Fleet Admiral	General of the Air Force
General (four star)	Admiral	General
Lieutenant General	Vice Admiral	Lieutenant General
Major General	Rear Admiral	Major General
Brigadier General	Commodore	Brigadier General
Colonel	Captain	Colonel
Lieutenant Colonel Major	Commander	Lieutenant Colonel
Captain	Lieutenant Commander	Major
First Lieutenant	Lieutenant	Captain
Second Lieutenant	Lieutenant Junior Grade	First Lieutenant
Sergeant Major of the Army	Ensign	Second Lieutenant
Command Master Sergeant	Master Chief	Chief Master Sergeant
First Sergeant	Petty Officer of the Navy	Senior Master Sergeant
Sergeant First Class	Master CPO	Master Sergeant
Staff Sergeant	Senior CPO	Technical Sergeant
Sergeant	Chief Petty Officer	Staff Sergeant
Corporal	Petty Officer First Class	Sergeant
Private First Class	Petty Officer Second Class	Airman First Class
Private	Petty Officer Third Class	Airman
	Seaman	
	Seaman Apprentice	

State Capitals

STATE	CAPITAL
ALABAMA	MONTGOMERY
ALASKA	JUNEAU (JOON-oh)
ARIZONA	PHOENIX
ARKANSAS	LITTLE ROCK
CALIFORNIA	SACRAMENTO (Note spelling)
COLORADO	DENVER
CONNECTICUT	HARTFORD (HART-furd)
DELAWARE	DOVER
FLORIDA	TALLAHASSEE
GEORGIA	ATLANTA
HAWAII	HONOLULU
IDAHO	BOISE (BOY-zee)
ILLINOIS	SPRINGFIELD
INDIANA	INDIANAPOLIS
IOWA	DES MOINES (duh-MOYN)
KANSAS	TOPEKA
KENTUCKY	FRANKFORT (FRANK-furt)
LOUISIANA	BATON ROUGE (BAT-un ROOJH)
MAINE	AUGUSTA
MARYLAND	ANNAPOLIS
MASSACHUSETTS	BOSTON (BAHS-tun)
MICHIGAN	LANSING
MINNESOTA	SAINT PAUL
MISSISSIPPI	JACKSON
MISSOURI	JEFFERSON CITY
MONTANA	HELENA (HELL-in-uh)

STATE	CAPITAL
NEBRASKA	LINCOLN
NEVADA	CARSON CITY
NEW HAMPSHIRE	CONCORD (KAHN-kurd)
NEW JERSEY	TRENTON
NEW MEXICO	SANTA FE (SAN-tuh FAY)
NEW YORK	ALBANY
NORTH CAROLINA	RALEIGH
NORTH DAKOTA	BISMARCK
OHIO	COLUMBUS
OKLAHOMA	OKLAHOMA CITY
OREGON	SALEM
PENNSYLVANIA	HARRISBURG
RHODE ISLAND	PROVIDENCE
SOUTH CAROLINA	COLUMBIA
SOUTH DAKOTA	PIERRE (PEER)
TENNESSEE	NASHVILLE
TEXAS	AUSTIN
UTAH	SALT LAKE CITY
VERMONT	MONTPELIER (mahnt-PEEL-yur)
VIRGINIA	RICHMOND
WASHINGTON	OLYMPIA
WEST VIRGINIA	CHARLESTON
WISCONSIN	MADISON
WYOMING	CHEYENNE (shy-ANN)

Nations of the World and Capitals

In broadcast newswriting unfamiliar foreign city names are usually omitted and the location of an event is related to the nation's capital city (300 miles southeast of Manila, rather than 35 miles west of Iloilo City). It is hoped this list will provide a quick reference to the general location of foreign nations and the pronunciation of them and their capitals. The information is current as of mid-1991. Pronunciations are generally "Anglicized" for American broadcasters. Native speakers from any of these countries would probably correct them. European ethnic, religious and political turmoil will undoubtedly cause some changes in this arrangement of nations, most notably, as this is written, in Yugoslavia. The individual states within Yugoslavia are included here. Stay tuned.

NATION	CAPITAL CITY
Afghanistan (S Central Asia)	Kabul (kuh-BOOL)
Albania (S Europe, Adriatic)	Tirana (tih-RAHN-uh)
Algeria (NW Africa)	Algiers (al-JEERS)
Andorra (W Europe, S France)	Andorra la Vella (an-DOR-uh luh-VAY-yuh)
Angola (SW Africa)	Luanda (loo-AN-duh)
Antigua and Barbuda (an-TEE-guh and bar-BOO-duh) (E Caribbean)	Saint John's
Argentina (S America)	Buenos Aires (BWAYN-ohs AIR-eez)

NATION	CAPITAL CITY
Australia (SE of Asia, S Pacific)	Canberra (KAN-bur-uh)
Austria (S Central Europe)	Vienna (vee-EHN-uh)
Bahamas, The (Atlantic, E Florida)	Nassau (NA-saw)
Bahrain (baw-RAYN) (Persian Gulf)	Manama (man-AM-uh)
Bangladesh (S Asia, E India)	Dacca (DAK-uh)
Barbados (bar-BAY-dohs) (W Indies)	Bridgetown
Belgium (NW Europe)	Brussels (BRUH-suhls)
Belize (buh-LEEZ) (Central America)	Belmopan (bel-moh-PAN)
Benin (buh-NEEN) (W Africa)	Porto-Novo (POHR-toh-NOH-voh)
Bhutan (boo-TAWN) (E Himalayas)	Thimphu (thihm-POO)
Bolivia (S America)	La Paz and Sucre (luh-PAHZ and SOO-kruh) La Paz is the capital-in-fact; Sucre is the constitutional capital.
Bosnia-Herzegovina (*see* Yugoslavia)	
Botswana (bawt-SWAHN-uh) (S Africa)	Gaborone (gab-uh-ROHN-ee)

NATION	CAPITAL CITY
NATION	**CAPITAL CITY**
Brazil (S America)	Brasilia (bruh-ZEEL-yuh)
Brunei (broo-NYE) (Island of Borneo)	Bandar Seri Begawan (BAN-dur SIHR-ee buh-GAH-wun)
Bulgaria (E Europe, Balkan Pen.)	Sofia (soh-FEE-yuh or SOH-fee-yuh)
Burkina Faso (W Africa)	Ouagadougou (waug-uh-DOO-goo)
Burma (*see* Myanmar)	
Burundi (boo-ROON-dee) (Central Africa)	Bujumbura (BOO-juhm-BOOR-uh)
Cambodia (SE Asia)	Phnom Penh (puh-NOM PEHN)
Cameroon (W Central Africa)	Yaounde (yaw-OON-day)
Canada (N America)	Ottawa (AW-tuh-wuh)
Canadian Provinces	
Alberta	Edmondton
British Columbia	Victoria
Manitoba	Winnipeg
New Brunswick	Fredericton
Newfoundland (incl. Labrador)	Saint John's
Nova Scotia	Halifax

NATION	CAPITAL CITY
Canadian Provinces (continued)	
Ontario	Toronto
Prince Edward Island	Charlottetown
Quebec (kweh-BEHK)	Quebec City
Saskatchewan	Regina (ruh-JYN-uh)
Cape Verde (VERD) (Atlantic islands, W Africa)	Praia (PRY-uh)
Central African Republic (Central Africa)	Bangui (BAHN-geh)
Chad (N Central Africa)	N'Djamena (Fort-Lamy) (ehn-JAHM-uh-nuh or FOR-luh-MEE)
Chile (S America)	Santiago (SAHN-tee-AH-goh)
China, People's Republic (Asia)	Beijing (formerly Peiking) (bay-ZHING) (pee-KING)
Colombia (NW S America)	Bogota (boh-guh-TAH)
Commonwealth of Independent States (formerly USSR) (E Europe, N Asia)	

Spellings and pronunciations are those in use by the Associated Press

Armenia (S Tier)	Yerevan (yer-uh-VAHN)
Azerbaijan (azh-ur-by-JAHN) (S Tier)	Baku (bah-KOO)
Belarus (beh-luh-ROOS (NW)	Minsk (MINSK)

NATION	CAPITAL CITY

Commonwealth of Independent States (continued)

Georgia (S Tier)	Tbilisi (teh-BIL-eh-see)
Kazakhstan (KUH-zahk-stahn) (S Tier)	Alma-Ata (al-muh-uh-TAH)
Kyrgystan (keer-gih-STAHN) (S Tier)	Frunze (FRUHN-zuh)
Moldavia (SW)	Kishinev (KISH-uh-nef)
Russia (N Tier)	Moscow (MAHS-kow or MAHS-koh)
Tadjikistan (tah-JIH-kih-stan) (SE)	Dushanbe (doo-SHAHM-buh)
Turkmenistan (turk-MEN-ih-stan) (SE)	Ashkhabad (ASH-kuh-bad)
Ukraine (SW)	Kiev (KEE-yef)
Uzbekistan (ooz-BEK-ih-stan) (SE)	Tashkent (tash-KENT)

Comoros (KAHM-eh-row) (islands off E Africa)	Moroni (mah-ROHN-ee)
Congo (W Central Africa)	Brazzaville (BRAZ-uh-vihl)
Costa Rica (Central America)	San Jose (SAHN ho-ZAY)

Côte d'Ivoire (*see* Ivory Coast)

Croatia (*see* Yugoslavia)

NATION	CAPITAL CITY
Cuba (Indies)	Havana (huh-VAN-uh)
Cyprus (E Mediterranian)	Nicosia (nih-kuh-SEE-uh)
Czech Republic (E Central Europe)	Prague (PRAHG)
Denmark (N Europe)	Copenhagen (KOH-pehn-HAH-guhn)
Djibouti (jih-BOO-tee) (E Africa)	Djibouti (jih-BOO-tee)
Dominica (dahm-ih-NEEK-uh or doh-MIHN-ih-kuh) (E Caribbean)	Roseau (roh-ZOH)
Dominican Republic (W Indies, Hispaniola island)	Santo Domingo (SAHN-toh doh-MIHN-go)
Ecuador (S America)	Quito (KEE-toh)
Egypt (NE Africa)	Cairo (KY-roh)
El Salvador (Central America)	San Salvador (sahn SAL-vuh-dohr)
Equatorial Guinea (GIH-nee) (W Coast Africa)	Malabo (mah-LAH-boh)
Estonia (NW Europe)	Tallinn (TAL-uhn)
Ethiopia (E Africa)	Addis Ababa (AHD-ihs AH-buh-buh)
Fiji (FEE-jee) (S Pacific)	Suva (SOO-vuh)

NATION	CAPITAL CITY
Finland (NW Europe)	Helsinki (hehl-SIN-kee)
France (W Europe)	Paris (PAIR-iss)
Gabon (guh-BAHN) (E Africa)	Libreville (LEE-bruh-VEEL)
Gambia, The (GAM-bee-uh) (W Africa)	Banjul (BAHN-jool)
Germany (Central Europe)	Berlin (buhr-LYN)
Ghana (SW Africa)	Accra (uh-KRAH or AK-ruh)
Greece (SE Europe)	Athens (ATH-unz)
Grenada (gruh-NAY-duh) (Caribbean, near Venezuela)	Saint George's
Guatemala (Central America)	Guatemala City (GWAH-tuh-MAHL-uh)
Guinea (GIHN-ee) (W Africa)	Conakry (KAHN-uh-kree)
Guinea-Bissau (bih-SOW) (W Africa)	Bissau (bih-SOW)
Guyana (guy-AN-uh) (N S America)	Georgetown
Haiti (HAY-tee) (shares Hispaniola with Dominican Republic)	Port-au-Prince (POART-oh-PRINZ)
Honduras (hahn-DOOR-us) (Central America)	Tegucigalpa (tuh-GOO-see-GAL-puh)

NATION	CAPITAL CITY
Hungary (Central Europe)	Budapest (BOO-duh-pest)
Iceland (N Atlantic, Arctic)	Reykjavik (RAYK-yuh-VIHK)
India (S Asia)	New Delhi (noo DEHL-ee)
Indonesia (ihn-doh-NEE-zjuh) (13,500 islands, SE Asia)	Jakarta (juh-KAR-tuh)
Iran (eer-AHN) (Middle East, S Asia)	Teheran (teh-ur-RAN or tay-RAN)
Iraq (eer-AK) (Middle East)	Baghdad (BAG-dad)
Ireland (W of Great Britain)	Dublin
Israel (IHZ-ree-ul) (E Mediterranean)	Jerusalem
Italy (S Europe, Mediterranean)	Rome
Ivory Coast (SW Africa)	Abidjan (A-bih-JAHN)
Jamaica (juh-MAY-kuh) (W Indies)	Kingston
Japan (E Asia)	Tokyo (TOH-kee-oh)
Jordan (W Asia)	Amman (uh-MAHN)
Kenya (KEN-yuh or KEEN-yuh) (E Africa)	Nairobi (nye-ROH-bee)

NATION	CAPITAL CITY
Kiribati (KIR-uh-bas) (S Pacific islands)	Tarawa (teh-RAH-wuh or TAR-uh-wuh)
Korea, North (NE Asia)	Pyongyang (PEE-yung-yahng)
Korea, South (NE Asia)	Seoul (SOHL)
Kuwait (koo-WAYT) (Middle East)	Kuwait City (koo-WAYT)
Laos (LAW-ohs) (SE Asia)	Vientiane (vee-EHN-tyawn)
Latvia (NW Europe)	Riga (REE-guh)
Lebanon (E Mediterranean)	Beirut (bay-ROOT)
Lesotho (leh-SOH-toh) (surrounded by S Africa)	Maseru (MAZ-uh-roo)
Liberia (lye-BEER-ee-uh) (SW Africa)	Monrovia (muhn-ROH-vee-uh)
Libya (LIHB-ee-uh) (N Africa)	Tripoli (TRIH-poh-lee)
Liechtenstein (LIHK-tuhn-SHTEYN) (W Europe, Alpine)	Vaduz (faw-DOOTZ)
Lithuania (NW Europe)	Vilnius (VIHL-nee-us)
Luxembourg (LUHX-uhm-burg) (W Europe)	Luxembourg (LUHX-uhm-burg)
Macedonia (*see* Yugoslavia)	

NATION	CAPITAL CITY
Madagascar (Indian Ocean, E Africa)	Antananarivo (AN-tuh-NAN-uh-REE-voh)
Malawi (mah-LAH-wee) (SE Africa)	Lilongwe (lee-LAHNG-way)
Malaysia (muh-LAYJZ-uh) (SE Asia and Borneo)	Kuala Lumpur (KWAH-luh LOOM-poor)
Maldives (MAL-dyvz) (islands Indian Ocean)	Mal'e (MAH-lay)
Mali (MAH-lee) (W Africa)	Bamako (BAM-uh-koh)
Malta (island, Mediterranean)	Valletta (vuh-LET-uh)
Mauritania (W Africa)	Nouakchott (nwahk-SHAHT)
Mauritius (maw-RISH-ee-uhs) (island, Indian Ocean, E Africa)	Port Louis (LOO-ihs, LOO-ee or loo-EE)
Mexico (Central America)	Mexico City
Monaco (MAHN-uh-koh) (NW Mediterranean coast)	Monaco-ville (MAHN-uh-koh)
Mongolia (E Central Asia)	Ulaanbaatar (OO-lahn-BAH-tor)
Montenegro (see Yugoslavia)	
Morocco (NW Africa)	Rabat (ruh-BAHT)
Mozambique (moh-zam-BEEK) (SE Africa)	Maputo (muh-POO-toh)

NATION	CAPITAL CITY
Myanmar (formerly Burma) (SE Asia)	Yangon (Rangoon)
Namibia (nuh-MIB-ee-uh) (SW Africa)	Windhoek (VINT-hook)
Nauru (nah-OO-roo) (S Pacific)	Yaren (YAHR-ruhn, uncertain)
Nepal (nuh-PAHL) (Himalayas)	Katmandu (KAT-man-DOO)
Netherlands (Holland) (NW Europe)	Amsterdam
New Zealand (S Pacific)	Wellington
Nicaragua (NIHK-uh-RAH-gwuh) (Central America)	Managua (muhn-AH-gwuh)
Niger (NY-juhr) (N Africa)	Niamey (nyah-MAY)
Nigeria (ny-JEER-ee-uh) (W Africa)	Lagos (LAY-gahs)
Norway (NW Europe)	Oslo
Oman (oh-MAHN) (Arabian Pen.)	Muscat (MUHS-kat)
Pakistan (SW Asia)	Islamabad (ihz-LAHM-uh-bahd)
Panama (Central America)	Panama City
Papua New Guinea (S Pacific, N Australia) (shares island with Indonesia)	Port Moresby

NATION	CAPITAL CITY
Paraguay (S America)	Asunción (aw-SOON-see-OHN)
Peru (S America)	Lima (LEE-muh)
Philippines (islands off SE Asia)	Manila (muh-NIHL-uh)
Poland (E Europe)	Warsaw
Portugal (SW Europe)	Lisbon (LIHZ-buhn)
Qatar (KAH-tuhr) (W Persian Gulf)	Doha (DOH-huh)
Romania (SE Europe)	Bucharest (BOO-kuh-resht)
Rwanda (RWAHN-duh) (E Central Africa)	Kigali (kih-GAHL-ee)
Saint Kitts and Nevis (E Caribbean)	Basseterre (bahs-TAHR)
Saint Lucia (LOOSH-yuh) (E Caribbean)	Castries (kuh-STREEZ)
Saint Vincent and the Grenadines (E Caribbean)	Kingstown
San Marino (SAN muh-REE-noh) (surrounded by Italy)	San Marino (SAN muh-REE-noh)
Sao Tome and Principe (soun too-MEH and PREEN-see-pih) (Atlantic islands off Central Africa)	Sao Tome (soun too-MEH)
Saudi Arabia (sah-OO-dee or SAH-dee) (Arabian Pen., Middle East)	Riyadh (ree-YAHD)

NATION	CAPITAL CITY
Senegal (sehn-eh-GAHL) (W Africa)	Dakar (duh-KAHR)
Serbia (*see* Yugoslavia)	
Seychelles (say-SHELL) (86 Indian Ocean islands)	Victoria
Sierra Leone (see-AIR-uh lee-OHN) (W Africa)	Freetown
Singapore (SIN-guh-pohr) (island off S Maylay Pen.)	Singapore (SIN-guh-pohr)
Slovakia (E Central Europe)	Bratislava (bra-tih-SLAH-vah)
Slovenia (*see* Yugoslavia)	
Solomon Islands (W Pacific)	Honiara (hohn-ee-AHR-uh)
Somalia (soh-MAHL-ee-uh) (E Africa)	Mogadishu (MAHG-uh-DISH-oo)
South Africa (S Africa)	Cape Town and Pretoria (Cape Town is legislative Pretoria is administrative)
Spain (SW Europe)	Madrid (muh-DRIHD)
Sri Lanka (shree-LAHN-kuh) (SE of India)	Colombo (kuh-LUHM-boh)
Sudan (soo-DAN) (E Sahara)	Khartoum (kahr-TOOM)
Suriname (SOOR-ih-nahm) (N S America)	Paramaribo (PAR-eh-MAHR-ih-boh)

NATION	CAPITAL CITY
Swaziland (SWAHZ-ih-land) (S Africa)	Mbabane (ehm-bah-BAHN)
Sweden (N Europe)	Stockholm
Switzerland (Europe, Alpine)	Bern (BURN)
Syria (E Mediterranean)	Damascus (duh-MAS-kuhs)
Taiwan (Republic of China) (Asia)	Taipei (ty-PAY)
Tanzania (tan-zuh-NEE-uh) (E Africa)	Dar-es-Salaam (DAHR-ehs-suh-LAHM)
Thailand (TYE-land) (SE Asia)	Bangkok (BANG-kahk)
Togo (W Africa)	Lomé (loh-MAY)
Tonga (S Pacific)	Nukualofa (NOO-koo-eh-LOH-fuh)
Trinidad and Tobago (tuh-BAY-goh) (S Atlantic off Venezuela)	Port-of-Spain
Tunisia (toon-EEZ-ee-uh) (N Africa)	Tunis (TOON-ihs)
Turkey (Asia Minor, Mediterranean)	Ankara (ANG-kuh-ruh)
Tuvalu (too-VAHL-oo) (SW Pacific)	Funafuti (FOO-nah-FOO-tee)
Uganda (yoo-GAN-duh) (E Africa)	Kampala (kahm-PAHL-uh)

NATION	CAPITAL CITY
Union of Soviet Socialist Republics (*see* Commonwealth of Independent States)	
United Arab Emirates (seven Arab countries) (Persian Gulf)	Abu Dhabi (AH-boo DAH-bee)
United Kingdom (England, Scotland, Wales and N Ireland) (NW Europe)	London
United States of America (N America)	Washington, D.C.
Uruguay (S America)	Montevideo MAHN-tuh-vih-DAY-oh
Vanuatu (van-uh-WAH-too) (SW Pacific)	Vila (VEE-luh)
Vatican (Roman Catholic city-state) (within Rome, Italy)	Vatican City
Venezuela (vehn-eh-zoo-AY-luh) (S America)	Caracas (kuh-RAH-kuhs)
Vietnam (vee-EHT NAHM) (SE Asia)	Hanoi (hah-NOY or han-OY)
Western Samoa (suh-MOH-uh) (S Pacific)	Apia (ah-PEE-uh)
Yemen, North (YEH-muhn) (Arabian Pen.)	Sanaa (san-NAH)
Yugoslavia (SE Europe)	Belgrade (BEHL-grayd)
Bosnia-Herzegovina (BOZ-nee-uh hurt-zuh-goh-VEE-nuh)	Sarajevo (sar-uh-YAY-voh)

NATION	CAPITAL CITY
Yugoslavia (continued) (SE Europe)	
Croatia (kroh-AY-shuh)	Zagreb
Macedonia	Skopje (skahp-YAY)
Montenegro (MAHN-tuh-NAY-groh)	Cetinje (setn-YAY)
Serbia	Belgrade
Slovenia (sloh-VEE-nuh)	Ljubljana (lee-oo-blee-AHN-uh)
Zaire (zaw-EER or ZAIR) (Central Africa)	Kinshasa (kihn-SHAH-suh)
Zambia (ZAM-bee-uh) (S Central Africa)	Lusaka (loo-SAH-kuh)
Zimbabwe (zihm-BAHB-way) (S Africa)	Harare (huh-RAH-ray)

APPENDIX VIII

Area Codes

By State, with Time Zones

Time Zone

Atlantic Time	New York plus one hour
Eastern Time	New York
Central Time	New York minus one hour
Mountain Time	New York minus two hours
Pacific Time	New York minus three hours
Alaska Time	New York minus four hours
Hawaii Time	New York minus five hours

STATE	AREA CODE	TIME ZONE
Alabama	205	(CT)
Alaska	907	(PT)
Arizona	602	(MT)
Arkansas	501	(CT)
California		(PT)
Bakersfield	805	
Fresno	209	
Los Angeles	213	
	310 and 818	
Sacramento	916	
San Diego	619	
San Francisco	415	
Colorado		(MT)
Boulder	303	
Colorado Springs	719	
Denver	303	
Durango	303	
Grand Junction	303	
Leadville	719	
Pueblo	719	

STATE	AREA CODE	TIME ZONE
Connecticut	203	(ET)
Deleware	302	(ET)
District of Columbia	202	(ET)
Florida		(ET)
Ft. Lauderdale	305	
Ft. Myers	813	
Jacksonville	904	
Miami	305	
Orlando	407	
Georgia		(ET)
Atlanta	404	
Rome	706	
Waycross	912	
Hawaii	808	(NY minus 5 hrs)
Idaho	208	(PT north, MT south)
Illinois		(CT)
Aurora	708	
Chicago	312	
Mt. Vernon	618	
Peoria	309	
Rockford	815	
Springfield	217	
Waukegan	708	
Indiana		(CT)
Evansville	812	
Indianapolis	317	
South Bend	219	
Iowa		(ET except northwest)
Council Bluffs	712	
Des Moines	515	
Dubuque	319	
Kansas		(CT, except MT west)
Dodge City	316	
Topeka	913	
Wichita	316	
Kentucky		(ET east, CT west)
Ashland	606	
Louisville	502	
Winchester	606	
Louisiana		(CT)
Lake Charles	318	
New Orleans	504	

STATE	AREA CODE	TIME ZONE
Maine	207	(ET)
Maryland		(ET)
Baltimore	410	
Cumberland	301	
Massachusetts		(ET)
Boston	617	
Cape Cod	508	
Springfield	413	
Worcester	508	
Michigan		(ET)
Battle Creek	616	
Detroit	313	
Escanaba	906	
Saginaw	517	
Minnesota		(CT)
Duluth	218	
Minneapolis	612	
Rochester	507	
Mississippi	601	(CT)
Missouri		(CT)
Joplin	417	
Kansas City	816	
St. Louis	314	
Montana	406	(MT)
Nebraska		(CT east, MT west)
North Platte	308	
Omaha	402	
Nevada	702	(PT)
New Hampshire	603	(ET)
New Jersey		(ET)
Atlantic City	609	
Newark	201	
New Brunswick	908	
New Mexico	505	(MT)
New York		(ET)
Albany	518	
Brooklyn	718, 917	
Buffalo	716	
Elmira	607	
Hempstead	516	
Manhattan	212, 917	
Syracuse	315	
White Plains	914	

STATE	AREA CODE	TIME ZONE
North Carolina		(ET)
Charlotte	704	
Winston-Salem	919	
North Dakota	701	(CT east and north, MT southwest)
Ohio		(ET)
Cincinnati	513	
Cleveland	216	
Columbus	614	
Toledo	419	
Oklahoma		(CT)
Oklahoma City	405	
Tulsa	918	
Oregon	503	(PT)
Pennsylvania		(ET)
Erie	814	
Harrisburg	717	
Philadelphia	215	
Pittsburgh	412	
Puerto Rico	809	(AT)
Rhode Island	401	(ET)
South Carolina	803	(ET)
South Dakota	605	(CT east, MT west)
Tennessee		(ET east, CT west)
Memphis	901	
Nashville	615	
Texas		(CT)
Abilene	915	
Amarillo	806	
Austin	512	
Dallas	214	
Galveston	409	
Houston	713	
Temple	817	
Tyler	903	
Utah	801	(MT)
Vermont	802	(ET)
Virginia		(ET)
Richmond	804	
Roanoke	703	
Virgin Islands	809	(AT)

STATE	AREA CODE	TIME ZONE
Washington		(PT)
Seattle	206	
Walla Walla	509	
West Virginia	304	(ET)
Wisconsin		(CT)
Eau Claire	715	
Madison	608	
Milwaukee	414	
Wyoming	307	(MT)

Canada and Mexico

Canada		
Alberta	403	(MT)
British Columbia	604	(PT)
Manitoba	204	(CT)
	807	
New Brunswick	506	(AT)
Newfoundland	709	(AT)
Northwest Territories	403	(MT)
Nova Scotia	902	(AT)
Ontario		(ET east, CT west)
London	519	
North Bay	705	
Ottawa	613	
Toronto	416	
Prince Edward Island	902	(AT)
Quebec		(ET)
Montreal	514	
Quebec City	418	
Sherbrooke	819	
Saskatchewan	306	(CT east and north, MT northwest)
Yukon	403	(PT)
Mexico		(ET southeast, CT east coast, MT west coast (PT Baja)
Mexico City	905	
Tijuana	706	

By Number

AREA CODE	STATE	AREA CODE	STATE
201	New Jersey	404	Georgia
202	Washington, DC	405	Oklahoma
203	Connecticut	406	Montana
204	Manitoba	408	California
205	Alabama	409	Texas
206	Washington State	412	Pennsylvania
207	Maine	413	Massachusetts
208	Idaho	414	Wisconsin
209	California	415	California
212	Manhattan	416	Ontario
213	California	417	Missouri
214	Texas	418	Quebec
215	Pennsylvania	419	Ohio
216	Ohio	501	Arkansas
217	Massachusetts	502	Kentucky
218	Minnesota	503	Oregon
219	Indiana	504	Louisiana
301	Maryland	505	New Mexico
302	Delaware	506	New Brunswick
303	Colorado	507	Minnesota
304	West Virginia	508	Massachusetts
305	Florida	509	Washington State
306	Saskatchewan	512	Texas
307	Wyoming	513	Ohio
308	Nebraska	514	Quebec
309	Illinois	515	Iowa
310	California	516	New York
312	Illinois	517	Michigan
313	Michigan	518	New York
314	Missouri	519	Ontario
315	New York	601	Mississippi
316	Kansas	602	Arizona
317	Indiana	603	New Hampshire
318	Louisiana	604	British Columbia
319	Iowa	605	South Dakota
401	Rhode Island	606	Kentucky
402	Nebraska	607	New York
403	Alberta	608	Wisconsin
403	NW Territories	609	New Jersey
403	Yukon	612	Minnesota

AREA CODE	STATE	AREA CODE	STATE
613	Ontario	806	Texas
614	Ohio	807	Ontario
615	Tennessee	808	Hawaii
616	Michigan	809	Bahamas
617	Massachusetts	809	Puerto Rico
618	Illinois	809	Virgin Islands
619	California	812	Indiana
701	North Dakota	813	Florida
702	Nevada	814	Pennsylvania
703	Virginia	815	Illinois
704	North Carolina	816	Missouri
705	Ontario	817	Texas
706	Georgia	819	Quebec
707	California	901	Tennessee
709	Newfoundland	902	Nova Scotia
712	Iowa	902	Prince Edward Island
713	Texas	903	Northeast Texas
714	California	904	Florida
715	Wisconsin	905	Mexico City
716	New York	906	Michigan
717	Pennsylvania	907	Alaska
718	New York	912	Georgia
800	Inward WATS	913	Kansas
801	Utah	914	New York
802	Vermont	915	Texas
803	South Carolina	916	California
804	Virginia	918	Oklahoma
805	California	919	North Carolina

International Dialing Codes
For foreign calls: 011-(country code)-(city code if any)-number

COUNTRY	CODE	COUNTRY	CODE
American Samoa*	684	Bolivia	59
Andorra	33	Brazil	55
Argentina	54	Chile	56
Australia	61	China (Taiwan)	86
Austria	43	Colombia	57
Bahrain*	973	Costa Rica*	50
Belgium	32	Cyprus	35
Belize	501	Denmark	45

COUNTRY	CODE	COUNTRY	CODE
Iran	98	Finland	358
Iraq	964	France	33
Ireland, Rep. of	353	French Antilles*	596
Israel	972	German Dem. Rep.	37
Italy	39	German Fed. Rep.	49
Japan	81	Greece	30
Kenya	254	Guam*	671
Korea, Rep. of	82	Guatemala	502
Kuwait*	965	Guyana	592
Liberia*	231	Haiti	509
Liechtenstein	41	Honduras*	504
Luxembourg*	352	Hong Kong	852
Malaysia	60	Indonesia	62
Monaco	33	Romania	40
Netherlands	31	San Marino	39
Netherland Antilles	599	Saudi Arabia	966
New Caledonia*	687	Singapore*	65
New Zealand	64	South Africa	27
Nicaragua	505	Spain	34
Norway	47	Sweden	46
Panama*	507	Switzerland	41
Papua New Guinea*	675	Tahiti*	689
Paraguay	595	Thailand	66
Peru	51	Turkey	90
Philippines	63	United Arab Emirates	971
Portugal	351	United Kingdom	44
Ecuador	593	Vatican City	39
El Salvador*	503	Venezuela	58
Fiji*	679		

*No city code necessary. City codes and additional country codes available from local operators.

REFERENCES

Brandeis, Louis, and Samuel Warren. "The Right of Privacy." *Harvard Law Review.* 4 (1890): 193.

Bremner, John B. *Words on Words.* New York: Columbia, 1980.

Carver, Craig. *American Regional Dialects.* New York: Columbia. 1987.

Elster, Charles Harrington. *Is There a Cow in Moscow?* New York: Collier, 1990.

------. *There Is No Zoo in Zoology.* New York: Collier, 1988.

Freeman, Morton. *A Treasury for Word Lovers.* Philadelphia: ISI Press, 1983.

Goldstein, Norm, ed. *The Associated Press Stylebook and Libel Manual.* New York: The Associated Press, 1990.

Code of Ethics. Washington, D.C.: Radio-Television News Directors Association, 1989.

Hecht, Ben, and Charles MacArthur. *The Front Page.* New York: Samuel French, 1955.

Hodges, Dr. Louis W. "The Journalist and Privacy." In *Social Responsibility: Journalism, Law, Medicine.* Lexington, Va: Washington and Lee University, 1983.

Hood, James R., and Brad Kalbfeld, eds. *The AP Broadcast News Handbook.* New York: The Associated Press, 1982.

Kilpatrick, James J. *The Writer's Art.* Kansas City: Andrews, McMeel and Parker, 1984.

Morris, William, and Mary Morris. *Harper Dictionary of Contemporary Usage.* New York: Harper and Row, 1975.

Rawson, Hugh. *A Dictionary of Euphemisms and Other Doubletalk.* New York: Crown, 1981.

Shaw, Harry. *Dictionary of Problem Words and Expressions.* New York: McGraw-Hill, 1975.

The Virginia State Bar. "Free Press–Fair Trial." Section 5 of *News Handbook on Virginia Law and Courts 6.* Richmond: Author, 1984.

Webster's Tenth New Collegiate Dictionary. Springfield, Mass.: Merriam-Webster Inc., 1993.

INDEX